ALSO BY JOHN G. MITCHELL

The Catskills: Land in the Sky
(with photographer Charles Winters)

Losing Ground

THE HUNT

THE
HUNT

John G. Mitchell

Alfred A. Knopf   New York   1980

Library of Congress Cataloging in Publication Data

Mitchell, John G [date]   The hunt.

1. Hunting—United States.   2. Wildlife
conservation—United States.   3. Hunting—Moral and
religious aspects.   I. Title.
SK33.M66   1980   799.2′01   80-7621
ISBN 0-394-50684-7

Manufactured in the United States of America

FIRST EDITION

For Cap and the Colonel
  Gone to the hunting grounds

Contents

Book One

THE GUNS
OF GAYLORD

My father shot and killed his first moose in New Brunswick in 1922. It was also his last, anywhere. The animal weighed eight hundred pounds after gutting and the antlers measured fifty inches across the full spread. The old man and his guide were a long portage from their canoe and a dozen miles out from the nearest roadhead when the big bull went down with a hole half the diameter of a man's little finger behind its shoulder. They gutted the moose in the shallow pond where it fell, quartered it, and carried everything edible or mountable to the canoe. The edible parts were long gone before my time. As for the moose's head, when I came of an age to notice such things, I found it mounted above the fireplace of our cottage in northern Michigan. Firelight flashed across the brown marbles of its make-believe eyes. Wherever I moved, the eyes seemed to follow. I spoke to the moose. I said: Moose, why do you watch me? Why do you look so sad when it no longer hurts? The moose did not answer. My father did not answer either, and I had asked him a more reasonable question. I asked him if killing moose is fun.

Perhaps there was no answer from the old man because he could no longer be sure how he felt about such things. Though he would live most of his life in it, he was not of the twentieth century. It seemed to me, for he was old enough to be my grandfather, that he was always back somewhere on the other side of the century, in a time of horses and bugles, among fresh memories of Cheyenne lances at the Little Bighorn and Krupp cannon at the Centennial Exposition in Philadelphia's Fairmount Park. He missed both of those events by three years, but not the great flights of passenger pigeons that still darkened the skies of Kentucky on summer mornings, or the diminishing herds of bison that would linger for a decade in Texas, though the last of that breed in Kansas was dropped in its tracks on the Santa Fe Trail the month he was born.

He was a country boy, and he learned to shoot early and well and possibly with some confusion as to what was or was not decent and right in the slaughter of wild animals; confusion, because he came of shooting age at the interface between traditions, between the extirpative excesses of the western mountain man and the newfangled restraints of the eastern aristocrat-sportsman. The bison were going fast then, and the pigeons would soon be gone forever, but not the old wrathy frontier appetite for killing. It would simply adapt itself to the law of the bag limit, so that in time most of my father's contemporaries would learn to be content slaying five of a species in a single day, instead of five hundred. My father was content with one moose for a lifetime.

I do not remember him especially as a hunter. There were occasional autumn trips after quail; and if you count the pursuit of fish with rod and reel a form of hunting, as I do, then there were summer trips in Michigan after trout and bass and walleyes as well. But he was not a hunter in the classic manner of those who are absorbed in guns and dogs and the vicarious fireside palaver of men impatient for the opening day.

Recognizing the old man's desultory attention to the blood sport, I am at a loss to explain my own early eagerness to taste of it. A country boy I was not, though woods and fields would be plentiful for a while yet in the suburbs where I grew up. I learned to shoot passably with a Daisy air rifle and a bolt-action single-shot .22, and later with shotguns of various gauges and vintages. I was about ten when I first shot a squirrel out of a beech tree in southern Ohio, and I was surprised how much lighter than human blood was the animal's as it splashed on the copper October leaves, and how sticky as it started to dry on the tip of my finger, and later how uncommonly tasty the thighs that came to table from the fat in the frying pan. I think I may have been sorry for the squirrel as I ate it, but only a little.

If I had stayed with it, I might have been more of a hunter. But somehow in the crucial years of post-adolescence there seemed always to be other distractions on autumn weekends, such as chasing footballs. More lasting by far were the later distractions of jobs and children—female children who would acquire their mother's loathing of guns and would stare at their father with ill-concealed contempt as he ineptly explained how he had once enjoyed walking in the woods with a rifle in the crook of his arm. What did he kill with the rifle? they wanted to know. Rabbits and squirrels, he answered. And they were sure good to eat.

My friends of recent years tend to be the kind who object to the killing of anything. They speak of a reverence for life. Rifles and shotguns, not to mention handguns, give them a certain claustrophobic tremor in the viscera. They have lived their lives against the background of a constant gunnery—murder, hijacking, assassination, and war. Their most unpopular war is the one in the woods. They do not understand, or do not want to understand, how anyone could possibly derive joy from shooting at animals. They see the hunter as a bumbling sadist, and they speak sardonically of protecting their constitutional right to arm bears. "If you can't play a sport," the old anti-hunting advisory goes, "then shoot one." But of course they wouldn't. It might entail using a gun.

Not all of my friends frown on hunting. I have sat together with a few for and many against, partaking of the domesticated flesh of an animal killed in a slaughterhouse by a man with a blunt instrument, and listened to the two sides arguing. Pro-hunter says that he, too, has a reverence for life, but no hang-ups about death. "How can you eat this beef," he demands, "and say it is wrong to hunt deer?"

"But no one shoots cows for sport," says the anti.

"You mean for *fun*," says her friend. And there's an echo for my ear.

Pro-hunter throws up his hands. "Telling you about hunting," he says, "is like trying to explain sex to a eunuch."

On which analogy the anti pounces like a quick cat. "It's cigars all over again," she says. "The gun is a phallic crutch. Correct?"

(In the matter of hunting or not hunting, everyone is so desperately eager to be considered correct. Yet there is such an overburden of dishonesty on both sides.)

"And what side are you on?" It is my north country friend, the attorney from Bay City. We are standing before the stone fireplace of the cottage in Michigan. It is his place now, gone from my own family's clutches for half a lifetime, a third-party ownership having fallen somewhere between. I do not think the children of the third party had much esteem for my father's moose. They put curlers to its beard and left it festooned with red ribbons. The Bay City family, moving in, restored dignity to the threadbare head.

Whenever I am in northern Michigan, I make it my unofficial business to detour into the old place, take passing advantage of my friend's hospitality when he is around, or trespass a little when he is not. This time I am on my way to Gaylord for opening day of the hunting season and I am not even sure which side I am on. My friend, a man of strong opinions, is waiting for my answer. I look beyond his face and see the birch fire crackling on the undersides of the brown marble eyes. And I wonder: Why is it that the moose still watches me like this? Since it no longer hurts.

Opening Day

Orange is the color of November in Michigan. Not the soft orange of aspen or maple, for the leaves have already fallen. I mean the harsh fluorescence of blaze orange that glows along the country roads and in the little towns up north on the fifteenth of the month. Orange caps and vests and jackets and jump suits are ubiquitous. Men without a patch of orange are viewed with suspicion and given wide berth. Even women and children who rarely venture beyond sidewalk or schoolyard wear orange, if not in joyous celebration of the time of year, then in wholesome respect for the value of their own lives. Orange is the uniform of the day and of the season. The day is Opening Day. The season, which will run until dark on the thirtieth, is the one in which 700,000 people in Michigan endeavor to shoot and kill 700,000 white-tailed deer. Relatives and neighbors of each hunter will keep asking: "Did you get your deer yet?" A hurtful question. By the first of December, only one in six will be able to say that he did.

The restaurants in Gaylord opened at five o'clock this morning, filled up by six, and emptied at quarter to seven. At seven there was sufficient light to see blaze orange dimly at fifty yards, and I could hear scattered shots in the woods far away after that. I drove east out of Gaylord on Michigan State Highway 32, heading for the village of Atlanta where there would be prizes for the first and largest of the day's kill. All the vans and pickup trucks that I had seen pulling out of Gaylord before me had suddenly vanished. I was alone on the highway. Now and then, the head of a woman appeared in the lighted kitchen window of a roadside farmhouse. But there were no men. For all I knew, I was the only man in the north who was not in the woods.

Gaylord is known as the "hub of the north," north meaning the upper third of the Lower Peninsula, not to be confused with the Upper Peninsula, or UP, which relates to the rest of Michigan in much the same cantankerous fashion as Alaska relates to the United States of America. Highway spokes go out from the hub to Traverse City and Charlevoix on Lake Michigan and to Rogers City and Alpena on Lake Huron; while the main spoke, Interstate 75, puts Gaylord within an hour's drive of the Mackinac Bridge, going north, and going a bit farther the other way, the cultivated outliers of a place contemptuously known to north people as "Down Below," meaning Grand Rapids and Lansing and Flint and, unavoidably, Detroit. On November 15, tens of thousands of hunters from Down Below arise after midnight and drive for hours in order to open the season up north at dawn. Most of them are home again in time for supper, without their deer. They are known as the sandwich hunters because, aside from taking one along for lunch, a sandwich is all the meat they are likely ever to traffic in or out of the north country.

The north is splendid country for *Odocoileus virginianus*, the white-tailed deer. It is mostly oak upland and cedar swamp country, as good for forage as for hideaway cover. Too far north or west and the hardwoods begin to run heavily toward maple and birch. But east of I-75, from Roscommon north into Cheboygan County and over Lake Huron way, the acorn crops do get prodigious; and with state wildlife managers manipulating habitats here and there, so do the annual harvest and reproduction of white-tailed deer.

The radio in the car this morning informed me that the deer population statewide is now estimated at one million, that about half a million deer hunters (of 700,000 licensees) are believed to be out for Opening Day, that in the course of the season five to ten will die of accidental gunshot wounds and another thirty of heart attacks, and that the surviving riflemen will spend upwards of $140 million this year on their sport. Dividing that last figure by the number of licenses, I came up with an expenditure of $200 per deer hunter. The average weight of a dressed-out, boned-out north country buck is sixty pounds. Successful hunters therefore end up paying almost four dollars a pound for their venison, a price that puts *O. virginianus* more or less on a par with beef.

No matter. It is a hunter's state. Michigan is second only to Pennsylvania in the number of licensed deer stalkers, and third behind New York in total hunting licenses of all kinds. In the 1940s and early '50s, Michigan was first on both counts. Part of the lingering enthusiasm for hunting here no doubt is related to the fact that no-trespass signs are relatively scarce north of Down Below. Public lands open to hunting include four national forests and a system of state forests and game areas the aggregate of which could swallow Connecticut twice with room to spare. Title to nearly a third of Montmorency County east of Gaylord is vested in the state, mostly within the metes and bounds of Thunder Bay River State Forest. From the buck pole in Atlanta, the county seat, a hunter may walk north or south and in half an hour be hunting on public land.

Atlanta is a town of five hundred people, with five gasoline stations, a drugstore, three saloons, a couple of supermarkets, two hardware and sporting goods stores, and a parking lot containing the chamber of commerce's buck pole, a tent-frame structure from which the hunters hang their deer. I arrived there at seven-thirty and introduced myself to Jim O'Bannon, the man in charge. O'Bannon and a friend named Hodge were sitting in a panel truck waiting for the first buck to come in. "Alpena got their first just after seven and none since," said Hodge, playing with the dial of a CB radio. "I never seen it so slow."

O'Bannon looked at his watch. "It's slow, all right," he said. "Guys been tromping through the woods for three days, checking things out, and the deer are spooked."

Was the herd in good shape in Montmorency County?

"We try to keep 'em fat," he said, and was about to go on when a pickup truck came into the lot with the tines of a buck's rack showing above the edge of the tailgate.

"Here it is," said Hodge, smiling. "First buck earns twenty-five dollars."

We got out of the panel and went over to the pickup. O'Bannon carried a clipboard. He took down the name of the hunter, Kurtis Dobbyn of Atlanta, and asked where he had killed the deer.

Dobbyn said, "Six miles east of town. He was chasing a doe. He couldn't have been more than a hundred feet away. I hit him with a thirty-forty Krag and he went right down."

Hodge and another man helped Dobbyn drag the buck to the pole. Two of them lifted it while the third, on a ladder, fastened a chain around the base of the rack. The deer hung with its head thrown back, revealing the incision Dobbyn had made across the animal's throat to bleed it out in the field. Still, blood fell from the open stomach cavity onto the dirt surface of the parking lot.

O'Bannon continued his story about keeping the herd in

good shape. "We feed 'em right in the backyard," he said. "Oats and corn. About two hundred pounds of each every month, September to June. Other families round here do the same." Dobbyn stood silently beside us, looking up at the head of his buck. "You bet they're in good shape," O'Bannon went on. "My wife likes to sit on the patio and watch 'em. Sure are pretty in the evening when they're into the feed."

For the men and women of Michigan's Department of Natural Resources (DNR), Opening Day is the longest day of the year. In district and area field offices throughout the state, switchboards are swamped with calls. Landowners complain about trespassers. Trespassers complain about inaccurate maps. Farmers mourn missing livestock. Friends mourn missing hunters. Violators plead ignorance of the law. It is an especially long day for the department's wildlife biologists, who must not only check out the age and condition of other people's deer, but, if they are so inclined, find time to check in their own as well.

Bob Strong of Gaylord is the chief wildlife biologist for District 5, a territory that embraces the eight northernmost counties of the Lower Peninsula. It is splendid territory in which to be so employed, for in addition to substantial numbers of deer there are also black bears and bobcats and coyotes and ruffed grouse and, in seasonal migration, woodcocks and waterfowl. There are hundreds of lakes and scores of streams, including the Jordan, Sturgeon, Pigeon, Black, Thunder Bay, and North Branch Au Sable. The Pigeon, flowing north to Mullett Lake, bisects the Lower Peninsula's largest and most esteemed wild area and gives the place its name—Pigeon River Country. Into this area some years ago the state imported a small herd of Rocky Mountain elk. The elk took to the country and are now believed to number four hundred. Since the 1960s, when hunting was permitted for two consecutive seasons, the elk have been protected. Their well-being is one of Bob Strong's most pressing responsibilities. Each deer season, half a dozen elk are found bullet-dead in the woods. If an animal's eyeteeth are missing, the killing was not an accident. A pair of teeth will fetch four hundred dollars for the watch chain of a member of the Benevolent and Protective Order of Elks. If the teeth are intact in the head, then it was yet another case of mistaken identity, some myopic rifleman from Down Below having believed as he squeezed the trigger that he was drawing down on the largest white-tailed superbuck ever sighted in North America.

On this particular Opening Day, Bob Strong was out of bed and Gaylord earlier than most men. He would not be heading for the Pigeon Country directly, but instead would turn a dog-leg around it, north and east past Onaway almost to Rogers City. In the acorn woods well off the highway he had found a deer trail with plenty of sign over the past few weeks, and now he would stake it out with his rifle for an hour or two on the chance that a buck might wander his way before sunup. The two of us had agreed to meet later at the DNR office near Atlanta.

Strong and I had already spent some time together the day before, moseying around Montmorency County in general and Lewiston in particular, which, with its motels, cafés, ammo shops, and deer camps large and small round about, appeared to be even more of a hunting man's town than Atlanta. Handwritten "Hunters Welcome" signs were displayed in every boardinghouse window, though I noticed the saloons tended to put certain conditions on hospitality. Their signs read: "No guns or knives allowed." Unarmed, we went into the Lewiston Hotel bar and took a table by the window, and presently Strong began to explain to me his theory of the Down Below workingman as deerslayer.

There had been periods during and after college at Ann Arbor when Strong himself wore a blue collar, working for the Buick Division of General Motors in Flint. It was a line job at first. Every move was by the clock, and the hands of the clock seemed afflicted with mechanical arthritis. Then it was a time-study job in which Strong observed and reported on how well or badly the men on the line responded to clocks and to the passing parade of Fisher Bodies. He heard the men talking, listened to their back-shop rap sessions to discover what it was that filled up their minds. A part of it was spectator talk, of ball games and girlie magazines. But more than anything else, the way Strong remembers it, the men on the line spoke of going north in November to a place without clocks, where there was bean soup for breakfast and bourbon for lunch and a passing parade of ten-point bucks.

"The talk kept them going," Strong was telling me in Lewiston. "Unless you've been on the line, you can't begin to imagine the unrelieved monotony of that kind of work. You've got to have a release."

"Maybe that's why deer hunting's so big in Pennsylvania."

"You mean coal and steel?"

"It has to be as dull as putting cars together."

"Nothing's as dull as putting cars together," said Strong.

I said, "For fifty weeks you talk about what you're going to do in less than two. But what's there to talk about, aside from deer?"

"Guns," said Strong. "They talk a lot about guns. And cartridge loads. Boots. Clothing. Staying warm. Getting lost. Anything about hunting. Anything that's different from what they're doing. They look forward to it. It's the one and only time of year when nothing is planned for them. It's important for people to have that."

"But aren't most of them one-shot sandwich hunters?"

"Some are," said Strong. "But some have camps. Five, six guys go in together and buy a few acres and put up a shack. That's camp. And some just come up for two or three days and hang out at a place like this. Those guys at the bar, maybe."

The men at the bar were drinking Stroh's beer from the bottle. Each wore an orange cap. There were several conversations in progress, and the one nearest me was about guns. Some orange-cap was saying that the .30/06 was too heavy for deer and his friend was responding that anything less was no better than a peashooter. The man in between pronounced them both full of scat.

I asked Strong how important it was for these men to go home with a deer. Did it hurt to get skunked?

"Sure it hurts," he said. "When you're young or beginning. But as the hunter gets older, the deer becomes less important.

Then, the real thing is the tradition. The hunt. It's something
you just have to do every year."

"What about you, Strong? Do you get a deer every year?"

"Just about," he said. "I sure as hell try, anyway."

On Opening Day, people in Gaylord know better than to ask
Harold A. Elgas if he got his deer yet. They used to ask, Opening Day and throughout the season, but that was before the
man began to think twice about hunting; and then, in a manner of speaking, to think of it not at all. The last time Elgas
went out Opening Day, some years back, he got a four-point
buck. He was on his way home after dark, traveling fast, and
the deer ran in front of his car. Both machine and animal were
totaled, as was Elgas's already slight interest in pursuing the
hunt.

Harold Elgas is president and chief executive officer of the
Gaylord State Bank, the city's oldest and largest financial institution. His office is on the second floor of the central branch
building on Main Street. The building itself is the architectural
leitmotif of the community. It is in the American alpine eclectic style, featuring modified A-frame, cut stone, exposed beams,
balconies, and flower boxes. Much of downtown Gaylord looks
like State Bank. It is a successful look, though somewhat anti-
septic; and if you happen to admire that kind of structural con-
formity, the man to thank for it is Harold Elgas.

In the next block west from State Bank, a historical marker
notes that the town was first settled in the 1860s by loggers,
who named it in tribute to one Augustine Smith Gaylord, the
attorney for the railroad that hauled their sawlogs off to
Saginaw. All of the north was lumberland then, mostly virgin
white pine. Cork pine, they called it. One giant tree, felled
nearby and shipped to Chicago, is said to have yielded fourteen
thousand board feet. The loggers worked fast; so fast, in fact,
that by the last decade of the century, when State Bank was
founded, all the cork pine was gone. Old-timers say it was such
a scalping you could stand on a stump south of town and see
clear to Grayling, twenty-eight miles away.

Through bust and boom, the people of Gaylord relied on the harvest of one natural resource or another. After the pines fell, so did the hardwoods, for tenpins and shoe lasts. Then, like other woods towns in the north, Gaylord went shabby. Storefronts began to sag along Main Street. People from Down Below passed through with closed eyes, hurrying toward new resorts on Lake Michigan, though some stopped to float a trout fly in springtime on the Pigeon, or to stalk an acorn-fattened buck in the fall. That was another kind of harvest, and for a long time it helped to keep the poor town in one piece. A buck pole was raised above Main Street each November. You could tell by its looks that Gaylord was a hunting man's town.

Harold Elgas came to Gaylord and its State Bank from his hometown of Cadillac in 1959. Already, a kind of municipal rigor mortis had begun to set in. There was talk of an interstate highway bypassing town—a bypass such that Down Below types would not even have to close their eyes, since they would whip right through at sixty miles an hour. On Main Street, stores were not only sagging; fifteen of them were tumbledown vacant. It was a piece of work cut out for Harold Elgas. Over the next decade, as president of the bank and chief factotum of the chamber of commerce and a new industrial development corporation, Elgas would mastermind the downtown renewal, the alpinization of skid row, and lure to town such major employers as Higgins Industries, Mayfair Plastics, and Champion International, whose annual production of sixteen-inch particle board (the banker proudly tells you) could stretch from New York to Los Angeles to Miami and home to Gaylord. The particle board is made of aspen, which regenerates rapidly in northern Michigan wherever oak, maple, and pine are no longer the dominant tree species. Thus does one harvest help to beget another. After clear-cutting, aspen stands provide fine browse for white-tailed deer.

There was yet another factor, beyond industrial development and flower-box cosmetics, in the greening of Gaylord. There was a sudden lust for north country recreations. People from Down Below would still whip right through on their way to the lakeshore pleasures of Petoskey and Harbor Springs, but now increasing numbers would stop here to pursue such land-locked diversions as golf (six courses), downhill and cross-country skiing (annual snowfalls exceeding 150 inches), fall foliage touring (colors comparable to northern New England's), and stalking the delectable morel mushroom (which sprouts from the forest floor in springtime profusion and is said to attract as many tourists as any other single quarry, activity, or event). Participation in these "quiet sports," as they are called in the north to distinguish them from the blood sports of hunting and fishing, has become the basis for big business in Otsego County, of which Gaylord is the seat. Such activities generate more than $30 million of annual income and provide at least one job of every five available in the county. And Harold Elgas is not un-aware of the benefits.

"The quiet sports bring greater returns to the community," Elgas told me in his office one afternoon. "Hunting is so different now. The men come up in campers, or to camps, with groceries from home, and they buy only gas."

I asked the banker how he felt about hunting now that he no longer went out himself after deer, now that he perceived it as being so different.

"It's not how *I* feel," he said. "It's the way people's attitudes are changing. Gaylord's becoming a real city. It's no longer a logging town."

"And people in a real city don't want to see deer hanging from a buck pole on Main Street?"

"They used to," said Elgas. "We haven't had a meat pole here for a number of years. People still hunt, though. If anyone at the bank wants to go out Opening Day, he gets the day off." Then Elgas told me about his two daughters.

"I know about daughters," I said. "They can get to you."

"Mine watched TV," Elgas said. "They got the idea every deer is named Bambi. And I began to wonder what is sport and what isn't."

"What did you decide?"

"I didn't," he said. "I only wish sometimes that someone would invent a camera shaped exactly like a gun. You take it into the woods, snap it to your shoulder, and pull the trigger.

Then you go home with a picture of the telescopic cross hairs on the deer exactly where the bullet would have hit him, if it was real."

Sitting in his office above Main Street, I tried to imagine Elgas in the woods on Opening Day with a .30/06 single-reflex bolt-action camera, manufactured not by Winchester or Remington but by Nikon or Kodak. Then I thought of all the bored men on the line in Flint, bolting Buicks together, and the men right here at Champion International, pressing particles into boards, and also bored, and I wondered if they would ever feel as comfortable—as released—with Nikon's .30/06 as they clearly are with Remington's. Still, as Elgas was saying, attitudes were changing fast, lumberland was getting to be more like the city, and, to top it off, there were all these new big-spending tourists in the woods, bloodlessly harvesting morels.

Bob Strong had not got his deer yet when I met him at noon of Opening Day at the DNR area office north of Atlanta. Neither had the resident biologist, Tom Carlson. But the two of them had just come in with someone else's deer. It was an eight-month-old fawn, shot through the hindquarters and left in the woods to be found and reported by another hunter. "It's hard for a man to admit a mistake," Strong said. "Especially one that's as pretty as this."

There had been a lot of shooting in the morning where Carlson had staked himself out, a hundred shots in the first hour. But neither biologist had seen many hunters with tagged deer. Possibly the lucky ones were taking their time hauling the carcasses out to the roads. Possibly they were trying not to become statistics in the seasonal summary of fatal coronary attacks. And it had been a slow morning as well at the buck pole in Atlanta. Now, Strong would peel off to check some camps near Lewiston, while Carlson and I would drive into Thunder Bay River State Forest. Driving, we talked about deer.

It is, this graceful ungulate with the raised tail like a flag of surrender, the predominant game animal not only of Michigan but of North America. Found in every state except Alaska and

Hawaii and possibly Utah, the whitetail ranges north into much of boreal Canada and south through Latin lands almost to the near side of the Amazon River. Though I did not hear Carlson himself on the subject, wildlife biologists like to speculate that the whitetail now numbers twelve million in the United States, many more than were present when Christopher Columbus hove to off Caribbean shores. There were, of course, no college-trained wildlife biologists in those days, and even if there had been, the only tallywhacker then available was the abacus; so we cannot know for certain that a population of fewer than twelve million deer was the case. But it is a likely case, given the forest primeval's proven inhospitality to wildlife in general and browser-grazers in particular. Whatever the animal's pre-Columbian numbers, they were surely sufficient even then to assure the whitetail of a certain preeminence—namely, as a primary source of protein and clothing among high-cheeked Algonquian hunters, the people of the deer.

Whitetails and pennyskin bow hunters had already struck a pretty good balance in North America over preceding hundreds, possibly thousands, of years. Cougars, wolves, and bobcats figured to some extent in the negative balance, and on the positive side of it was the ancient people's practice of putting the torch here and there to the forest to provide better browse in the resulting clearings. As European settlers pressed inland, the point men and flankers themselves became people of the deer. Their buckskin shirts and leggings were as much the sartorial symbols of the old frontier as their wolfskin caps. But the scouts were followed by farmers, who axed out new clearings. Into them the farmers led cows and sheep and goats and pigs until such time as almost everyone in America, including the high-cheeked ones, had to be counted out as people of the deer, for now they were beef eaters, cow killers, and it was no longer necessary to slaughter deer as well in order to stay alive.

In historic times in Michigan, the whitetail experienced boom or bust in response to changing uses of the land by humans and cyclical trends in the weather; and, to be sure, before biologists began to understand the dynamics of wildlife populations, in response to too much or too little pressure by blue-eyed beef-eating gun hunters. There were high times for the herd in the slash-covered clearings after the cork pines fell, after the hardwoods were toppled for tenpins; and higher times yet when the farmers moved in and planted the clearings to corn. But there were low times when farmers could not pay their taxes, when the banks foreclosed, and the cornfields reverted to runaway birch and to jack pine.

"The herd was pretty low in the late sixties," Carlson was saying as we drove south from Atlanta. "But then we had two seasons, seventy-one and seventy-two, when you could take bucks only, no specials on does, and five easy winters in a row. That was good. Last winter wasn't good. Deep snow and subzero. They say the one coming up won't be good either. That's the way it goes with deer. That's why our habitat work's so important."

Bob Strong had already told me about the habitat work. In Michigan, he explained, one dollar and fifty cents from every deer license fee is allocated to deer management. It adds up to more than one million dollars a year, and most of it goes into timber cutting, brush clearing, and the planting of winter rye. Winter rye is especially useful to whitetails in early spring, before the native forbs and grasses come into their own. In some areas, rye purchased by license money is what saves the yearling from starvation in April so that it may die in the notch of a gunsight come fall.

Knowing the age of a deer killed in either fashion is important to Bob Strong and Tom Carlson, and to their department. It is so important to the management function that both biologists spend a good part of each hunting season prying open the jaws of dead whitetails and peering into their mouths to ascertain age by the wear and tear on the teeth therein. Nearly all of the deer taken in District 5 are yearlings and two-and-a-half-year-olds. At Greasy Creek in Thunder Bay River State Forest, Carlson and I came upon a party of five hunters from the Saginaw–Bay City area. They had three bucks strung up in a grove of birch trees. The hunters stood in a semicircle, with folded arms, and solemnly watched as Carlson looked into the mouths of the whitetails. When he was finished, he turned to them and said, "Not a one over two and a half."

"See there," said one of the hunters. "They just don't live very long in Michigan, do they?"

Then the sound of five quick rifle shots came to us through the darkening woods. I looked in that direction and saw the new moon—a harvest moon—hanging low and yellow in the treetops.

On my way back to Gaylord I stopped by the buck pole in Atlanta. A dozen whitetails were hanging there now, and a fine-looking ten-point buck had just been added to the lineup. Its owner was a tall young man with sideburns and soft eyes. He sat tensely on the tailgate of his vehicle with one boot propped up on an Indiana license plate. It seemed for a while that he could not take his eyes off the antlers of the deer. Then a small sevenish sort of girl stepped from the crowd that had gathered in the parking lot and placed her hands quickly on the back of the ten-point buck. The girl wore an orange jacket. Taking her hands from the deer and placing them in the pockets of her jacket, she turned to the hunter from Indiana.

"Why do you kill it?" she asked.

The hunter appeared to be stunned by the question. He looked from the face of the girl to the tines of the buck, then back to the girl. Finally, he said to her, "I kill it because there are too many of them. Because if I don't, it will starve."

The sevenish sort of girl stood there with her hands in her orange pockets. Watching her, I got the feeling that she had heard that one before.

Hunting Hypotheses

Twice a decade, the U.S. Fish and Wildlife Service conducts a telephone and mailed-questionnaire survey from which it extrapolates a statistical profile of hunting in America. The survey seeks to discover how many people hunt, how often they hunt, and how much money they spend in the process of going afield. One suspects the results may be comforting to those who would defend hunting from its critics on socioeconomic grounds. Last time around, the Service discovered that there were 20.6 million hunters; that the ratio of hunters, by sex, to total population was 21 out of 100 men and 2 out of 100 women; that the hunter's average household income was $14,700; that 56 percent reside in urban areas; that deer hunting accounted for the greatest number of days of participation in a single year (103 million), followed by rabbit hunting (88 million days), squirrel hunting (69 million days), and quail hunting (47 million days); and that hunters in the year of the survey and in the course of hunting spent $1.2 billion on food and drink, $1.8 billion on equipment, and $2.1 billion on transportation. The survey, in fact, reveals everything you ever wanted to know about hunting but for the one thing you may be afraid to ask: Why in this day and age do 20.6 million Americans still want to hunt?

Part of fearing the question is knowing there may be 20.6 million different answers, given the hunter's individuality; and knowing, too, that most of the answers would be imprecise, given the record of hunters' rationalizations over the years. Possibly the most profoundly honest explanation I ever heard was: "I hunt because it is something I like to do." No fooling around on that one.

Yet so much of the motivational rhetoric is defensive and wincing. I have talked with hunters from every region of the nation and sooner than later there is one in every crowd who attempts to convince me that hunting is a public service to wild animals. I hear the young man of sideburns and soft eyes telling the little girl in Michigan that he kills the buck in order to spare it the agony of winter starvation. He might have added, as many do, that nature is remorselessly cruel. I perceive brigades of orangemen as angels of mercy in the November woods, thwarting nature's bitchy ways with 170-grain softpoint bullets.

Do they really believe it? I suppose some hunters do. Being

kind to animals with rifle or shotgun is one of the articles of
faith of the hook-and-bullet press, though individual editors
know better. Surely, if one wishes to look at it anthropomor-
phically, nature *is* cruel. Animals do die of disease and starvation, especially when their numbers exceed the carrying capacity of their habitat; or, more to the point, when their numbers
are manipulated to exceed that capacity. Therefore, it is rea-
soned, since such quadrupedal predators as wolves and cougars
are no longer present to bring the game herd into balance, and
since in any event the bullet is more merciful than the fang, it is
left to the hunting man to provide the full and necessary measure of predation. Hunting man must arise in the cold before
dawn, dress and arm himself expensively, travel long miles into
the country, trudge steeply up hill and down vale, shoot unerr-
ingly, immerse hands and forearms in the steaming guts of the
fallen beast, then wrestle the meat all the way home to the
freezer. And all of this, for what? For the sake of the animal?
For the advancement of wildlife euthanasia? It hardly seems
possible. And it is not.

Most hunters do not really know why they hunt, and some
probably would not want to know if it ever occurred to them to
wonder. The writer John Madson and his colleague Ed Ko-
zicky once observed in a pamphlet for the Winchester Arms Division of the Olin Corporation that "hunting is a complex affair with roots too deep to be pulled up and examined. If a
hunter is asked to explain his sport, he can no more rationalize
hunting than he can describe emotion." Still, scholars and investigators have pursued the question relentlessly over the
years, emerging from their studies with one motive or another
quantified as the core root. Thus, from Wisconsin and Colorado one ascertains that it is a love of the outdoors that most
strongly attracts the hunter to his sport, while from Maryland,
at least among deer hunters there, comes word that suspense
and challenge are the most significant attractions. Other studies find that companionship—the camaraderie of the group—is
a value of importance equal to or greater than the adrenal high
of the hunt itself. Yet how easily these motive values can be
separated from the act of hunting. Take away hunting, and one

can still love the outdoors, encounter challenge there, and enjoy the company of good friends. So, why do men hunt?

Among the most active researchers delving into the motives of the American hunter is Stephen R. Kellert, a behavioral scientist at the Yale School of Forestry and Environmental Studies in New Haven, Connecticut. Kellert on this Opening Day had come out to northern Michigan, as I had, to prowl the back roads and buck-pole places, talking with hunters and game officials. We had planned informally to meet in the field; perhaps too informally, for we missed each other in Lewiston by hours and would miss each other again by a day down near Baldwin, where I would be heading at the end of the week. I was doubly disappointed, being an admirer of Kellert and his work. At the same time, I think I may have felt a measure of relief. For his most recent efforts to examine American attitudes toward wildlife, Kellert had taken a couple of vicious raps from knee-jerk scriveners of the sporting press, and I wasn't all that sure I wanted to be caught with him alone on a game trail in Michigan. Not that any hunter would consider an orange-breasted sociologist fair game, though open season on the species might not be unlikely in one or two other states I know.

Stephen Kellert had not set out specifically to discover why men hunt, or even to study hunters as a special group. When he began his work in 1973, under contract to the U.S. Fish and Wildlife Service, his aim was to construct a typology of attitudes toward wild and domestic animals that might reflect the full spectrum of human motives for getting involved in animal-related activities. Hunting, of course, was one such activity, but so was bird watching, and ownership of pets and attendance at rodeos and membership in animal welfare organizations. Kellert wanted to discover how various types perceive animals and possibly how their attitudes might be distributed throughout the U.S. population as a whole.

The researcher started with sixty-five carefully selected individuals representing every region of the country, every kind of relevant institution, and every point of view. There were intensive open-ended interviews. From them, he was able to identify seven basic attitudes toward animal and wildlife resources. Not all of the attitudes were mutually exclusive, so that typically a number of them could be held in varying degree by the same person. Nonetheless, one basic attitude or another would generally dominate an individual's perception of the animal world.

According to the Kellert typology, there is an individual who is said to be naturalistic. He or she has a strong attraction to wildlife (pets being regarded as inferior beasts) and to the outdoors. The greatest satisfaction is in direct, personal contact with wild places and things, and one is not above seeking such contact as an escape from the tick-tock assembly lines of urban life.

The second type is more intellectual and detached about the natural environment, which he tends to view as a system of interdependent parts. Affection for habitat is likely to be stronger than for a species that occupies the habitat, as one might favor the whole over any one of its parts. Kellert defines this type as one who is basically ecologistic. It is a type that tends to run on the scarce side of rare.

Humanistic and moralistic types, the third and fourth categories, are not at all rare. The former tends to personify the individual animal, more often a pet than a wild one, so that empathy for Rover or Tabby is extended to creatures less familiar. The other type is concerned for the welfare of all animals, and, standing on ethical principles, opposes activities that result in the death or exploitation of any wild beast. Both types run plentifully through the ranks of anti-hunting organizations.

The fifth character in Kellert's cast is the utilitarian who views animals as providers of material benefit to humans. The sixth is one who, taking a leaf from the Book of Genesis, would have dominion over the beasts of the earth, thereby exercising a sense of superiority and competitive skills. Hunters galore turn up in either role. And finally there is a character described by Kellert as negativistic, a person largely alienated from the natural world and desirous of avoiding animals out of fear, superstition, indifference, or dislike. These, then, are the basic seven.

Actually, Kellert came up with two more types—the aesthetic and the scientific—but neither is of relevance to the question of what may or may not motivate men to the hunt.

Having established a pattern of identifiable attitudes, Kellert structured a questionnaire to be administered by the Gallup Organization to a random sample of Americans. In personal interviews lasting forty-five minutes, more than five hundred respondents were queried on their reaction to wildlife and the natural world, their knowledge of animals, their social and demographic characteristics, their animal-related activities. Kellert found that hunting could not be counted as a single activity. Among those who qualified as past or present hunters (37 percent of the national sample), there were conflicting and diverse perceptions. Some hunting types seemed to have more in common with bird watchers than with bang-away bird shooters. Others came on like U-boat commanders upping their periscopes at Noah's Ark. It seemed "simplistic and even foolish to discuss hunters as a whole," Kellert admitted in one interim paper. So, wisely, he eschewed the single-image hunter and concentrated instead on the composite faces of three: the meat hunter, the recreation hunter, and the nature hunter.

Anthropologists inform us that members of our family, the Hominidae, have been meat hunters for at least half a million years and maybe even two million years. And that—a hundred thousand generations within the outside guess—is a far piece of time over which to hone the racial appetite for flesh. There is no clear evidence that either *Homo erectus* or Neanderthal hunted woolly and fearsome game in order to indulge a personal attraction to the great outdoors or to seek diversion from the tedium of a dark and voiceless cave. They hunted in order to eat; and eating, survived.

Preceding *erectus* were a couple of pre-humans known as *Ramapithecus* and *Australopithecus*. The latter no doubt slew a small animal now and then, thereby qualifying as a meat hunter, too, and explaining why small canine teeth developed beside the molars it may have inherited from *Ramapithecus*. For its part, which came earlier, *Ramapithecus* was an absolute bust as a meat hunter. Its jaw lacked incisors and it likely grubbed for bulbs and grass stems on open savannas. So much for our last-known vegetarian missing link. At this end of the evolutionary time frame, one encounters a first cousin, Cro-Magnon, dentured in a modern sort of way, though almost wholly carnivorous since caribou and mastodon fared better than berries at the tundra edge of the great Würm ice.

All of which accounts for more than 99 percent of Hominidae's tenure on the planet. In the fraction left over, the Neolithic farmer begets the nuclear agribusinessman, who sits on the school board, approving the admissible texts. And the texts say that civilization dawned on the man with a hoe. The older way is now so easy to forget.

Yet we are beseeched not to forget. In his writings, the Spanish philosopher José Ortega y Gasset, hunting man's most eloquent interpreter, warns us not to forget that once we were beasts. Look to our carnivore's fangs for evidence, he says, though of course there are vegetarian's molars as well. In fact, writes Ortega y Gasset, man "combines the two extreme conditions of the mammal, and therefore he goes through life vacillating between being a sheep and being a tiger." In America, I suspect, the sheep clearly have it.

Of the three basic hunting types examined in Stephen Kellert's study, the meat hunter loomed largest. Nearly half who had hunted within the past five years said that their primary reason for so doing was to obtain provender for the table. As a group, meat hunters tended to include a disproportionate number of people who were over sixty-five, earned less than six thousand dollars a year, and had been raised or lived presently in a rural area. They scored high on the utilitarian scale, especially insofar as that attitude was reflected in responses to questions of harvesting game, trapping for profit, and controlling predators. "Deer have to be harvested," one respondent told his interviewer. "It's not a whole lot different than going into the field and harvesting apples every year. You cultivate animals for what their purpose is, the same as cultivating a crop." I hear an agrarian echo there and suddenly I wonder why it is that the tiger begins to sound like the sheep.

Kellert concedes that other investigators have questioned the finding of so large a percentage of meat hunters in a single sample. Other surveys, both regional and state by state, have turned up scant evidence that wild game is anything more than an occasional and unimportant source of food in the hunter's household, whatever the high degree of ritual appreciation. Kellert's sample, however, was not confined to licensed hunters, as the other studies were. In most states, restricting the sample to licensed hunters automatically excludes senior citizens and rural landowners, the two hunting subgroups most likely to shoot primarily for the pot.

Chances are that shooting for the pot is more symbolic than economic. A case could be made here and there for modified subsistence life styles, for hunting and gathering in ways altogether ancient but for the precision rifle and the gasoline engine, at least as such ways are pursued by recluse Appalachian mountaineers and Native Americans roundabout Alaska. But that is something apart from Kellert's findings. His meat hunters for the most part could subsist on McDonald's hamburgers if they had to. They choose instead to supplement the burger with venison and goose. They are surrogate Pilgrims homeward to Plymouth, Kentuckians down from the Cumberland Gap. They are, as Kellert and others perceive them, unconsciously reenacting the last tableau of the American frontier tradition. They are coming home from the wilderness with the fat of the land in one hand and their self-reliance in the other.

And possibly, too, some self-professed meat hunters are only fooling themselves and the pollsters in the interest of making love, not war. Everyone loves a provider. Even Cleveland Amory, founding father of the Fund for Animals, says he can find no fault with the man who hunts in order to eat. But God help the man who hunts in order to sport.

· · ·

There is some confusion over the word "sport." Perhaps it has too many meanings, for my dictionary gives it twenty-six listings, starting with the noun defined as an "athletic activity." The third entry refers to a diversion, a recreation; the eighth, to "sportsman," which is defined elsewhere as one who engages in some open-air sport, such as hunting or fishing, and who exhibits qualities of fairness, courtesy, and good humor. The seventeenth definition is of a verb, "to play, frolic, or gambol, as a child or animal." Each of these definitions reflects in its own way an aspect of hunting. If we take away diversion, which covers a multitude of graces and sins, we are left with three different perspectives on what sport hunting in America is all about. The athletic perspective is Stephen Kellert's, based on behavioral research. The well-tempered-sportsman perspective is that of the hunter himself, based on soul-searching talks with the mirror on his wall. And the playful-child perspective is one that is shared, but for different reasons, by anti-hunters as well as some pro-hunters who believe there is nothing craven or inhuman in having one helluva childish good time, even at the expense of an animal's life.

The concept of play goes a long way back, even to the harder times of the Pleistocene. "It was in the play of words that abstractions developed," observed the Canadian biologist C. H. D. Clarke, "and many of these had their origin in the chase." In his classic essay "Autumn Thoughts of a Hunter," Clarke noted that with abstractions the world of make-believe assimilated the business of reality, giving rise to the "divine games" of magic, ritual, religion, and the law. And even while the chase was still the chief business of survival, "hunting became a game to be played according to the rules, and man would sooner fail in his hunt than succeed by breaking the magic circle."

By some scholarly hindsight accounts, fun and games went out of fashion when men put away their spears and took hoes to the field. Where the free hunter had resembled the sprightly stag, the dour farmer soon mirrored the beast of burden. The joy of sex became the labor of procreation, if only to keep the bunkhouses filled. There was a plague for all seasons. In Cromwellian England, bear baiting was outlawed—not, according to Clarke, because the Puritans believed it gave pain to the bear "but because it gave pleasure to the spectators." From Urals to Alps, the privilege of hunting was denied to the peasants; came the revolutions, the first fences to fall were the ones around the noblemen's deer parks. In America, after the Civil War, eastern gentry hunted for "sport"; society branded them ne'er-do-wells. Workers in France were chastised in the press—having won a reduction of the workday, they "wasted" their newfound leisure by the Seine, fishing with cane poles. . . . "Little boys," the Friend of Animals is saying in my ear. "Little boys who never grow up."

"But if certain things take me back to my childhood and I enjoy it that way," says a hunter in Indiana, "there's nothing wrong with that. Is there?" And I tell him: Nothing wrong with that at all. He smiles, but I do not think he believes me. Maybe he does not even believe himself.

Few hunters perceive themselves as joyful players of the game. Most have been conditioned, by mentors and media, to something more serious. They are sportsmen. They used to belong to rod-and-gun clubs but now they belong to sportsmen's clubs. Fairness, courtesy, and good temper are the rules of the house. Membership is open to good conservationists only, and good conservationists take their sport seriously. What is conservation? Conservation is the wise use of natural resources. It is growing trees in order to chop them down. It is chopping them down in order to grow deer. It is growing deer in order to shoot them down. It is shooting them down in order to spare them a ghastly death. And it is paying special fees and excise taxes that, according to the National Shooting Sports Foundation of Riverside, Connecticut, in large part have "kept America as green as it is today." This is the sportsman; color him green, over the orange. He believes in himself absolutely.

The joyful player and the conservationist-sportsman are breeds apart from the sport hunter Stephen Kellert encountered on the computer printouts of his behavioral study. To avoid confusion, Kellert renamed his subjects dominionistic/sport hunters, after the high scores they attained on that attitude scale. For brevity I shall rename them once again, as recreation hunters.

Though outnumbered by the meat hunters, this group comprised 38.5 percent of those who had hunted in the past five years. It was a more socially diverse group, with slight tendencies toward urban residence and prior service in the armed forces. On the whole, the recreation hunters did not emerge either as great outdoorsmen or as middling conservationists. They reported little activity in the backpacking or bird-watching areas. They scored close to rock bottom in a knowledge-of-animals test; their ignorance of natural history and wildlife biology was exceeded, among major activity groups, only by anti-hunters. Competition and mastery over animals, Kellert observed, "in the context of a sporting contest, appeared to be the most salient motivational elements of [their] interest in the hunting activity." They viewed wilderness, in response to one question, as "an obstacle to overcome." They were negativistic, showing a lack of affection for animals in their responses to questions. Relative to other activity groups, they tended to regard most wildlife as dangerous and cats in particular as vicious, to report less desire for close contact with animals, to support limitations on "undesirable" animals, and to reject the notion of pets as a major satisfaction in life. The successful hunt, noted Kellert, "was one in which the animal as a target provided opportunities for revealing special capabilities." There was a certain concern with prowess and masculinity— "not in the narrow sense of asserting one's sexual virility, but more as a means to express a broader interest in displays of aggressiveness, strength, courage, boldness, physical endurance, and hardiness." In short, the hunter as Jock.

Proportionately, Kellert did not encounter in his study a great number of nature hunters, so called because of their high scores on the naturalistic attitude scale. Only about 17 percent of the respondents qualified in this category. Compared with individuals in the other two hunting groups, a member of this one was more likely to be under thirty, to be college-educated, to have a higher income, to know more about animals, to have greater involvement in backpacking and camping activities, and to hunt more often. There was a desire to participate intensely in nature, to be directly involved with wild creatures in their natural habitats. Nature hunters, noted Kellert, viewed themselves as predators and relished the role for the awareness of natural phenomena it forced upon them. In one report, Kellert illustrated this point with a quotation from Ortega y Gasset: "When one is hunting, the air has another, more exquisite feel as it glides over the skin or enters the lungs; the rocks acquire a more expressive physiognomy, and the vegetation becomes loaded with meaning. All this is due to the fact that the hunter, while he advances or waits crouching, feels tied through the earth to the animal he pursues."

In such a relationship, according to Kellert, this rarest of hunters perceives his prey with "affection, respect, and, at times, even reverence." He is therefore confronted with "the paradox of inflicting violence" on a world he admires and cherishes. He, alone among hunting types, is compelled to rationalize the death of the animal.

One of the most plausible examinations of the hunting paradox was advanced some twenty years ago by Paul Shepard, Jr., the human ecologist, in his essay "A Theory of the Value of Hunting." Noting that advocates of hunting were being figuratively slaughtered by articulate opponents, and that these critics had "an accusing finger on the morality of the act of killing," Shepard urged that the old hairy-chest explanations, which might have appealed to Teddy Roosevelt or Ernest Hemingway, be junked. "The answer," he wrote, "is not a matter of forcing the admission that we are all human bipedal carnivorous mammals, damned to kill, but consists in showing . . . that the superb human mind operates in subtle ways in the search for an equilibrium between the polarities of nature and God. To share in life is to participate in a traffic of energy and materials the ultimate origin of which is a mystery, but which has its immediate source in the bodies of plants and other animals. As a society, we may be in danger of losing sight of this fact. It is kept most vividly before us in hunting."

Shepard then went on to suggest that "it is only a biased opinion that death is the worst of natural events." Such a view, he wrote, "ignores the adaptive role of early death in most animal populations" and "presumes naïvely that the landscape is a room-like collection of animated furniture."

Most of Stephen Kellert's nature hunters would have to agree with Shepard's perspective on the death of animals. They might agree as well with Durward L. Allen, the noted authority on predator-prey relationships, whose view is downright impassive. "The reality," said Allen in a personal interview, "is that you've got to have mass production and mass slaughter, or the whole thing is going to pot. Life and death are the stock in trade of nature. There's no use sobbing about it, because we're all a part of it. It is not a matter of an animal being killed. The issue is *when* it's going to be killed. . . . A wolf that tears into the anal region of a moose and gets one tooth into the coelomic cavity may be inoculating it with a pathogen that will cause peritonitis. And that moose will stand around and be killed by only one or two wolves ten days later. This all is a part of the system. Nature deals in unlimited time. And the whole thing is eminently respectable. Why, there isn't anything in nature that isn't respectable, even though some of us are small enough to get murderous with mosquitoes and blackflies."

Thinking later about all these examinations and explanations, I realized there was nothing whatsoever clear-cut about the American hunter and why he hunts. And since I had missed Stephen Kellert in Michigan during the deer season, I decided to telephone him in Connecticut to compare notes when I got home. I told him I had encountered—at the edge of the woods around Gaylord, Atlanta, and Lewiston—a few meaty utilitarians and a diverting surfeit of dominionistic sports.

Kellert wanted to know about the other kind.

"If you mean your nature hunters," I told him, "they must

have been hiding. You're talking about an endangered species. I met maybe two or three, and I guess you already know about one of them."

"Who's that?" Kellert asked.

I said, "A hunter named Mummert."

Something for Pride

Douglas Mummert lives with his wife and two children in a home off Coger Road just outside Gaylord, Michigan. He is a regional sales representative and driver for the Peet Packing Company of Chesaning, Down Below; and on this morning of the second day of deer season, a large refrigerator truck is parked in his driveway near the wire pens where his Walker hounds sit, waiting. Douglas Mummert is also a hunter. He is a hunter with scant use for snowmobilers, trail-bikers, four-wheelers, fancy-pants gadgeteers, New York television producers, Pigeon River oil drillers, and orange-capped dilettantes. Mummert would scrap them all if he had his way—his preferred way being afoot, running, with the baying of hounds up ahead somewhere in the sultry season for bear, or stalking alone over fallen leaves in the month of the deer, with a rifle and no dogs and a wind from the Soo bearing the scent of blue ice and a promise of snow, later on, for tracking. But today Mummert won't be having his way. Nowadays, a hunter cannot live by the chase alone, at least not in Michigan. Nowadays, with a wife and two children in the house and dogs in the pens, a hunter—this hunter, anyway—must arise in the cold before dawn, dress himself in a white butcher's coat, and, at the wheel of a big silver truck, travel long miles to the supermarkets and party shops of Bellaire and Mancelona and Kalkaska and Grayling with eight thousand pounds of Playtime frankfurters, Vienna bulk sausage, kielbasa, Braunschweiger, bologna, cooked ham, bacon squares, pork loins, and Kenosha beef. "Farmer Peet's People Pleasin' Meats," it says right here on the side of the truck. I swing up into the cab beside Mummert and we are on our way.

We are traveling west through big-barn country where potatoes and milk cows do well enough to supplement the protein imports from Farmer Peet's and other places Down Below. Mummert himself once thought of farming in this country, but not for long. In the 1950s, as he recalls, there wasn't enough money in north Michigan farming "to stuff in your ear." Nevertheless, one uncle managed to do it. Mummert himself grew up in Petoskey, where his father worked for twenty-five years at the cement factory. What with four children to feed, the father worked hard at cement and there was never much time left over for hunting. In Petoskey, then as now a city much larger than Gaylord, one does not come home tired from work through the front door and, grabbing a rifle, step out through the back into huntable woods. It's possible at Brutus, over near Burt Lake, where the uncle had his farm and young Mummert took learning from him in the ways of the woods and of hunting. Douglas's first hound was a beagle called Frankie. They ran rabbits together. Then, for fifty dollars, including the freight, the boy imported a Walker from Calloway County, Kentucky, and, having named it Cal, ran coyotes all over Emmet County. "Working with dogs," Mummert says now with an affirmative wag of the head, "I just love it. Turn 'em loose, and I go. I just keep going. I can't quit. And guess I never will."

The silver truck rolls on through the sand hills of Antrim County, heading for Dingman's Market in Bellaire, where the butcher is waiting for his order of pork shoulders and boneless Australian beef. I watch Mummert at the wheel. All right. He may be a hunter, but he does not look to me like any jack-pine savage. For a man of middle years and tough conditioning, his features seem almost too delicate: high cheekbones accentuating the ivory smoothness of his skin, slender wrists, quick lucid eyes. The eyes catch my scrutinizing stare and deflect it. "I know at least one thing for sure," he says. "A man needs something to give him pride. Hunting can do that for you. It does it for me. It puts me in an environment I like. I love to walk the woods. Getting deeper in it, though, something gets pumped up in me. Not just pride. The adrenaline. It flows. It's a good feeling."

Mummert moved to Gaylord in 1960 to take the job he holds with Peet Packing. He works strictly on commission, calling on accounts west of I-75 two days a week, and on those east of the interstate, in such towns as Atlanta and Lewiston, twice a week also. This leaves three days for walking the woods and running the hounds. In addition, there are four weeks of vacation. One is taken in the spring, for cutting and splitting the twelve cords his Ashley wood stove will consume the following winter off Coger Road. A second week is taken for fishing. And the final two weeks are reserved for fall hunting, mostly for bear on the Upper Peninsula. With wood for heat, with fish and wild game for part of the protein budget, with home-grown cabbages and potatoes wintered in the root cellar, Mummert says he is trying to set his family up so that eventually it might function on a self-sufficient basis. "Or as close to self-sufficient as we can get," he adds. "That would be something else, for getting pride."

Mummert parks the truck in back of Dingman's Market and we unload boxes of pork and beef and stack them on a dolly. Mummert is checking his order pad. There is a man in blaze orange hunting clothes coming our way. An older man. He is weaving. He is holding a deer's tail in one hand and a spike horn in the other. The neck of a whiskey bottle protrudes from a pocket of his jacket. He wants to tell us something but we cannot understand what he is saying. Mummert has the grim look of a curbside traveler sidestepping dog-doo. We push the dolly inside. The butcher explains. It is only Pete, the local character. The butcher tells us that Pete, drinking, imagines the craziest things. For example, ever since yesterday afternoon, Pete has been going around with the deer tail and the spike horn telling anyone who can understand him that his was the first buck taken out of Bellaire. "And a few years back," the butcher recalls, "Pete had a buck in a wheelbarrow on Main Street on Opening Day. Where he gets the deer or the deer tail sure beats me. But they're not his animals. They just couldn't be."

Mummert seems anxious to get back on the road. He takes a new order from the butcher and we go out to the truck. After a long while of silence on the road to Torch Lake, Mummert at last says, "Now that's just tailor-made, isn't it?"

"Isn't what?"

"The drunk hunter with a deer tail dripping blood."

"But he's not for real. He's a clown."

"It doesn't matter," says Mummert. "That's the impression people get, that some people *want* to get. There are too many Petes out there, real and unreal. Now, if Irv Drasnin could get hold of that one, there'd be another massacre for sure."

I tell Mummert not to worry, since a second massacre couldn't possibly be any worse than the first one.

Irving Drasnin is the television producer who, in 1975, brought to the American public through "CBS Reports" a remarkable documentary film entitled *The Guns of Autumn.* I say remarkable, in that the film possibly stirred up as much prim concurrence and outraged dissent as any documentary produced since the passing of Edward R. Murrow. The program touched a nerve. It reached to the innards of a republic gutted by the dark memory of Vietnam and found part of the body politic a-twitch as never before over the prospect of deadly violence. And another part of the corpus was found a-twitch over something else: strong moves in the U.S. House of Representatives that year to restrict the private possession of arms. *The Guns of Autumn,* of course, had nothing directly to do with either Saigon or the Saturday Night Special, those being only code words in the vocabularies of people more concerned about happenings closer to home. In fact, the guns of CBS's autumn were the long guns of American hunters—guns shown being sighted, for the most part, not on the wild species most commonly taken, such as rabbits and squirrels and upland birds, but on game-ranch bison and exotic deer imported from abroad, and on black bears in Michigan, baited to the garbage dump or chased up a tree by Walker hounds. The bear chase was the *pièce de résistance* of the first half hour of the program, and it featured a hunter from Gaylord named Douglas Mummert.

In the cab of the truck, Mummert is talking now about *The Guns of Autumn* as we head for Torch Lake. He is apologizing for, as he puts it, crying in his beer, but all the same, after these several years, he is still angry. It was, he says, a misrepresentation of intent. They had come to him, these television people, saying they wanted to show the American hunting tradition as it truly was on the eve of the bicentennial. And since that was a good thing to show, he had allowed them to follow him into the woods of the Upper Peninsula, with his hounds and Ben, the younger son; and they hunted for three days until, finally, the dogs crossed a fresh scent and took off, baying, with Mummert behind them; and when the bear went up in the tree, Mummert's people did not kill it right off but obligingly waited for the camera crew's breathless arrival. In the woods, Mummert had spoken about the meaning of hunting and how he figured it had to build character and pride; but somehow in the editing process in New York City, that part of it fell in the cutting room, and what went into the can instead were phrases about hunters who sometimes "get into the juice a little bit" and why, after the bear is shot out of the tree, the hounds are turned loose for a good chew. As if the dead bear, in its own happy hunting ground, would ever know the difference.

Now we are approaching Alden on Torch Lake. Mummert says, "I know my ethics didn't appear to be proper the way they showed them on that program. But I hunt according to the rules and regulations that the DNR sets up for me. That's the way I presented myself to CBS. And they just cut me apart. They just made me out as a slob hunter."

"Slob" is a popular code word in its own right, especially when it is applied to hunters, as it so often is nowadays, and not always without reason. I cannot testify under oath as to whether or not the word can justly be applied to Doug Mummert. A lot of good people I trust say he has always been anything but; and having spent some time with him, though too much of it in a meat truck and too little afield, I am inclined to guess that Mummert probably stands about as far away from Slob Hunter as any man can get and still have hounds and guns and the lean, hungry look of the human carnivore. And besides, there are so many different kinds of slobs you would need a Stephen Kellert and the Gallup Organization to sort them all into their proper categories—violators such as jacklighters not being counted here since they are not slobs; they are criminals. Offhand I am thinking, with Mummert's help from the driver's seat, that there are four or five types of classic slobs whom everyone knows, such as the sign shooter, and the truculent trespasser who believes there is still a thing called the free hunt, and the daytime drunk with a loaded rifle, and the litterbug, hunters in general tending to be second only to off-road vehicular recreationists as the sloppiest slobs in the great out-of-doors. But we already know about these antisocial types.

For my own part, I am more concerned about the *social* types, who possibly should not be branded as bona fide slobs, for they are more to be pitied than scorned. I mean the road hunters. I mean the indolent ones in their orange jump suits and white space boots, waddling along the side of the road with sidelong glances of fear and loathing toward the terrible and unfamiliar woods; or, driving along that same road in search of a cluster of parked cars, and then timidly putting into the woods there, as if logic dictated that somehow there might be success as well as safety in numbers.

Some cynical observers of the road-hunting scene say you can tell how savvy and daring a man is by how many rolls of toilet paper he carries to mark his way in and out of the woods. The writer Bil Gilbert believes the phenomenon is strictly sar-torial. "That only the most prime sports can bear up for very far or very long under a sixty-pound Deer Hunt costume," he once observed in print, "may be the principal reason so many of them seem to be hunting closer and closer to open roads." And it is not all speculation and hearsay. In 1971, University of Michigan researcher Richard E. McNeil reported on a survey of several hundred hunters using a Roscommon County tract with sand roads running through it. McNeil found that 75 percent of the hunters acknowledged penetrating the forest no

more than a quarter mile from the nearest road, while 25 percent said they went up to half a mile. Lest the casual interpreter of that finding conclude that, in any event, one in four of
the hunters was a veritable Natty Bumppo, McNeil added:
"The author is certain the average hunter overestimates the
distance he travels in a straight line from the road."

Off a sand road in Lake County, Michigan, I once encountered a jump-suit hunter seated in a folding aluminum chair
with a .30/30 rifle across his lap. By off the road, I mean barely,
like five yards. The road ran alongside an electric power line, so
that the land was cleared of all brush and trees for thirty yards
on either side. The man had placed his chair on the downslope
of a hill. His field of fire was open, into a gully and up the other
side, for a distance equivalent, let us say, to four or five rolls of
toilet paper, unrolled. I stopped to chat, figuring he was lonely
and from Down Below. He was, and from Lansing. He looked
sad. I asked him what the matter was. He said he was dis-
couraged because the weather was turning cold and the chair,
with its plastic straps, was uncomfortable. And he wished that
more hunters were in the woods to chase a deer or two into
range along the power-line clearing. I asked him, then, how he
was with the .30/30, not to make small talk but because he
seemed to be holding the rifle on his lap in a curious way. "I
guess *I'm* pretty good," he said, looking down at the hands that
would have to do the shooting. "But maybe *it's* not. I just don't
know, 'cause I never shot it."

After Alden and Torch River comes the town of Mancelona,
Glen's supermarket and the IGA, four cases of smoked ham and
two of Kenosha beef. It is high noon. Mummert knows it is
high noon from the way he feels and the cant of the shadow
beside his truck. Mummert refuses to carry a timepiece. "I
won't be a slave to one," he says. "No, sir. I just won't have
anything to do with clocks."

Supermarkets occupy enormous spaces in northern Michigan. I suppose they do that everywhere; but here, in towns of
sparse hundreds or thousands of people, they seem to sprawl

out of all proportion to need, and one wonders how so many survive so handsomely. Mummert says it is all a measure of modern merchandising. The little mom-and-pop groceries cannot compete. They either convert to party shops or they go broke and fall through the cracks. We mull that over for a while, heading for Kalkaska. We mull merchandising and packaging and technology and how these things have changed not only the business of food but the business of pleasure outdoors, including hunting. And mulling that one, I recall what Aldo Leopold long ago had to say about the coming of the gadgeteer:

"He has draped the American outdoorsman with an infinity of contraptions, all offered as aids to self-reliance, hardihood, woodcraft, or marksmanship," wrote Leopold, "but too often functioning as substitutes for them. Gadgets fill the pockets, they dangle from neck and belt. The overflow fills the auto trunk, and also the trailer. Each item of outdoor equipment grows lighter and often better, but the aggregate poundage becomes tonnage.... The American sportsman is puzzled; he doesn't understand what is happening to him.... It has not dawned on him that outdoor recreations are essentially primitive, atavistic; that their value is a contrast value; that excessive mechanization destroys contrasts by moving the factory to the woods or to the marsh." As his end-case, Leopold asked us to consider the duck hunter who arrives at his blind in a steel boat with an outboard motor, who is warmed by canned heat, and who calls the flock to his composition decoys on a factory caller. As the birds approach, the hunter opens fire at seventy yards, "for his polychoke is set for infinity, and the advertisements have told him that Super-Z shells, and plenty of them, have a long reach." A pair of cripples "scale off to die elsewhere," and Leopold wondered if his end-case was truly hunting or "just feeding minks."

Leopold sounded that lament nearly forty years ago, long before the advent of the hunter in his all-terrain vehicle or snowmobile ("Those roarin' sons a bitches," says Mummert through clenched teeth), and longer yet before the angler in his carpeted bass boat with the fish-scanning sonar device. Now, alarms are being sounded all over the place. "Has anyone stopped to ask," wonders Daniel A. Poole, president of the Wildlife Management Institute, "what new technological developments the good Lord has hung on deer or elk or any other wildlife in these past decades to better equip them to cope with the technically augmented sportsman? Where does application of technology exceed the bounds of sportsmanship?" Poole has no absolute answer; neither did Aldo Leopold. Yet the hook-and-bullet press, the champion of good sportsmanship, is still as Leopold found it years ago—"billboard for the gadgeteer." One advertisement, cited by Poole, offers a shotgun sight for "the man who doesn't have time for long hours of practice. Mount it on a gun, zip into the field, get your birds, and be home in time for lunch."

"That's it exactly," Mummert is saying in the cab of the truck. "They're turn-on and turn-off and they're living by the clock. My mom wonders why, when I hunt with other guys, they're always the older ones, like Sarge Anderson. Well, just look at most of the younger ones. They're on that time schedule. They're always looking at their watches because they told their wives they'd be home for lunch."

Kalkaska is an oil town, if you can conceive of such a thing in northern Michigan. It lies just south of a ruler's edge placed diagonally across the north country from Manistee on Lake Michigan to Rogers City, on Huron. The edge defines one of the state's most promising oil- and gas-bearing geologic formations. Shell, Amoco, and a number of independent producers have wells in the area; Otsego County is said to be the second most active oil-producing county in the state. Part of the action is taking place in and around the Pigeon River Country. It is a circumstance that does not especially trouble some of the county's hunters. As for Doug Mummert, it sends him straight up a wall.

"Big Oil moves in and opens up country like that," says Mummert, taking his hands from the wheel in a gesture of palms-up surrender, "you just wouldn't believe the mess."

Mummert is president of the Pigeon River Country Association, which, with the West Michigan Environmental Action Committee, among other groups, opposes further drilling on state forest lands in the area. (The Michigan Supreme Court has since ordered a ban on oil exploration in the state forest, principally in the interest of protecting the elk herd.) Thus, Mummert says he finds himself "in bed with the environmentalists," a position considered highly compromising by some of his friends. In fact, a few members of the Northland Sportsmen's Club in Gaylord regard Mummert as if he were some kind of ecofreak hippie. These sports are not only untroubled by Big Oil's presence around the Pigeon Country, they are downright unhappy the presence isn't larger. After all, when oil comes, can roads be far behind? Mummert from time to time speaks out in favor of closing some roads already existing in the Pigeon Country. Some colleagues in the local club are not likely to second the motion. "What the hell are you trying to do, Mummert?" they wrathfully want to know. "Ruin our hunting?"

Kalkaska is behind us now, and we are heading east, for Grayling. I am telling Mummert not to worry too much about the oil boosters in Gaylord, for they are not unique. There are hunters like that everywhere. They have no use for wilderness. Take away their mechanized access and you have ruined their sport. During the U.S. Forest Service's Roadless Area Review and Evaluation proceedings, hunters in some regions were among the feistiest opponents of enlarging the national wilderness system. In Smoky Mountain country, before a television news camera, one hunter threatened to put the torch to the forest should the government see fit to declare it wilderness, though possibly he was only looking for an excuse to improve the deer habitat.

"But how do you fight the majority?" Mummert is wondering. "The majority's dictating right here to our DNR. They want more deer. They want easy fish." We roll across a bridge over the Manistee River. "They want big canoe traffic on all the rivers. I've got a canoe, but it's getting so I'm ashamed to put it into the water. Everywhere you turn, there's—"

A jolt. Something has hit the side of the truck. Mummert's right foot goes for the brake, his eyes to the side-view mirror. "Be damned," he says. "We got one."

"Got what?"

"Got a deer," he says, and pulls the truck to a stop on the shoulder of the road. I jump out on my side and start back. The deer is about fifty yards behind us, lying in the grass on the opposite shoulder with a broken neck.

"Fifteen thousand go like this in Michigan every year," Mummert says. "Figuring all the miles I do, it's a wonder I never hit one before."

"You didn't hit it. It hit you."

Mummert looks into the woods beside the road. He figures there must be hunters nearby, stirring things up. Two hunters are already beside us. They were coming the other way in their car and saw the deer go straight into the side of the truck. One of them says, "You didn't have to work very hard for this one."

"I'm not taking it," says Mummert. "You go ahead."

"But it's yours."

"No," says Mummert firmly. "It is not mine. Not this way." Whereupon the two others declare ownership of the carcass.

We walk back to the truck. Under the place where it says "Farmer Peet's People Pleasin' Meats," Mummert runs his thumb and forefinger lightly along the steel underframe, then holds them up for my inspection. Between his fingers is a single deer hair.

The Second Season

There are three seasons for deer in Michigan, as in most of the other eastern whitetail states. There is the blaze orange firearm season in the last two weeks of November. There is a brief December season in which a handful of nostalgic types revert to muzzle-loaded ball and black powder. And there is the bow season, which generally runs through all of October, the first two weeks of November, suspends itself while the riflemen are afield (most bow hunters putting in time with rifles as well), and then, resuming, plays out another two to four weeks in the final month of the year. Bow hunters number about 175,000 in Michigan, and they can be counted upon to take upward of 20,000 deer, a success rate barely half that of the riflemen but better than twice that of the muzzle-loaders. Because of the numbers involved rather than where it happens to fall across the calendar, the bow season is sometimes referred to as the second season. It is a season of special significance around Grayling, where Doug Mummert makes his final deliveries of the day, because Grayling, until recently, was the home of Bear Archery; and the prideful fact of the matter is that Bear bows and razorhead arrows are practically as common in the whitetail woods of the north as are Fisher Bodies on the freeways of Detroit.

As hunting tools, the bow and the arrow are enjoying something of a renaissance these days, though Robin Hood and Hiawatha, were they around, would hardly recognize the instruments for all their twentieth-century refinements. No more the longbow of English yew, laminated imitations of which still linger around the archery range, and no more the shortbow of hickory, though some recurve models are still manufactured from American maple. Now, most of America's two million bow hunters come equipped with a device that looks like something William Tell might have invented, in consultation with the National Aeronautics and Space Administration. It is the compound bow. It is designed to reduce human muscle strain while increasing foot-pounds of energy applied to the arrow in flight. It is a thing, in one model or another, of thermal-bonded epoxy-resin Fiberglas limbs, magnesium alloy handle, plastic-coated steel aircraft cables, Dacron string, eccentric wheels with roller bearings, and such accessories as the bowsight with micrometer windage adjustment and yardage pin corrector, the burr-like rubber silencer to still the game-spooking *twang* of the bowstring, and camouflage bow sleeves with Velcro fasteners. Sherwood Forest was never like this.

To anyone who has never pulled a bowstring, compounded or otherwise, bow hunting is a puzzlement. Here are men and women who would seem to be reaching directly for Paleolithic vibrations, for hunting in its purest, most aesthetic form. Yet here are all these pulleys and cables, these alloys and epoxies, forever getting in the way of the pristine experience. What does it all mean? It probably means that the staunchest aesthete is not succumbing to the allure of the compound bow and will continue to use his old recurve until such time as either bow or bowman falls apart. And it means, too, I think, that bow hunters get what bow hunters want, most of them preferring the easy pull to the aching arm, and having extra time in the woods with a chance, in such states as Michigan and Pennsylvania, to take a bonus deer from the second season. Still, for all the compromising technology, and for all its sedentary ways— most successful hunters sit it out in a blind—bow hunting for deer, or anything else for that matter, is about the most challenging blood sport available to outdoorsmen at a price most outdoorsmen can afford to pay. "There's nothing quite like it," says Fred Bear, not without prejudice, for he is founder and chairman of the archery company that bears his name. "You can learn more about hunting in a week with a bow than in a lifetime with a rifle."

A lifetime is about what Bear has already invested in his business and his sport. Now in his mid-seventies, he is the woods archer emeritus of America, a legendary figure among those who admire his past publicized big-game hunting feats, and a cursed one among those who would join Cleveland Amory in dubbing him "Grand Dragon" of the bow hunt. I first met Bear at his factory in Grayling, on a drizzling day in September when faces seemed longer than one might reasonably blame on the weather. Everyone in town seemed to have a long face, and Bear soon explained why. His company (actually not *his* now, but rather a subsidiary of Walter Kidde & Company, Inc.), the largest non-government employer in Grayling and Crawford County, would be heading by year's end for the Sun Belt, for Gainesville, Florida, to be exact. Bear and his people were going to miss the north country. After brown trout in the Au Sable River, largemouth bass in the Oklawaha would take some getting used to; and worse, for there were rumors that the

Floridian whitetails were stunted. "Where you fellas goin' to hunt next year, Florida?" said one Michigan sporting goods dealer to an aide of Fred Bear. "Hell, I've seen dogs bigger than Florida deer." North country folk have a certain way of punishing the deserters.

Fred Bear was not always a Michigander. He was a Pennsylvanian first, in mountain country, and a rifle hunter born and raised to be just like his rifle-hunting daddy. At twenty-one, he moved to Detroit. He worked as a wood pattern maker. He was twenty-five before it ever occurred to him that some men still hunted with bows. He learned as much from a silent movie. The bow intrigued him. He tried tournament archery first, and he was good, scoring tops or second almost every time. In the basement of his home, he designed and built his own bows. He met the master archer Art Young, who had been bow hunting in Alaska. Bear's hobby was becoming his obsession.

When the Depression finally caught up with him, Bear was out of a paying job. But there was still the workshop in the basement, full-time now, and the tournament victories that called attention to his product. By 1944, Bear had moved his bow-and-arrow operation twice in Detroit, each time for more space for expansion. And two years later he moved it to Grayling, for space again, but also for propinquity to the fish and game of the north country. He began to write for the outdoor magazines. Readers were fascinated with his accounts of taking the wily whitetail Indian-style; before long, some readers would try it themselves, with Bear bows.

He had a genius for self-promotion and began to exercise it in the 1950s in a series of hunting films, invariably starring Fred Bear, with supporting credits going to the creatures that would die in the final frames. Over the years, in one or another of almost twenty films, he would be seen in Alaska ("Bowman faces thousand-pound [Kodiak] bear across twenty feet of open beach"), in British Columbia and the Yukon ("What happens when a daring bowman meets a truculent grizzly?"), in India ("In search of Sher Kan, the great Bengal tiger"), and in Mozambique, where the supporting cast included impalas, waterbucks, warthogs, lions, and one bull elephant zapped through the liver with a single razorhead arrow. With prints of his films circulating to Scout troops and service clubs, with Arthur Godfrey's microphone following him to the ends of the earth, with features in *Time* and *Life* magazines and the producers of ABC-TV's "The American Sportsman" clamoring for his on-camera presence, and with his own likable, lanky, craggy-faced, cracker-barrel backwoods charm, Bear at last had something going for himself and for the sport of bow hunting. His bows, arrows, and accessories represent a third of the U.S. market in production and sales. And the Fred Bear Museum, the repository of all his personal trophies, and still located in Grayling, the last I heard, draws one hundred thousand visitors a year.

The September rain splashed against the windows of his office as we talked that first time. He was saying that things were changing everywhere. Even Mozambique, he said—"shot to hell, and no game left." But the whitetails were still running down in Ogemaw County, at Boyer's Grousehaven near Rose City, and why didn't I join him there for a few days of hunting in October? It sounded like a good idea, I said. But since I didn't bow-hunt, and he did, would there be time enough to continue the conversation?

"There'll be time enough," Bear said. "I don't carry a bow much in the woods any more."

"Why not?"

Bear leaned back in his chair and sighted me in along the ridge of his aquiline nose. "Oh, I suppose it was all those years, and trips," he said. "Every damn time I went hunting, I had to *kill* something." He stopped then and turned his face toward the rain, and in a voice so soft and low I could barely hear it, said at last, "I figure you know damn well what I mean."

Grousehaven is a 3,000-acre hunting preserve in the Rifle River watershed, fifty miles southeast of Gaylord. It is owned by Bill Boyer, a retired vice-president of General Motors Corporation. Boyer and Bear have been friends for a quarter century; and, in recent years and in the second season, the hospitality of the host has been extended as well to Bear's bow-making associates, to his top salesmen, and, on occasion, to such scriveners as come guaranteed not to deplete the enclave's inventories either of liquor or of white-tailed deer.

At the time of my visit, the Boyer-Bear guest list included a number of Bear Archery's top sales people. Most of them were billeted in the main lodge. It was classic camp: stone fireplace, heads of trophy sheep and deer among obsolete skis and snowshoes on the unfinished walls, ancient photographs yellowing with age, furniture of attic value and uncertain vintage. It was, as some chauvinist once observed of hunting camps in general, "a place too good for women." It had the mixed qualities of a locker room with socks on the floor and a Victorian study with snifters of cognac and fine cigars. Here, the bar was on a sideboard, well stocked and accessible twenty-four hours a day. One framed homily on the wall advised: "Avoid the New Year's Rush—Drink Now!" Another depicted a cadaver with a smoking whiskey bottle. "Yah mean you guys brought *guns?*" read the legend. For a man with neither bow nor gun, the prospects seemed entirely promising. Yet sobriety was rampant.

In camp, with all his stories, Bear is a good man to be with. But he is even better in the woods, for savvy. We went out from the lodge one morning and moseyed around a leatherleaf bog and up over a hill covered with oaks and sweet fern until we came at last to a deer trail with fresh tracks. Bear squatted beside the trail and said, "Looks like there's some traffic here." He motioned me to follow him. "Last week the factory supervisors were out here and they took eighteen deer. That's a lot of kicking around. Deer know they have to play it safer now." He stopped abruptly and leaned over the trail. "Damn, that's a good deer," he said. "But it's running now. The wind's behind us. It's going for the swamp." Up ahead, thirty yards or so, the land dipped toward a stand of tamarack. There was a golden light in the woods and the air smelled of leaf litter and humus. Bear threw up one hand and waved it in a farewell salute to the unseen buck. And in the passing moment of that gesture, I suddenly pictured this same man in Mozambique, throwing up one hand to loose an arrow into an 8,000-pound elephant.

It was getting on toward lunchtime when we returned to the lodge. On a picnic table out front, Al Dawson and Saffell Blackburn, both from Bear Archery, were butchering a buck that had been taken two days earlier and had hung for the interim, for firming the meat, in a shed nearby. Dawson, a professional butcher before he got into sales, was wielding his knife with impressive skill as he told a small audience around the table of the American hunter's waste of wild meat.

"You wouldn't believe it," Dawson was saying. "Back home a rifle hunter comes into the shop with a two-hundred-pound deer shot three, four times maybe, with a big three-hundred Magnum. When he comes back later for the meat, I hand it to him in a little paper sack and his jaw drops. 'What happened to all the rest of my meat?' he wants to know. And I have to tell him that his meat got all et up by Magnum bullets."

The way Dawson told it, with support from Blackburn, a rifle bullet causes massive tissue damage along the plane of the wound. Unlike the razorhead arrow, a soft-point bullet does not slice its way through the flesh—it tumbles. "Most people who don't like venison," said Dawson, "have eaten meat that was treated badly by the hunter, or that shouldn't have been saved in the first place because it was spoiled by blood. Blood is what causes the spoilage almost every time. A deer killed by gunshot dies of shock, but by arrow, of hemorrhage. By arrow, the meat gets bled in the field."

Inevitably, any hunters' dialogue concerning the impact of an arrow on flesh must lead, as this one did, to the question of the bow and arrow's relative efficiency—relative, that is, to the rifle and bullet—and to whether or not bow hunting contributes to a disproportionately high loss of crippled animals. There is a recurring allegation that bow hunters leave as many deer in the woods, wounded, as they take out, dead. Not infrequently, the charge is made by a rifleman who resents the bow hunter's longer season. The bowmen at Grousehaven were saying baloney to this; and my own subsequent rummaging around in the literature failed to turn up any substantial evidence to support the theory that bow hunters, proportionately, cripple any more animals than riflemen do. In fact, one of the few studies of crippling loss from bow hunting, among deer in Wisconsin, found that loss to be only about 10 percent of the bow-hunting harvest.

Part of the prejudice against bow hunters harks from a time when most of them hunted with tournament-type bows, strung for draw weights of thirty pounds or less (meaning less velocity for the arrow), and with arrowheads barely one evolutionary notch this side of the Stone Age. Some of these early archers were among Fred Bear's first customers. Beside the picnic table now at Grousehaven, Bear recalled the disadvantage of hunting with a conventional bow, though he himself has never abandoned his recurve for the compound. "To a deer," said Bear, "the *twang* of a bowstring in the forest must be a terrifying sound. The arrow from a conventional bow is traveling about a hundred and twenty-five miles an hour. But the speed of sound is nearly eight times faster. Deer have involuntary muscular reactions. A standing deer squats first in order to leap. That's when the arrow goes over its back, or makes a high wound. And that's why we have the compound now. More velocity, and more hitting power."

"From tree blinds," Bear salesman Joe White put in, "and that's how most of us hunt, the average deer is taken at about twenty yards. At that range, the arrow has more penetrating power than a thirty-thirty, and it goes clean through."

I said, "If it saves crippling losses, then I guess your compound technology isn't so bad after all."

"You don't have to worry *too* much about the technology," said Fred Bear. "Now, about the people who use it—that's something else."

At breakfast next morning in the lodge, some of the hunters were talking about the Murphy boy. The Murphy boy was a negative celebrity. On Sunday of the previous week, Sunday being Opening Day of the second season, young Murphy was moving through heavy brush down Saginaw County way. He was wearing a white sweat shirt and a red vest, and he was bent over. The other bow hunter in the brush said later that the Murphy boy had looked like a deer. The arrowhead entered the boy's neck and lodged in his head, so that in all likelihood he never knew what hit him. Murphy thus became Michigan's first bow-hunting fatality in three years.

For some curious reason probably having to do with the darker side of human nature, hunters and newspaper editors and occasional journalists seem to be fascinated with the seasonal mortality tables of the chase. Hunters tend to hunker around the breakfast table trying to see who is best at turning the other fellow's stomach on the gruesome details. Newspaper editors tend to regard hunting horror stories as being among the most attractive items available during the slow, generally non-catastrophic, autumn months. And occasional journalists occasionally wonder whether gut- or head-shot hunters might be less fascinating if there were more of them.

The total number of hunting fatalities in Michigan—I mean people shot to death, not those falling out of tree blinds or asphyxiating themselves with propane gas at night in their trailers or suffering cardiac arrest trampling, winded, uphill— has averaged about fifteen a year over the past decade. Factored into the number of licensed hunters of every kind in Michigan, that represents a death rate of about 1.25 per 100,000 of hunter population. By way of contrast, the national death rate for drowning is about 3.1 per 100,000 of *total* population, which perforce includes dry-land types who don't or won't go near the water. How many fishermen are among the drowners? There isn't one statistician with the foggiest idea. A drowned fisherman is so undramatic, compared with a shot hunter.

At the breakfast table, it was Fred Bear's turn for telling stories. He had his listeners on a moose hunt in British Columbia. One of the hunters there mistakes another for a moose. It is bad enough that the bullet goes through the groin of the mistaken identity, though without killing him, but then it has to pass fatally on through the chest of a second hunter standing behind the first. "That fellow who fired the shot," said Bear, shaking his head from side to side. "They had to stop him at the edge of a cliff with a flying tackle."

Then a man named Bob Errett spoke across the table, saying: Turkey season can get dangerous in Virginia. A female hiker was dispatched on a wilderness trail by a man on a ridge with a telescopic .243. That's right. In *turkey* season. Al Dawson spoke up next. In Pennsylvania, he said, it just didn't pay to be a varmint shooter. The varmint-shooting population was losing four or five members every year. "You're prone," said Dawson, "shooting at distances of three hundred yards or more. At three hundred yards all you see in the scope is this round thing sticking up from the ground. It looks like a 'chuck. Only it turns out to be another 'chuck hunter's head."

For all the accidental killing, the rate keeps going down, thanks in part to the blaze orange requirement imposed by some states during firearm deer season, and thanks, too, to such hunter-safety education programs as are mandatory for those under sixteen (as in Michigan and Pennsylvania) or for first-time hunters of any age (as in New York). Still, in more than half of the states, safety training remains strictly voluntary; and in only eighteen of the states with either mandatory or voluntary programs is wildlife identification a part of the regular curricula. Which may explain why some hunters cannot see much difference between a moose and a human being.

I once tried to enroll in a hunter-safety program, in Connecticut, where such training is only halfway mandatory; that is, you are exempt if you have held a valid hunting license from another state within the past ten years, even from a state, I should add, wherein the only prerequisite is an assumption that the applicant possesses a functioning trigger finger. Connecticut, of course, is not among the more active hunting states. In fact, in southern Connecticut, where I live, the peer pressure *against* hunting is intense. Some hunters I know, to avoid their neighbors' scorn on autumnal Saturday mornings, stash their guns in their cars under cover of darkness, attire themselves in the morning in stadium tweeds, announce they are getting an early start for the Yale Bowl, and dare change into their hunting frocks only after they're deep in the boondocks north of the Merritt Parkway.

And so it happened that in my search for a hunter-safety course nearby, a state official directed me to Funk (which is an alias, for I do not want to embarrass the man, and besides, he is my townsman). I telephoned Funk and said I wished to enroll in his next hunter-safety class. Since it was September, I figured the courses would be running full and I might have to wait. I had to wait, all right. But not because the courses were running full—because they were running empty. The first time on the phone, Funk said he expected to pull a class together in a week or so. In a week or so, I telephoned Funk again. He said he'd give me a call when he got the class pulled together. "In a week or so?" I asked. "Just about," said Funk, and never called back.

I do not mean to ridicule the anemic status of Connecticut's hunter-safety program or the loneliness of any of its volunteer instructors. Under the circumstances, it seems remarkable that Connecticut should feel it still needs any such program at all. What the saga of my friend Funk points up, I guess, is the increasing lack of interest in hunting among young people who live in states that are essentially urban. There is a leveling out, now, along the recruitment curve. Nationally, the number of licensed hunters creeps a little higher each year; but in proportion to the total population, the hunter as subgroup begins to show a net loss. The new generations are not quite the same as Fred Bear's. Nowadays, there is no such thing as a man-child born and raised to be just like his hunting daddy. Because nowadays Daddy's got competition.

There is a man in Gaylord, a seventyish sort of man I happen to know, whose life in retirement has been devoted to trout fishing and gunning for grouse in the woods of the Pigeon River Country. In his den are twenty-five splendid bamboo fly rods and a brace of side-by-side shotguns that would honor the gun case of an Old World nobleman. And this man is not rich—at least not in currency. His children are grown now, with their own children, living in faraway places where the grouse no longer flush to the point. I mean places that have come to be known as metropolitan. Places where there are swimming pools and basketball courts and hockey rinks and community concerts and photography classes and travel agents with packaged tours to ski resorts and tropical beaches. Places where, in the recreational scheme of things, there are now convenient alternatives to the rod and the bow and the gun, to the stream and the forest. And one day in his den in Gaylord, the man of the twenty-five fly rods and the brace of elegant shotguns said to me, "So what's to become of all this good stuff when I pass along?"

I was thinking of that my last morning at Grousehaven, walking the trails with Joe White of Kentucky. White has an eight-year-old son. At home near Bowling Green, they like to prowl in the woods together. I said I guessed, at eight, the boy must be getting anxious to hunt. "No," said Joe White. "He says he doesn't want to hunt. And I'm not pushing him." I said it was still too early for that in any event, and that maybe the boy would change his mind. "Yeah?" said Joe White. "I sure hope you're right."

Cops and Robbers

Between the daylight and the dark, mid-January, when the night is beginning to fall, comes a pause in the north's occupation that is known as the bear hunter's ball. Actually, it is known better as the bear *banquet*, which is held the day after the ball, on a Saturday, at the Knights of Columbus Hall in the alpine village of Gaylord, Michigan. Bear hunters from throughout the state gather to exchange information, listen to speeches, swap tall tales, crown a queen, and partake of *Ursus americanus*, prepared to a fare-thee-well in the Knights' kitchen and served up in sliced roasts and sausages with heaping portions of salad and mashed potatoes. To my own palate, the sausage is delicious, and, given a choice, I guess I'd choose roast bear over

bottom round as often as I could get away with it and still have
confidence that ursine populations would be sustained in the
north country.

Some two hundred men and women were seated at the
banquet I attended; but while that seems an impressive number, I am told that twice as many might have turned out in the
old days, when the affair was held at Lake City, near Cadillac,
and one could look up at the head table and see a dozen state
legislators and maybe even the governor himself, or at least a
delegate from his inner circle. It used to be that way. It used to
be, before city folk Down Below got anthropomorphic about
bears from watching Gentle Ben and Grizzly Adams, and also
before the bear hunters started quarreling among themselves
over methods. Now, in Gaylord, there was one member of the
Natural Resources Commission and three state legislators, and
if the hunters at the banquet weren't exactly quarreling among
themselves, it was only because those who disagreed had wisely
decided to cool it at home. For my part, I had certain feelings
about bear-hunting methods. I had been on one hunt in September on the Upper Peninsula, and had talked about bears at
some length with Doug Mummert in Gaylord. I had listened to
the speeches. And somewhere along the way—just where, I'm
not quite sure—I think I may have come to feel a little like the
McCaslin boy in William Faulkner's "The Bear," at the point
in the story when, first blood having been drawn from the great
ghost bear of the Yoknapatawpha, the boy realizes that he
stands at "the beginning of the end of something." And knows
even then that he will not grieve for it.

In Michigan, there are essentially three ways to bag a black
bear. You can stand and hunt, you can walk and hunt, or you
can run after dogs and hope that they, hunting, will chase a
bear up a tree. Those who walk and hunt are rare, for the simple reason that, of all three methods, this one is the least likely
to produce a dead bear. Alive, the black bear has a shrewd nose
for human shenanigans, and a fair ear, and only the most for-
tuitous circumstances of wind direction and cushioned footfall
stealth allow the hunter to get the jump on a bear in this fashion. Some bears, however, are killed on the Upper Peninsula by

wandering archers or riflemen during their respective seasons for deer. For the most part, these are venatic windfalls, and they account for fewer than one in ten of the bears taken. Except for those who believe that bears should be taken under *no* circumstance, no one objects much to the hunter who moseys. And no one grieves for him, either.

The man who stands to hunt, or sits or lies down, according to his mood and the disposition of his blind, is the one who generally hunts over bait. In baiting, the idea is to start early, well in advance of Opening Day. Apples dipped in molasses make a splendid bait, though almost anything will do, bears being omnivorous scroungers. Once a bait is taken, it must be replaced without fail, and before long the bear's visitation is so punctual that one may almost predict the precise five-minute slot within which it will die on the first day of the season. About six hundred bears, some three quarters of the total kill, are dispatched in this fashion each year. The dog hunters, devotees of the third methodology, deplore the fact that baiting is even practiced in the north, much less sanctioned by the rule books. The baiters, in turn, condemn the doggers' tactics, running their hounds all over hell and back and chasing *their* bears off *their* baits. Between the two sides, there had been much recent bad blood, as I would presently discover at the Knights of Columbus Hall in Gaylord.

The dean of north country doggers is Carl T. Johnson, a Cadillac insurance man, longtime member of the state's Natural Resources Commission, and past president of the Michigan Bear Hunter's Association, which he helped to organize at a time when hound dogs round about were almost as rare as visiting hyenas. As early as the 1930s, Johnson had run hounds after bobcats; but bears seemed too crafty and tough. Then, in 1946, the *Outdoor Life* writer and editor Ben East appointed Johnson field commander of the state's first organized bear hunt; and after that, as the commander recalls it, "the sport caught fire." In more ways than one.

The preferred hound for bears in Michigan is the Walker,

though some packmasters favor the Bluetick. Douglas Mummert runs with Walkers, and so does Carl Johnson, who no longer keeps a pack of his very own. The Walker name goes back to the early nineteenth century, to Willy Walker of Garrard County, Kentucky. According to one account, Willy and Wash Maupin liked to put their English foxhounds after deer and gray foxes, but time and again the craftier red fox outsmarted them. So Willy and Wash decided to do a little outcross breeding to improve the strain. Possibly the most significant contribution to that endeavor was not by the Walker family but by Wash Maupin and George L. F. Birdsong of Thomaston, Georgia. Round about midcentury, an unidentified gentleman returning to Kentucky from the Deep South by way of the Cumberland Mountains of Tennessee intercepted a great and phenomenal hound in pursuit of a deer, and, tethering the feral dog on a leash, took it home with him and presented it as a gift to Wash Maupin. Meanwhile, in Georgia, George L. F. Birdsong had imported from England three splendid dogs named Fox, Rifler, and Marth. One way or another—though one suspects there was only one way about it—the genes of Birdsong's three imports as well as those of the Maupin hound, dubbed Tennessee Lead, meandered on through generations of hounds owned by Walkers. So that, in all likelihood, there was a shadow of Fox or Rifler or Marth, and possibly of Tennessee Lead as well, across the genetic coding of the very best bear hound that Carl T. Johnson ever owned.

The dog's name was Snip. Snip could follow a scent anywhere and displayed an uncommon haughty feistiness in the presence of bears. As a result, Snip would be packed off periodically to the veterinarian for suturing of the claw wounds. After each mauling and convalescence, Snip would return to the hunt, not wiser, alas, but haughtier than ever before. In the end, a bear sank its teeth into Snip's head, breaking that particular branch of the Walker hound lineage. Sometimes Carl T. Johnson gets dewy-eyed telling it.

Man and dog and bear have been going around in circles together almost since the adaptive offspring of captive wolves first learned to heel for their spear-toting Neolithic masters.

The method of pursuit hadn't really changed that much even when Faulknerian heroes went into the sloughs of the American Southeast with buckboards and wall tents, though McCaslins and Compsons carried breech-loaders, not spears. But by the time Carl T. Johnson got to running Walkers after the Black Ghost of the Muskegon and the Tahquamenon Rogue, the old ways were beginning to take on a distinctive modern tenor. Aldo Leopold had heard it nearby in the woods of Wisconsin. "The voice of Bugle Ann," he wrote, "mingles with the honk of the flivver." Had he lived another twenty years, Leopold might have added that the honk of the flivver mingles with the crackle of the CB radio.

On the September hunt in which I participated, on Michigan's Upper Peninsula, there were at any one given time at least seven flivvers and as many CB radios, eight dogs, and a platoon of hunters numbering up to seventeen, all variously armed and under the command of Commissioner Johnson. The commissioner himself was armed with a converted British Army .303 rifle, and he spoke proudly of the weapon as one that had killed more game than any other gun in Michigan.

We opened the tenth of September on the Baraga Plains, UP, near L'Anse on Lake Superior's Keweenaw Bay. It was sunny and warm the first day, which was good for tracking; raining hard the second, and windy the third, which were not good for tracking or for much of anything. On the afternoon of the third day, I packed out for the Lower Peninsula. On the morning of the fourth, I learned later by telephone, Johnson's troops finally got their bear. It was neither a ghost nor a rogue, just a plain old potlicker with the fat beginning to coalesce under the pelt for the coming winter. And that was all of it. One potlicker in exchange for a couple of cartridges, a few sweat-lathering races for feist dogs, heaven knows how many gallons of flivver gasoline, and about four hundred man-hours of fun. I even guess, too, that the bear had fun; or at least until such time in the race when the man-smell came to it and the dogs, closing in, put it up into the branches of a tree. Which, for all manner of men and creatures involved, proved to be the beginning of the end of something.

To hunt bears with such a group as Carl Johnson assembled at Baraga is to participate, after all these years of presumed maturity, in an elaborate game of cops and robbers. Almost all of the essential elements are at hand: the resources commissioner as police commissioner, the DNR flivvers as patrol cars with official emblems embossed on the sides of the front doors. There are the radios, and the inter-vehicle dialogues, in code ("Portable J? This is Straight Arrow. Have you found anything?"). There are the dogs, though, alas, not bloodhounds. There are the regular beat cops, riding around in the prowl cars until such time as the dogs have picked up a bandit's trail, and then deposited at a certain point along a sand road in the event the fugitive might come into the open there. In addition, there are sleuths, who neither stand a sand-road watch nor crash through the underbrush after the dogs, but who simply prowl around on their own looking for the elementary deducibles and turning up in unlikely places just when the rest of the force least expects them. To be a sleuth is to be a moseyer. We had only two or three in our game: Carl Imhoff, a veteran bear hunter from Down Below, driving his Cadillac fearlessly over the roughest roads on the UP; his friend the First-Timer; and Leon Peck, a silent and solitary fellow from Marshall.

Penultimately, there is the athlete who follows the dogs through miles of rough country; possibly, in parts of the UP, through some of the wildest deadfalled, cedar-swamped, spruce-bogged country in North America. To follow the dogs, you have to be as tireless as Commissioner Carl Johnson—tireless still, for all his seventy years—and as tough as Tom McMannus, the packmaster from Traverse City. But you are a player only in the presence of the others. Once you are into the woods, running, with the dogs bugling on a fast scent, the fantasies fall behind, for the chase is in deadly earnest, and you are the hunter.

This leaves the bear, as robber. There is no other role left for it. But what is the crime? Some players of the game believe no prima facie case is necessary. It is enough to know that the robber is capable of raiding an orchard or bowling over a beehive, both of which acts would be construed as misdemeanors if perpetrated by a human, but are considered felonies of sorts—not only that, capital crimes—when committed, as they often are in the north country, by a bear. Also, once or twice or more in this century, a black bear on the UP has been known to fetch up and kill a human child. Therefore, if one chooses to strain at the limits of logic, every mean robber may be seen as a latent murderer. Among certain players of the game, one detects beneath the sporting veneer a kind of vigilante righteousness, as if the security of the human community depended on their ability to apprehend robbers with preemptive strikes.

"You just could not possibly leave this animal at large." It was Commissioner Johnson's voice. The entire force—beat cops, dog men, sleuths—had rendezvoused the first afternoon in a fern bower at the edge of a mixed stand of tamarack and hemlock. The commissioner was leaning against the front fender of a flivver, addressing the men. "You could not do it," he said. "Before long, the bear would be doing so much damage that he would be placed on an elimination list. We cannot have that. Man and animal must have a balance of some kind. That's why we have game seasons, to determine the number of animals that we can keep in the woods. So that people coming after us will be able to see bear."

The men in the fern bower nodded agreement. And the commissioner said:

"Now, the Bible tells us that man should have dominion over the fowls of the air and the cattle that roam the hills and the game and the wild animals. And I believe that, because man is superior. He should manage the wild animals just as he does a herd of cattle. We have a season. We say we're going to take so many bear. Now, when the bear get down to a level, the Game Division comes up and says, 'You have to stop, you're taking too many bear.' And it's the same thing as a farmer. He says, 'Now wait a minute. I've got to take so many cattle out of this field or they're all going to die. But only so many.' So we are benefiting these animals when we protect them and manage them properly."

Among the men in the fern bower was the quiet moseyer Leon Peck. Possibly because he was *so* quiet—not only in the

woods but about himself, if anyone bothered to ask—it was in-
evitable that there would be stories to fill in the gaps. By one
account, old Leon Peck was never officially invited to the commissioner's hunt. He had just heard about it somewhere, and
the next year drove up from Marshall in his battered Ford
pickup truck. No one much minded, since Peck was so damn
shy; and year after year, uninvited, he showed up in his truck to
join the hunt on Opening Day. One year, for reasons unknown,
Peck did not appear on that day, or any other day of the hunt.
The other men were disappointed, and worried.

"Maybe he don't know where to find us," someone suggested, inasmuch as they were hunting in a different county.

"Maybe he's sick," said another, noting Peck's advancing
years.

On Opening Day of the following year, one of the regulars
came around a bend in a trail and there was Leon Peck, leaning against a big oak tree, smiling. "Where the hell *were* you last
year, Leon?" said the hunter. "You had us worried half to
death."

"You didn't see me?" Leon Peck said.

"Hell no, I didn't. And no one else did either."

"Well, I saw *you*," said Leon Peck. "Saw it all, just sneak-
in'."

Carl Johnson had finished citing the Bible as the source of
game-management wisdom, and he came over to Leon Peck
now, and said, "Leon, next year you better write me in advance
and find out where we're going to start the season. We might
not be up here at Baraga. You won't know where to find us.
You're getting too old to be flying wild."

Leon Peck said nothing, but you could see he wasn't buying
it. Then John Robertson of the DNR put in: "Don't go worry-
ing about Leon, Carl. Fact is, if we don't get a bear up soon, we
ought to put Leon out in the woods, give him an hour or so,
then sic the dogs on him."

"*Dare* you," said Leon Peck.

Whereupon, I made a decision. I decided that if I should
ever grow up, I mean as a bear hunter, I want to be like Leon
Peck. Or better yet, like the Man from the West. On the UP

there are stories about the Man from the West, apocryphal stories perhaps, because no one seems to know the Man's name, or where in the West he comes from. But they swear he *is*. At Ironwood and Ontonagon and Crystal Falls and Seney and Newberry, they tell more or less the same tale—of this Man coming out of the sundown, across Wisconsin in September, with a pair of feist dogs and a donkey stashed in the back of his truck, and a curious bundle, long and narrow and wrapped in tarpaulin. They say that the hair of his head is the color of rust, and his beard, black as swamp muck. But no one has ever heard his voice. Hunters always seem to see him from afar, coming in by truck; or, out of it, mounting the donkey and riding off into the forest with the strange bundle in one hand and a pair of leashes, attached to the dogs, in the other. Yet no hunter, as far as I can ascertain, has confessed to seeing what happens next. They only *know* what happens next. They know that when the hounds strike a fresh scent, the Man from the West dismounts, tethers the donkey to one tree and the dogs to another, and then takes off his clothes, every last stitch straight down to the skin, except for the sneakers on his feet. He stands there naked in the filtered sunlight of the forest and slowly unwraps the tarpaulin from the long, narrow object. The object, of course, is a spear. Homemade, it has a steel head ten times the size of a Fred Bear razorhead arrow, and just as sharp. The head is lashed to the shaft with rawhide. When the dogs see the spear, unsheathed, they set up a frantic howling. The Man from the West folds his clothes into the tarp and straps the new bundle to the back of the donkey. And only then does he unleash the dogs. He gives them a head start of ten, maybe fifteen minutes, and then he, too, takes off, running with the spear, the old way. Hunters who tell this story stop there, never knowing how many bears, if any, the Man from the West has taken in such a fashion; although some hunters wonder whether a naked spearman, even with two dogs, is any match for a bear in the woods, much less superior to it.

· · ·

"We better take a stand," Doug Mummert was saying at the bear banquet in Gaylord, "or we're sure going to lose it all. Every last bit of it." The hunters nodded agreement. There was bad news from the UP. People near L'Anse were talking of bringing a ban down on dog hunting. People were saying that dog hunters trespassed and left their hounds behind in the woods to rip off the deer. "A fella that would do that sort of thing got to be a nonresident," said a Michigan hunter. "It's those fellas from down south for sure." And to make matters worse, now the baiters wanted a split season, with *them* getting the first half. "There's just no limit on those baiters," Mummert was saying. "All they want to do is domesticate the bear." The dog hunters nodded. Their president, Jack Gretzinger, then took the floor, saying, "If you take a fair-chase position, that means no more CB radios." To which Mummert, the technology hater, replied, "So be it." (Mummert on occasion uses walkie-talkies in the woods. "I'm not proud of it," he once told me. "But they sure cut down a lot on running around in the cars, and that saves gasoline.")

Later, after the plates had been cleared away, Mummert and I sat talking with Commissioner Johnson and State Representative Thomas Anderson, head of the House Conservation, Environment, and Recreation Committee in Lansing, and David Arnold of the DNR, and Bob Strong, the Gaylord district biologist, and Merrill L. (Pete) Petoskey, a former director of the state's Wildlife Division. Mummert was not happy. "There's very few of my type that want the old-time hunt," he said. "We're getting left out of the bottom end. All these masses that are participating in these modern sports, like the snowmobile, are getting the attention. There's no room for me no more."

Representative Anderson brought the dialogue back to bears, and dogs. "There is almost an *incensement* when you talk with some people about hunting with dogs," he said. "I find it on the legislative floor. We had a bill up to reduce the number of dogs you can run. And the bill passed. The reason we got some votes for it was because it was a trend in the direction of no dogs at all. I know this. Everybody knows this."

David Arnold said, "I guess there's no other sport in Michigan that generates as much emotion and acrimony as running bear with dogs."

"Where's it generate from, David?" asked Pete Petoskey.

"This is the spooky part about it," said Arnold. "Most of the steam is coming from the hunters themselves. They've got to realize what they're doing and be more tolerant of each other because it's only a small step from not hunting bear with dogs to not hunting bear."

Then Commissioner Johnson put in, saying, "Remember this. When we started hunting bear with dogs there was an outcry all over the Upper Peninsula. I went up to Escanaba. The supervisors were wanting to close bear hunting with dogs. A lady got up, and I said, 'What does your husband hunt with *his* dogs?' And she said, 'He hunts rabbit.' I said, 'You mean to tell me he goes out and runs that rabbit that can't hurt anybody, with *dogs?* And then we hunt bear that do a lot of damage, kill sheep, do that, and we only take the surplus of the bear, and your husband is immune to criticism while we are criticized?' She sat right down and there wasn't another word out of her."

Bob Strong said there was big trouble in Atlanta between the baiters and the dog hunters. "When we first opened bear hunting here in the Lower Peninsula, it was mainly the dog hunters that kept the sport going," said Strong. "But with the advent of the sportsman's license [an all-inclusive permit] and a better life for everyone, why, we created a bunch of guys that like to set and shoot bear. And now they outnumber the dog hunters. And the condition we have around Atlanta is that there are about four guys who hunt with dogs, a couple maybe shaky in their ethics, and it's caused a real problem around there."

"Who kills the most bear?" asked Pete Petoskey.

"That's not the point, Pete," said Strong. "These bait hunters are really up in arms. If it came to a vote right now in that part of the country, why, the dog hunters would lose nine to one, easy."

"This is the sort of thing where nobody wins," David Arnold said. "When society is looking at the hunter, the hunter should be awful careful about what he says against his brother."

Doug Mummert raised his hand quickly to break in. He said, "But isn't there usually a right and a wrong to everything?"

"It's not always that clear," said Pete Petoskey. "Sometimes there's a middle. Somewhere."

Clear-cuts

On the fourth day of the first week of deer season (firearms), I said goodbye to Doug Mummert and Bob Strong and Tom Carlson—none of whom had yet got his deer but all of whom would in the week following, Mummert taking his at Brutus just as the rest of the family was about to sit down in the farmhouse to Thanksgiving dinner. I drove south through Kalkaska and Carl T. Johnson's city of Cadillac to Baldwin in Lake County, which is still north country, though barely, since it is getting on toward Down Below. I wanted to go to Baldwin to spend some time with DNR wildlife research biologist Edward Langenau, Jr. Langenau and his colleagues were in the area gathering data for a study of human responses to experimental clear-cutting for deer habitat improvement. Actually, the project was designed to assess the natural responses of plants and animals to clear-cutting as well, but Langenau's team was concentrating on the human element in general; and, this week, it was concentrating on the deer hunter in particular.

Here and there along the way, going south, I could see good examples of the DNR's basic premise about north country deer habitat—the premise being that natural succession is squeezing it out. For the most part, the wildwood of the north is trending toward a climax forest type, which in Lower Peninsula soils means oaks, mainly. Not that deer disdain acorns. On the contrary, deer thrive on acorns. But the trouble with acorns is that the good crops come only every three or four years. And the trouble with oaks is that they tend to shade out most of the fruit-bearing shrubs and smaller trees that are beneficial not only to deer but to grouse and songbirds. Aspen is a smaller tree favorable to deer for browse and shelter. But in a successional race with oak, aspen loses every time. Aspen loses enough times and you have a forest that is splendid for squirrel shooters but lousy for deerslayers. Now, in the old spear-toting and muzzle-loading days, before the double-bit loggers, no one had to worry about the forest getting to be too much of the same thing. Wildfires took care of that. But the human condition in wooded country nowadays is such that wildfires are no longer in popular demand. Instead, we get clear-cuts—entire blocks of forest cut clear of everything.

In the DNR project, eight nine-square-mile sites were selected on state forest lands in Roscommon, Kalkaska, and Lake counties; and within them, in the years 1972 through 1975, some 18,500 acres were clear-cut in variable patches ranging from 3.5 percent of the site (on an annual cut basis) to 75 percent of the site (on a one-shot cut basis). After cutting, DNR researchers over the years proceeded to monitor the responses of the new-growth vegetation, of deer and snowshoe hares and grouse and woodcocks, and of people either owning property in the area or of a type described by Langenau in one interim report as "the most influential forest recreationist in northern Michigan: the firearm deer hunter."

Edward Langenau, whom I found late that afternoon bivouacked with three other scientists at a motel north of Baldwin, is a bright young Ph.D. out of Michigan State University and the United States Army, Vietnam Class of 1969. In Vietnam, as an Army paramedic, Langenau interviewed GIs to ascertain if they were fit for combat. Now he interviews firearm deer hunters to see what kind of clear-cuts are fit for hunting. "I got into this," said Langenau, "because I decided that wildlife biologists know a great deal about deer but hardly anything about people." And I said there were probably a lot of young wildlife biologists elsewhere in America who would make the same wise choice if only their old-guard superiors would let them.

After talking with Langenau and his colleagues and reading some of their reports, I am inclined to tread carefully among the fragments of their preliminary findings, if only because it is an ongoing project and the data gathering is not yet complete. Still, it is probably safe to suppose that deer are indeed finding their range vastly improved in and around some of the clear-cuts; that aspen in some places is regenerating three times faster than oak in others; and that if grouse could be grateful, they would be, if only for all the sunlit nannyberry and thorn apple brush that has sprouted where once there was only the fern under red oak shade.

As for the hunter, suppositions get trickier. During three years of monitoring the clear-cuts, the research team sent questionnaires to some four hundred hunters known to have visited one or another of the sites. Responses showed that sites clear-cut of a quarter or half of their timber attracted proportionately more "immigrant" hunters—an immigrant being one who did not hunt there the previous year—than sites shorn of three quarters of their timber, suggesting there may be a threshold level for hunter tolerance of large-scale clear-cuts. Most respondents, however, felt that the clear-cuts would increase the number of deer; and having more deer was more desirable than having undisturbed scenery.

Next, Langenau and his teammates conducted a number of informal on-site interviews. Here the reactions were decidedly mixed. On the positive side of it, some hunters were delighted with the cuts because, now, it was "easier to see the deer," there were "lots of stumps to sit on," and the clearings "pulled the deer out of the swamps." In the ambivalent middle, one hunter reported with no visible distress that, in the early morning, oak stumps look like deer. "I shot two of them yesterday," he said. Meaning stumps. And on the negative side, the responses ranged from suspicion that there were "too damn many hunters around now" to a complaint that cutting operations had left "holes in the ground you fall into." At one campsite early one morning, the interviewers came upon a young man sitting in front of a campfire reading a book—a skin book, I would imagine, inasmuch as the interviewer later described it as pornographic. In any event, the other hunters in this particular party were out of camp. What did the solitary reader think of the cuttings? "What cuttings?" the young man replied. "I don't care about cuttings or much about shooting a deer. I'm here for the stuff in the evening. When we cut for the bars, to town."

Much is made of the stuff in the evening, especially around Baldwin. The headline on page three of the Detroit *News* on Opening Day had read: "'Dear' herds are flocking north, too." The dateline was Idlewild, a small run-down resort community a few miles east of Baldwin. The "yoo-hoo girls," according to the news item, had arrived on schedule from Down Below and from Ohio to hunt the hunters. A year earlier—"after Idlewild's year-round male population became angry about having their wives pushed aside by prostitutes while shopping for groceries, or worse yet, propositioned by deer hunters who didn't distinguish between good women and the other kind"—state police dropped into town and arrested eighteen of the nonresident oldest-professionals. It caused quite a stir, such that this year the police were predicting an even larger turnout, if not of hookers, then surely of hunters.

I do not know why it is exactly that hunters seem always to attract this kind of notoriety. Perhaps it is because they are supposed to be in the woods, doing other things. Perhaps it is a part of the pop-psych palaver about hunting man's sexuality. Who knows? And who *cares?* Yet I couldn't help wondering, that night at Baldwin with the Langenau team, seeing the spillover action outside the barrooms, why, if adults must be boys, they have to pretend to be hunters as well.

The pretense sometimes gets to things a little more important than the exchange of proscribed favors between consenting adults. Sometimes it gets to how the deer tag of a pretender-to-the-hunt winds up on the rack of a poacher's buck—a buck jacklighted at night, then shot from the window of the violator's pickup truck, his foot on the clutch and the engine running. Now how could that possibly happen, except in an exchange of proscribed favors between the pretender and the poacher? One hundred dollars cash for one four-point buck. It's under the tarp in the back of the truck. Then, home is the hunter, home from the hill. With his stag, and his alibi.

There was a stakeout at a roadhouse near Baldwin the night I was there. Lawmen had a reliable tip that a poacher was negotiating the sale of two deer to a couple of sports from Down Below, a couple who, for one reason or another, did not want to arrive home empty-handed. I sat with one of Langenau's men in a DNR panel truck parked on a road several miles from the stakeout, waiting for the radio message that would tell us the "bust" was in progress. It never came. The word on the radio was: Scratch it. Yet that same night, state police dropped in nearby, to Idlewild, and managed to arrest nine hunters on charges of soliciting acts of prostitution. Three of them, who pleaded guilty, were sentenced to nine days in jail and a fine of $150 each. The poacher, had he been caught, would have faced a stiffer sentence, though barely.

On the afternoon of the fifth day of the first week of deer season (firearms), I said goodbye to Ed Langenau—who had not got a deer yet, and would not, since he hunts game birds only—and drove south through White Cloud and Sparta into Down Below. The fifth day was Sunday. The traffic was heavy, almost bumper to bumper on State Highway 37, because most of the first-week deer hunters were heading for home; but slow-moving also because of a few who would not make it. Near Ramona there had been a collision, head on in the northbound lane. Two bodies were on stretchers at one side of the highway, under white sheets. On the other side stood the morbid curious, in blaze orange. I looked at the stretchers and thought, then, of the deer that had broken its neck near the bridge on the Manistee River, against the side of Mummert's truck. And I thought, too, of the old man on the clear-cut hill.

He was sitting alone in his car the day that Langenau found him, looking out over a great swale of stumps and top slash from a recent cutting. He appeared stunned. The last time he was here, his view had been of a second-growth forest, with hardwoods getting on toward fifty years. The old man knew how old the trees were without even counting the rings on the stumps. He knew because he had been here, the first time, right after the loggers passed through. So he had seen it cut once, had lived with it for half a century growing, had come each year to take deer and birds and berries and firewood from it, and now, this. Langenau looked at the old man sitting at the wheel of his car. Then Langenau did not look at him, for the old man was crying.

They had come upon men like this before, though perhaps not showing their feelings quite so openly. They had delved into the behavioral literature and decided to call such men "fixed site" hunters, to describe them as being "site-tenacious." Somehow, they felt, the word "territorial" was not entirely accurate. It sounded too aggressive. Perhaps such a word was suitable only for those few who were so site-tenacious that they would peg warning shots over the heads of intruders on their turf. But in the aggressive sense, no; territoriality did not apply to the old man on the hill. Better to perceive him as a man come back to his home range. But now, this.

On the hill, the old man told Langenau how, after the logging the first time, the hunting got better each year. Each year there were more deer and more woodcocks, even as the stumps began to rot around their edges and the slash turned to duff and the suckers shot up into trees.

"The younger people," said the old man, "they'll sure have good hunting here soon enough."

But what about him? Langenau wanted to know. How did he feel about the new cuttings, for himself?

"They make me feel old," said the man. "They make me feel that it's time to quit."

Langenau left shortly after that, so I can only guess. I guess that, after a while, the old man started the engine of his car, turned it around, heading south probably, and drove out of his home range through the top slash and the stumps with rings for epitaphs to wherever it was he would spend the rest of his own huntless years, Down Below.

Book Two

IN ANOTHER COUNTRY

December is the hunter's month in Texas. Even in the Brush Country down toward Cotulla and Artesia Wells and the Rio Grande beyond, the morning air then is getting crisp enough to snap between your fingers, and triggers can get frosty to the touch at 6 a.m. County to county, hunting seasons vary somewhat, but for the most part that is rule-book time for taking white-tailed deer, wild turkey, javelina, and quail; bear, too, where the land is timbered to its liking, and squirrel, which tends to be fair game, most river-bottom places, any time. Once, deer grew big in the Brush Country, *muy grande*. In the Hill Country, over Kerrville way, not so big as so many; more deer out there on the Edwards Plateau, some folks say, than in all of North America when sunlight first glinted on Spanish armor. Which is a wonderment to me, since so much of central Texas is already aswarm with black-buck antelope, ibex, aoudad and mouflon sheep, and axis, fallow, and sika deer, all imported not by the Spanish, who brought only horses and pigs, but by Anglo ranchers gone prickly over the negligible trophy value of native game.

There are natives and exotics among the hunters as well. In the east, in piney-wood and post-oak savanna country, some hunters and their kin tend to lean a bit toward down-under Dixie or Appalachian ways of being, which have less to do with black-eyed peas and bib overalls than with a certain positive attitude about the privileges of poachers and trespassers in other parties' woods. Yet west beyond the blackland prairies, getting on toward high-plains grass or trans-Pecos chaparral, one might encounter broad-brimmed rawhide types whose granddaddies trafficked in longhorn steers and, for culling the human herd, shared hair-raising reciprocity with Comanches in open seasons during which all bag limits were mutually waived. And between the hill people and the plainsmen are the city-slick hunters of Houston and Dallas and San Antonio, some being Texan but others being immigrant newcomers from the Snow Belt, who hunted freely on public lands back home in Michigan or Montana and are now somewhat surprised to find that almost all land in Texas is private, and huntable only for a fee. Things run to extremes in Texas, or seem to.

It is generally felt, among those whose views on life, liberty, and the pursuit of happiness fail to accord with the views of hunters, that Texas has done more than its share to cast guns and hunting in a bad light. The evidence against Texas is mostly circumstantial. For example, these witnesses would bring before us the ghost of Davy Crockett, saying that he represents the archetype of the savage frontier hunter, and that the inspiration for all modern American violence somehow derives from under his coonskin cap. Crockett did indeed once confess that he was "wrathy to kill a b'ar," and then proceeded to kill one hundred. It matters little that he was of Tennessee, and did most of his killing there. His accusers remember only that he hobnobbed with Sam Houston and died at the Alamo. Armed Texans ever since have swaggered a bit more heavily than nature intended; but so have more than a few non-Texan writers in attempts to caricature them.

And before us comes the ghost of Lee Harvey Oswald, an exotic from Louisiana. He hobnobbed only with himself (or with his co-conspirators, if you want to go that route) and a 6.5-mm. Mannlicher-Carcano rifle at a window on the sixth floor of the Texas Schoolbook Depository in Dallas, now second only to the Alamo as the state's most-visited shrine. The rifle was a World War II military weapon of inferior design. It consistently misfired with European ammunition. Confiscated by our side, the Carcano with American ammunition was advertised and sold as a sporting rifle, for deer. For deer, it was dreadful. For Dealey Plaza, it was right on the mark. So we remember Oswald as a native Texan; the Mannlicher-Carcano, not as the gun that lost a war for Italy, but as the "deer rifle" that started the war in America over the right to bear arms.

Hunting the Hunter

I have come to the airport at Tyler—Tyler being the Rose Capital of the World, in East Texas—to place myself voluntarily in the custody of Jerry Owens, who is a native of the Lone Star, a constable of Anderson County nearby, a sometime private detective, and an agent of Cleveland Amory's Fund for Animals. The Fund has much clout among humane organizations; it is the capital of grief for hunters in America. Owens is the Fund's solitary staff person in Texas, but because of his background in criminal justice and his fortitude in ticklish situations, he has served as Amory's chief confrontation troubleshooter from Maine to California. In Texas, he wears a Stetson hat and cowboy boots. There is a large-caliber revolver in a holster on his hip. In his sedan are a siren, a two-way radio, and a 12-gauge sawed-off Winchester pump gun, loaded with slugs, standing upright in its rack beside the gearshift. "When you're cruising the back roads at night, looking for poachers," says Owens of the shotgun, "it sure is good to know that it's there."

Owens grew up with guns in cattle country near Fort Worth. He remembers his granddaddy standing in the kitchen with a shotgun, saying, "I gotta get us somethin' for supper," and the old man coming home later with four or five squirrels for the stewpot. But Owens never knew the old man to kill anything when there was meat in the house, and inasmuch as cow meat was always cheap and plentiful in those days, there were few occasions to stock the larder with wilder flesh.

From the airport we drive southwest toward Anderson County and Owens points out to me how all the farms along the way are posted against trespass by hunters. Some of the

signs read: "Wildlife Management Area—State of Texas."
Owens explains that the land in reality is private, that the state
issues these signs to landowners because, in this part of Texas,
anything less official-looking tends to be ignored. "As constable, I bust more hunters for criminal trespass than for anything
else," he says. "And I feel for some of them. All those guys sitting in their offices and factories wanting to get back to the way
it used to be, to the way it *ought* to be. But they can't pull it off.
Something's gone wrong. All the land is posted. They don't
have the time to get to the land that isn't. They have this new
rifle and they want to shoot it. That's how cows get shot. Sure,
there're accidents. There's plain old frustration, too. And then
there're the ones who don't even have the time to learn the difference. There was a hunter here a while back, shot a farmer's
mule and insisted it was a deer. And he would have packed the
carcass off over the owner's protest but for the fact that the
mule weighed a thousand pounds."

Listening to Owens, I cannot decide whether he is a cop
moonlighting as an animal protector or an animal protector
moonlighting as a cop. He had started out wanting to be a veterinarian. At Texas A & M, he paid for his tuition by raising
hogs and working part-time summers for the sheriff's department. ("Did you know," he said, and I did not, "that in Texas
the only person empowered to arrest a sheriff is the constable?") He graduated with a degree in animal husbandry and
went to work as a nutritionist at the Dallas zoo. He felt that the
animals were being neglected, so he filed a legal action against
the city and retired, for job security, to the sheriff's department. Some time later, he was licensed as a private investiga-
tor. Among his clients was the Corpus Christi office of a national humane organization, which was then looking into
questionable slaughterhouse practices. Next, Owens was retained to investigate a ring of fighting-bulldog entrepreneurs.
His work resulted in a number of criminal indictments, and
Cleveland Amory invited him to join the staff of the Fund for
Animals. On behalf of the Fund, Owens has investigated and
exposed illegal trapping of black bears in the Southeast and the

use of live rabbits for training greyhounds in California, among other practices regarded as nefarious in humane circles.

Down the road, ahead of us, a hawk glides low over the tops of some post oaks. I ask Owens why it is so many rural Texans have so little use for predators.

"They want to believe they still live on the wild frontier," he replies. "I guess it helps a little to believe the hawks and coyotes are out to get you."

I point out that this put frontier Texans in the same league with Albert Schweitzer. Owens reacts as I knew he would. "Schweitzer was against killing anything."

But he wasn't against killing snakes and birds of prey, I say. In Africa, he had a gun. And he used it to shoot snakes and raptors. He figured it was justified in defense of domestic animals. Yet apparently he felt so strongly about the right to life of a moth that he would close the windows of his study on the hottest nights rather than risk a moth's life in the flame of his kerosene lamp.

"Good animals and bad animals?" says Owens.

"That's the way some people see it. And others draw their lines according to the temperature of the creature's blood."

"Fish," says Owens.

Yes, fish. And I am telling him that I cannot understand how so many people can be opposed to hunting birds and mammals and at the same time have no negative feeling whatsoever about fishing for fish. The *muy grande* Texas writer J. Frank Dobie once quoted a letter published on the editorial page of the Dallas *Morning News*. According to Dobie, the correspondent allowed as how the bald eagle "was chosen as our national bird because it gains an honest living. It is a fish-eater. The golden eagle, on the contrary, is a bird of prey. The founders of our republic wanted no predator eagle as an American emblem. . . ." Possibly fish are not considered prey by some people, and possibly the criterion for empathy in any event is the threshold of pain. A study of human perceptions of wildlife some years ago found that almost all of the respondents agreed that rabbits felt pain, while barely half agreed that fish could.

"Take your pick," I am saying to Owens. "Would you rather be a bass with a hook in your jaw, five minutes dying at the end of a tight line, or a rabbit with a bullet through the brain?"

"Thanks for the options," says Owens.

Insofar as Americans may be divided along pro- and anti-hunting lines, there is no accounting for their real numbers. One extrapolator of my acquaintance figures the general population is divided into three parts: about forty million people favoring hunting, about forty million feeling somewhat or strongly against it, and one hundred and forty million not much caring one way or another about hunting, mainly because they do not much care one way or another about wildlife and wild country. My friend the extrapolator does not insist on absolute numbers, only the relative proportions, give or take a 5 percent here and there.

I accept the forty millions on either side of the silent majority because I believe that being for or against hunting has to do with a great deal more than whether one goes armed into the woods or contributes personally of time and money to the anti-hunting establishment. It has a lot to do with how an individual perceives America, such perceptions tending nowadays to get split along urban-liberal and rural-conservative lines, though cross-strains do occur with sufficient frequency to keep the distinction gray and blurry.

Still, from the city one is likelier to take a view of an ordered society in which authority is centralized, decisions are made by benevolent white-collar bureaucrats, and meat is rendered painlessly between cellophane and cardboard. In such a view, hunting has to appear somewhat barbaric. The rural perspective is altogether different. It beholds a society in which those governed least are governed best, the frontiersman is hero, life is competitive, nature is cruel, and meat is rendered violently by bullet or blade. Hunting is a valid part of this system, and those who would restrict or proscribe it can only be regarded with suspicion and contempt.

Under more exact quantitative scrutiny, as when one sizes up the rolls of institutions on either side of the issue, the number of players begins to dwindle, especially on the anti side. The pros often claim twenty million hunters, but it is a meaningless number, for it does not represent a cohesive bloc. There is cohesiveness only among the two million hunters who belong to grass-roots sportsmen's clubs affiliated, through state umbrella groups, with the National Wildlife Federation; among the hunters enrolled in the 1.1-million-member National Rifle Association; and possibly among another million hunters who belong to such other pro organizations as Ducks Unlimited, the Izaak Walton League of America, and Safari Club International.

Against these three to four million stands a much smaller army of active anti-hunters, numbering fewer than one million and belonging for the most part to the Humane Society of the United States, the Fund for Animals, the Friends of Animals, and the Animal Protection Institute of America, among some two to three dozen humane groups marching collectively under the banner of animal liberation.

Even as sociologists have classified American hunters according to their primary motive for pursuing game—for meat, for sport, or for immersion in nature—so, too, have they attempted to distinguish the varieties of anti-hunter. There seems to be consensus that anti-hunting sentiment runs in three directions. It runs strongly, first, toward the idea that hunting is cruel, that hunted animals react to the chase in terror, that wounded animals suffer excruciating pain, and that dead animals leave the equivalent of sorrowful widows and orphans in their passing. A second direction finds that hunting is unethical; that it is, in the words of Joseph Wood Krutch, a perfect form of "pure evil" and a "damnable" pleasure, that it degrades both the practitioner and society at large. And the third casts the hunter as spoiler of ecological balances and extirpator of endangered species. No doubt I oversimplify the taxonomy of the anti-hunter by shaving it so closely, given the probability that there are shadings of all three attitudes in nearly every staunch anti-hunting individual. Still, three types do emerge with sufficient distinctions to justify labeling the first as anthropomorphic, the second as moralistic, and the third as hyperbolic.

From personal encounters with the breed as well as sorties through the literature of anti-hunting, I surmise that the anthropomorphic types perceive wild animals much as they might view a menagerie of cats and dogs and gerbils and pet-store parakeets. I suspect, too, that they tend to fantasize the natural world as a kind of idyllic pastoral stage upon which no animal ever suffers or dies except at the hands of a cruel and inept hunter. There is generally less concern for the species than for an individual animal, and the furrier its coat and the wetter and browner its eyes, the better. Walt Disney is the patron saint of the anthropomorphic types. For the most part they tend to live in big cities, where they keep their big dogs on short leashes in small apartments.

The moralistic anti-hunter is a breed apart. What most concerns him is not the perceived suffering of a hunted animal but rather the "uncivilized" behavior of the hunter. Possibly to justify their belief that killing wild animals is indeed uncivilized, some moralists purposefully place recreation and subsistence hunters in the same lineup with leg-hold trappers, varmint shooters, predator poisoners, seal clubbers, whalers, and assorted other killers whose procedures are even more distasteful to the public. To the extreme moralist, all of it is hunting and it is all wrong. And on occasion, a few display their real feelings about both man and beast. (I was talking once with a woman who grew up in New York City and now lives in a Connecticut hill town where deer feed on her front lawn in April and in November get shot at by hunters in the woods. She said she loved the deer. And the men who shoot at them? "Those bloody lousy hunters," said the woman through clenched teeth. "They're no better than animals.")

As for the third type of anti-hunter, I use the modifier "hyperbolic" advisedly, for his argument is richly steeped in extravagant overstatement. In claiming that hunters upset the natural balance by causing species extinctions, the hyperbolist plays somewhat the same game as the moralist: He resorts to the lineup. He places the sport hunter next to the market hunter of yore and hopes that the audience won't notice the difference. In his book *The Politics of Extinction* (Macmillan, 1975), Fund for Animals lobbyist Lewis Regenstein writes: "It is thoroughly documented that over the years hunters have been responsible for helping to wipe out numerous species of wildlife." Citing the U.S. Department of the Interior as his source, Regenstein then lists the elk, Carolina parakeet, heath hen, passenger pigeon, timber wolf, and cougar as species made extinct in the eastern United States "due in part or in whole to over-hunting."

Of the six species, two—the heath hen and the passenger pigeon—were indeed hunted to extinction; but not by twentieth-century sport hunters toting firearms, rather by nineteenth-century market hunters armed with whatever was handy, including nets and clubs. As for the elk, it was gone from Pennsylvania and most other eastern states by the 1870s, a decade generally remembered as having fostered only the most tentative beginnings of recreation hunting in North America. Moreover, what really finished the elk in the East was not so much the rise of the hunter as the decline and fall of its wild habitat. The Carolina parakeet, done in by nineteenth-century hunters? To some extent, yes. But the parakeet's greatest executioner was the agriculturist, for the simple reason that the parakeet devastated orchards, even as the wolf and the cougar on occasion raided livestock inventories and thereby brought bounties down on their heads. Yet for all the hyperbole, Regenstein at least acknowledged that hunting was not the only factor in pushing species to the brink. In an earlier book, *Death as a Way of Life* (Little, Brown, 1970), the other grand hyperbolist, Roger Caras, declared that "hunting has been not just 'a major factor' in the endangerment or extinction [of dozens of animal species] but the *only* major factor."

Over the years, studies of one kind or another have shown that the anti-hunter I identify as anthropomorphic is probably the most numerous of the three, and that the hyperbolist is probably the rarest. In a report for the Michigan Department of Natural Resources, researcher William W. Shaw sampled a cohort of supporters of the Fund for Animals. To ascertain the respondents' relative concern between the issues of perceived cruelty and human ethics, Shaw asked: "Which bothers you more about hunting: the suffering of animals that have been shot or wounded [or] the idea that humans can get pleasure from an activity which involves killing a living animal?" The responses showed 60 percent bothered more by the suffering of animals, 22 percent bothered more by the idea that humans derive pleasure from killing, and 18 percent bothered equally by both. Then Shaw asked which was more bothersome: the suffering of animals or "the idea that due to hunting, there may be less wildlife." Again the anti-hunters indicated more concern on the cruelty issue, 73 percent, compared to 16 percent concerned about "less wildlife," with 11 percent bothered equally by both issues.

Shaw's conclusion that cruelty as an issue looms larger than either ethics or ecological impact was more or less corroborated in a 1976 study commissioned by the National Shooting Sports Foundation. The foundation retained the advertising firm of Batten, Barton, Durstine & Osborn to conduct what is known in the trade as a problem-detection study among respondents selected (strong pro- and anti-hunters were screened out) in four major metropolitan areas. BBD&O presented a list of 115 problems to its respondents and asked them to score the problems in order of their relative importance and frequency. Ranked by combined importance and frequency, the top five problems detected were: (1) *hunters kill other hunters accidentally,* (2) *wounded animals die a slow death,* (3) *wounded animals die a painful death,* (4) *hunters don't have to know anything to buy a rifle,* and (5) *leaving a wounded animal to die is sadistic.* Based on these and other findings, BBD&O concluded that "the public is revolted by the perceived suffering of hunted wildlife, but perceives this suffering to be the result of the hunter's ineptness and don't-care attitude rather than intentional cruelty on the part of the hunter."

In Anderson County, East Texas, cruising along in the constable's blue sedan, I suddenly wonder what all the anthropomorphic, moralistic, hyperbolic young women volunteering in

Cleveland Amory's headquarters on New York's Fifty-seventh Street would think if they could see Jerry Owens now with the pistol on his hip and the shotgun in its rack beside the gearshift. Amory's Fund for Animals lists Owens as having a residence and telephone in Arlington, Texas, situated about halfway between Dallas and Fort Worth. Owens, his wife, and their two children did indeed live in Arlington for a number of years, quietly minding their own business, except for Owens's investigative work and his increasing involvement in matters of interest to Cleveland Amory. Then, one evening, or rather over a number of evenings, Jerry Owens picked up his ringing telephone and realized that sooner than later he would be moving away from Arlington, because a good-ole-boy voice at the other end of the line was passing along some information in no uncertain words, and the words were threatening. Now Owens and his family live a hundred miles away in Anderson County and he prefers that I do not mention the name of the town; though inasmuch as he holds public office, as constable, I suspect any good ole boy could track him down without much trouble. And I also suspect it would not pay any good ole boy to try.

We drive up a long dirt track through open fields to a fortress-like ranch house at the top of a hill. "This is where I hide out," Owens says. "There's good cover up here in the oaks and you can see pretty far down the hill for whoever's thinking about coming on up."

I tell Owens that with all the young people joining the animal protection movement and swelling its ranks, he shouldn't worry so much about the other side. "I don't," he replies. "But sometimes I worry about the movement. Sure it's growing, in numbers. But in action, it's dying. You can sell bottles of air for just so long."

The animal protection movement—the "Kingdom of the Kind" as Margaret G. Nichols, a *Field & Stream* editor, once called it in a critical study—encompasses an array of organizations so diverse and in some cases so fiercely competitive that one risks nothing worse than exaggeration in comparing it with the feuding fiefdoms of southern Europe in Borgia days. I do not mean to impugn here either the motives or the goals of these various groups, or to imply that many from time to time have not joined hands in common efforts to make life, or at least death, a little easier for some of the non-human creatures that inhabit the earth. Intergroup rivalries, one notes with regret, are not unknown in the environmental movement either; or, for that matter, among the ranks of any other broadly based cause. It just seems to me that some champions of animal welfare have lately been spending more time protecting their institutional flanks than the hides of the creatures they are pledged to protect. "It boils down to a crazy battle for supremacy," says Margaret Nichols. "The movement is riddled with professional jealousies."

Much of the envy is directed at Cleveland Amory and his Fund for Animals, founded in 1967 and a relative newcomer in the company of such landmark groups as the American Humane Association (founded in 1877), the Humane Society of the United States (1954), and Friends of Animals, Inc. (1957). Until recently, adman Belton Mouras's Animal Protection Institute (1968), based in Sacramento, California, gave Amory's Fund a run for the media and the money. But the Institute became more of an embarrassment than a pacesetter within the movement when the California attorney general's office in the mid-1970s began investigating allegations that Mouras's advertising agency benefited financially from Mouras's Animal Protection Institute ad campaigns (Mouras having since divested himself of interest in the agency). Thus, within what most observers consider the radical left wing of the movement, the major rivalry is now reduced to a one-on-one scrap between Amory's Fund and Alice Herrington's Friends of Animals.

Friendly words rarely pass between Herrington and Amory. Amory is too much the proper Bostonian to excoriate his rival, but Herrington is a self-described "farmer's daughter" from Wisconsin, and while she concedes that Amory is a "pretty fair" spokesman for the movement, she wonders petulantly why he "always looks like an unmade bed." Amory envies Herrington's multimillion-dollar budget, most of which goes into the spaying of domestic animals. Herrington envies Amory's consistent good press and the credit given to or claimed by the Fund for victories she believes were engineered by others, including her own organization. "I just hate to see the do-nothing groups getting all the credit," Alice Herrington said after a federal judge ordered a moratorium on porpoise kills by Pacific tuna men. The newspapers had identified the Fund as the spearhead of the effort that led to that decision; what irritated Herrington was the unmentioned fact that it was her organization, not Amory's, that had pressed uncompromisingly and alone for the total moratorium.

Amory's posture on sport hunting has mellowed in recent years, but it has not moved from the basic position that hunting by his definition is not a sport. He no longer spins the old acerbic yarns that laced his 1974 manifesto, *Man Kind? Our Incredible War on Wildlife.* But he has not closed the book on his "Hunt-the-Hunters Hunt Club," a mythic "world-wild" organization dedicated to the proposition that hunters are a renewable resource, a crop to be harvested, a herd to be trimmed for its own good. As Amory used to tell it, the club's motto was: "If you can't play a sport, shoot one." But not during the hunter's dating season, and please don't drape the trophy over the hood of your car. Once, in a review for *TV Guide,* Amory described a drama revolving around attempts to rescue a hunter from a mountain ledge. Wrote Amory: "I was cheering for the ledge."

Such swingeing comments invariably brought out the hired guns on the other side. Amory was "a man with a nonstop mouth," wrote Clare Conley in *Argosy.* "A lace-curtain Beacon Hill eco-fake," wrote John Madson in *True,* adding that an insult from Amory was "like being run over by a baby buggy." Moreover, anonymous saboteurs harassed the old curmudgeon, especially in Texas. Despite numerous pleas for a correction, the Dallas *Times-Herald* for many months managed to identify the author of the syndicated column "Amory's People" as Cleveland Armory. Amory said later he figured that, given the fact this happened in Dallas, it had to be a Freudian slip.

Most reasonable people exposed to the apocryphal violence

of the hunting wars do not seem to be affected much by the overblown rhetoric. But not everyone is reasonable. Jerry Owens, after all, has been driven by threats into semi-hiding in the hills of Anderson County. And from the other extreme, a reader of *Audubon* writes in dead earnest in the May 1979 issue that the only way to be "fair" to hunters is to "pursue, terrorize, trap, torture, and shoot them with their own bullets and arrows. Then leave them to hobble wounded until they die."

Alice Herrington's bias against hunting is a bit more intellectual than Amory's, although her publications, like his, tend to dwell on the presumed suffering of hunted animals and thereby play to the emotions of her anthropomorphizing constituents. Almost alone among the radical-left animal-libbers, Herrington seems to understand that wildlife needs habitat as well as human kindness, and she scorns the woods managers who would manipulate ecosystems, explaining that "Remington Arms doesn't like climax forests because deer can't climb trees." She is likewise alarmed over the genetic dangers inherent in the traditional hunter's quest for the trophy specimens of game species. "In Pennsylvania," she says, "they don't have deer any more. They have over-sized bunny rabbits with spike antlers." But this is cerebral stuff for anti-hunters of the rank and file; they appreciate Herrington better when she declares that the only game regulation she'll ever lobby for is "an open season on hunters."

Herrington's authentic lobby and legal hit squad is the Committee for Humane Legislation, based in Washington, D.C. Among the committee's latest attacks on the hunting establishment is a lawsuit demanding of the U.S. Fish and Wildlife Service that environmental impact statements be filed on all projects funded under the Pittman-Robertson Act. Enacted in 1937, the measure provides for an 11 percent excise tax on sporting arms and ammunition (and, by amendment since 1971, for a similar tax on handguns and archery equipment). The levies over the years have raised nearly one billion dollars, and the money has been allocated to the states not only for wildlife management projects but for game habitat acquisition and research as well. The litigation presumes that impact-statement scrutiny will leave the Pittman-Robertson program with bad environmental marks.

Herrington is also behind a move to ban all hunting on public lands. In a direct-mail appeal for signatures supporting such action, she leads off her "Dear Friend" letter by asking: "Are you held spellbound by the brilliance of a cardinal in the snow?" and then neatly segues to the statement that "these [among other] independent, beautiful creatures fall prey to man's traps, guns, poisons, and clubs—as many millions do every year." Elsewhere in the letter and the preamble to the petition, she manages to convey the patently false impression that the National Wildlife Federation is "funded by the armaments industry" and that non-hunters are somehow officially "excluded" from public lands during "the killing season."

When the hunting chips are down, the farmer's daughter from Wisconsin overreaches even Cleveland Amory—and knows how to hit the tender places. A number of years ago a herd-thinning deer hunt was proposed for the Great Swamp National Wildlife Refuge in New Jersey. Herrington responded with a newspaper advertisement, an open letter addressed to "Rod Hunter, Sports Columnist." Across the top of the ad, the headline challenged hunters in general to "Make it 'Dear' . . . Not 'Deer' . . . will you . . . won't you . . . can't you?" A cheesecake photograph of actress Gloria DeHaven appeared beside the text, and below it, the signatures of Miss DeHaven, Lauren Bacall, Gretchen Wyler, Ali McGraw, June Havoc, Patrice Munsel, Sheila MacRae, Betsy Palmer, and Joanne Woodward. The gist of the message was that these alluring signatories were "not turned on by a show of masculinity which takes place in the forests. . . . We like guys whose virility holds on better proving grounds." Amory, the man who would have had us hunt hunters except during their dating season, thought that was going too far. He told his colleagues at the Fund for Animals that Alice Herrington was hitting the hunter "below the belt."

From the shrill, free-swinging left wing of the animal protection movement, anti-hunting sentiment ranges across a field of decreasingly feisty institutions toward a middle ground exemplified by the Humane Society of the United States and its soft-spoken president, John A. Hoyt. Hoyt abhors sport hunting, but he is not abrasive about it. In fact, his society's position is downright benign compared with the radicals' pronunciamentos. The society's goal, it is written, is "to develop, largely through education and the exposure of the unnecessary cruelties involved in much of the public hunting as conducted today, a generation of adults who will no longer have any wish, desire, or willingness to kill any living creature purely for pleasure and recreation."

Right of center, as perceived by the true animal-libber, the movement falls off its own edge, as the earth did in pre-Columbian times. Here one begins to encounter the environmental organizations, which for the most part view wildlife as a part of the whole rather than an end in itself, and which, to the everlasting consternation of Cleveland Amory and Alice Herrington, tend to tolerate regulated sport hunting in pragmatic acceptance of the facts of life, and death, and politics. For example, the Sierra Club—founded by John Muir, who traveled the high country unarmed but nevertheless reported great value in biscuits shortened with bear grease—is "not opposed to sport hunting outside of approved sanctuaries such as national parks, provided it is regulated," but adds, perhaps in deference to its increasingly urban constituency, that "more and more people are finding ways to value wildlife in other terms." The Wilderness Society "subscribes to hunting as a legitimate use of wilderness in national forests and certain wildlife areas." And the National Audubon Society—named after John James Audubon, who, according to Cleveland Amory, "shot five birds for every one he ever painted"—"has never been opposed to the hunting of game species if that hunting is done ethically and in accordance with laws and regulations designed to prevent depletion of the wildlife resource." The society's policy statement adds, however, that "we do not advocate hunting. . . . Our objective is wildlife and environmental conservation, not the promotion of hunting."

Possibly the only organization that might not fit into one or another of such niches as left and center and out-of-this-world is Defenders of Wildlife, a Washington, D.C.-based group with a rapidly expanding membership (45,000 at last count) and what would seem to be a foot in both the humane and environmental camps. "I suppose we're the most radical of the rational," says John W. Grandy, Defenders' executive vice-president. "We're not anti-hunting; we're just awful hard on it. We don't want to destroy the system. We want to make the things that are wrong with the system work. We're looking for ways to instill a new wildlife ethic." Defenders specializes in push-and-shove, often in court, with federal and state wildlife agencies, especially those which, in Grandy's words, "go in to kill one kind of animal so they can have more of another."

One might think that the pro-hunters would be better organized than the antis, but they are not. Institutionally, the pros are in disarray. Their spokesmen explain it by saying that it is the hunter's nature to be individualistic and parochial; that, as a rule, hunters do not respond to broad sweeping attacks on their sport, and are more likely to spar casually among themselves over the practical specifics of seasons and bag limits than to take up cudgels in ideological battle with the Cleveland Amorys of America. Where the institutional antis seem to be handicapped by sibling rivalries, the pros suffer for lack of long-range vision. No one group appears to know or care much what the other is doing. There are tactics for fighting the brush-fire wars against Alice Herrington, but no overall strategies for winning public acceptance—or tolerance—of the hunting tradition.

Toward that end, the large membership organizations are almost wholly ineffective. The National Wildlife Federation, with many non-hunters among its 3.5 million members, makes a deliberate effort *not* to get embroiled in the hunting wars. In fact, in its widely circulated "Should We Hunt?" brochure, the Federation explains that "we have neither opposed nor recommended hunting to our members, holding that the question of whether to hunt is one that each individual must decide for himself." The bulk of the message, of course, is that regulated hunting is a proper and sometimes necessary wildlife management tool. Nevertheless, the Federation says it deplores the continuing controversy over hunting and urges its members not to waste their time and energy arguing while "shopping centers and marinas" supplant wildlife habitat. In practice, this sound advice filters down to reach mainly the Federation's backpackers and bird watchers, while its hunters look elsewhere for direction. Mostly they look to the Federation's state affiliates, many of which are delighted to argue the hunting issue with truculent vigor. Possibly the most effective of the fifty affiliates is Michigan United Conservation Clubs, Inc., an organization with 110,000 members, twenty-eight full-time staff employees, and a budget of $1.7 million.

Safari Club International, headquartered in Tucson, Arizona, claims nebulous hundreds of thousands of members in the United States and Canada and projects as its twin objectives "the protection of the rights of hunters and the conservation of wildlife." The *1979 Conservation Directory* (published by the National Wildlife Federation) illuminates the latter goal by explaining that the Safari Club seeks to promote wildlife conservation "through selective trophy hunting of aged and infirm animals." Exactly how one determines an animal's age and infirmity through a telescopic sight is not made clear. Exactly how the club seeks to protect the rights of hunters is not clear either. As for the organization's public image, I can only report on the view from here. The view is of nostalgia inside a stuffed shirt under a pith helmet, and two hands. One hand is holding Richard Haliburton's 1920s classic, *The Royal Road to Romance,* while the other clutches a smoking .458-caliber elephant rifle.

The image in other views may be even less charitable, for it wasn't too long ago that a letter on Safari Club International stationery arrived at the U.S. Department of the Interior, seeking permission to import "hunting trophies" of a number of endangered species, including one hundred cheetahs, twenty-five tigers, ten snow leopards, ten white rhinos, five gorillas, and five orangutans. Club officials later insisted that the letter was written without their knowledge or consent, but that in any event the writer had no intent other than to dramatize some perceived imperfection in the Endangered Species Act. I heard a different version of the story in San Antonio, Texas, which happens to be hometown for Game Conservation International, a similar fraternity of trophy hunters, some of whom hold the Safari Club at about the same level of esteem as Alice Herrington holds Cleveland Amory. "Those Safari Club people," said my informant at Game Coin, as the Texas group is known acronymically (as well as in deference to the wealth of some of its Lone Star members), "they're nothing but a bunch of rabbit hunters." I asked him: If the Safari Clubbers were indeed only rabbit hunters, why would they want to import trophies of tigers and rhinos and orangutans? The San Antonian stared at me for a long time, and then he said, "Hell's bells, hain't you ever seen a trophy room with nothing but rabbits? After a while on the wall, they get to looking kinda lonely all by themselves."

For a lonely while, Game Coin sponsored a spinoff organization known first as the Legal Defense Fund and later as the Sportsmen's Alliance, whose mission was "to protect the U.S. hunting public against infringement of its civil rights." The Alliance, however, never got off the ground. Its mission has since been assumed by the Wildlife Legislative Fund of America, based in Columbus, Ohio. The Fund's chairman is G. Ray Arnett, a past president of the National Wildlife Federation and former director of the California Department of Fish and Game. Both Ohio and California figured in the organization's genesis, for it was in those two states that founders of the Fund defeated efforts to ban the leg-hold trap. But the Fund's association with the trapping issue is not regarded joyously by all who would support its stance on hunting. Alice Herrington herself says she now finds her Friends "in bed with hunters in some states" because of the damage inflicted on hunting dogs by leg-hold traps.

And finally, rounding out the cast of players on the pro-hunting side, one arrives among the quieter communicators, such as the Wildlife Society, a professional association and publisher of the *Journal of Wildlife Management;* the Wildlife Management Institute, sponsor of the annual North American Wildlife and Natural Resources Conference; the National Shooting Sports Foundation, a public relations outfit supported by the sporting arms industry; and the International Association of Fish and Wildlife Agencies, which, in turn, has spawned an offspring called AWARE, meaning "America's Wildlife Association for Resource Education." AWARE is attempting to put together a prime-time television series that "will tell the real story of fish and wildlife conservation." An appeal for financial support, according to one spokesman, "has not been a howling success."

Most rational pro individuals and institutions realize that their collective best interests will not be served simply by raising money for new lobbying and public relations efforts. They know that the hunting establishment must, as the saying goes, begin to clean up its own act. But how—when trespass in some regions is almost epidemic, when the most common rural road sign is the one peppered by shot and shell, and when some state game agencies in total disregard of public sensitivity require the deer hunter to truss his homeward buck to the hood of his car, among other traditional hunting gaffes? Cleaning up the act is easier said than done. "People's traditions," says retired Remington Arms Company president Philip H. Burdett, "are not easily changed by somebody else's rules."

Jerry Owens and I have been mulling over the pros and the antis for a couple of days now in East Texas, and we have been talking, too, with Texas people who may feel pro about their own kind of hunting but who are downright apoplectic anti about the way some other people go about it during deer season, shooting dogs and cows and mules in simple-minded error or arrogant mischief. Inasmuch as the wearing of blaze orange clothing is neither mandated by game law nor considered even remotely fashionable in Texas, and since I have none to wear in any event, I decide it is time to move on to where the shooting might be more discreet and selective. Owens wants to know where my itinerary will take me next. I tell him San Antonio, the Brush Country, and Kerrville, the Hill Country. By way of Dallas, first.

And straightaway Owens says to me, "Keep your head down."

The Gun at the Window

The news on the radio in my rental car this morning informs me that a sniper is at large once again somewhere in Texas. Somewhere nearby, probably, since I am approaching the outskirts of Dallas and the sniper's two victims are said to have perished in Irving, the next town over, heading west. The victims were riding in separate cars. The sniper presumably selected them at random and shot both from a highway overpass. The voice on the radio is telling me that the bullets that struck the two men have been recovered. Pending the results of a ballistics test, the unrecovered weapon has been identified as a deer rifle. A *deer* rifle? I hear a bell ringing. It is not on the radio; it is in my head. Snipers with deer rifles give me this feeling of déjà vu.

Over the years, I resisted making straight connections between the gun and the hunting issues. I believed that the two could be viewed apart and separate, with few loose threads. I knew that some anti-hunters favored stringent gun controls and that a few anti-gunners favored curbs on the chase. But for myself, I could see not even a looping link between the urban mugger's zip gun and the outdoorsman deep in December woods; or, for that matter, between the assassin of a President and a rifle that in other hands happens to be used to assassinate deer. Reasonable people assure me the issues are best viewed apart, and kept that way. But as I noted before, not everyone is reasonable.

The eminently reasonable Alaskan wildlife biologist David Klein once observed that the anti-hunting fervor has at least "some of its roots in the symbolism associating the gun with crime and violence." In the public eye, wrote Klein, "the gun has increasingly come to represent the tool of criminal violence and the weapon of seemingly pointless wars which degrade humanity; it is seen as a direct agent of death or destruction. When large elements of society are turning against expressions of overt aggression, the gun, whether in the hands of the criminal, the soldier, or the hunter, symbolizes aggression; therefore the hunter by association becomes a primary focus for anti-aggression appeals."

Unreasonably, the symbols sometimes get turned inside out, so that the gun and the bullet by association become the foci for anti-hunting appeals. Alice Herrington draws her own provocative conclusions about the source of excise-tax monies in a piece entitled "Some Things You're Not Supposed to Know About Hunters." "The Mafia and other underworld characters," she writes, "probably buy as many guns and bullets as hunters do and thus the Mafia appropriately supports hunters. And every time a president is assassinated or a citizen murdered, the hunting world reaps an 11 percent reward if the bullet came from a rifle, and 10 percent if from a handgun." By Herrington's definition, Mafiosi and other underworlders must therefore number close to twenty million and collectively shoot up a storm of lead—say, about fifty rounds per person per year, which is either one helluva lot of target practice or plenty of contracts on pigeons plucked for the city morgue. Following her reasoning, I figure that Lee Harvey Oswald's excise-tax contribution to the hunting world in 1963, for both rifle and ammunition, was less than $2.75.

Possibly the most astonishing straight-line connection ever attempted between the gun-control issue and the question of hunting was one which appeared some years ago in a Friends of Animals publication under the by-line of Cyril Toker, a fiery polemicist for the animal-libbers. Part of Toker's thesis goes like this:

> The wanton savagery that is being visited upon helpless wild creatures must, inevitably, be turned on us. No longer

can this criminality be ignored by an indifferent and unconcerned populace. Day by day the toll in human lives
grows larger. Why, you may ask, are we to hold the hunter
responsible, in significant measure, for the death that stalks
our streets and ravages our homes? There are two reasons
why the hunter must be broken if we are to escape, ourselves, from the menace of the gun. The hunter has, in the
first instance, promoted, disseminated, and incalculated
[*sic*] a philosophy of brutal violence within the very fabric
of our society. Sadistic cruelty and utter contempt for the
sanctity of life have been glorified. The minds of the young
have been subverted and distorted by these perverts. They
have sought to raise yet another generation in their
image—strangers to pity, devoid of compassion, the person-
ification of all that is vile and contemptible within the
human frame. Are we to wonder why truth does not exist in
their code? Are we to be amazed when those who have been
reared in the school of violence come forward, their lust to
kill unsatiated, to point the gun at those who stand beside
them? And why, we ask, is the gun always at hand? Because
the hunter has, in the second instance, ensured that every
effort to achieve gun control shall be frustrated. Are we to
expect that those who kill for pleasure, that those who hold
life so cheaply, will allow the cries of widows and orphans to
disturb them? Surely not.

Cyril Toker has spoken. Amen.

I drive into downtown Dallas, run an obligatory errand,
make a business call, and, on the way out, pass by the Texas
Schoolbook Depository at Dealey Plaza. And I stop, because
bells are ringing somewhere between my ears. There are tourists on the sidewalk, looking up, staring at the corner window
on the sixth floor. Me, I stare at the tourists and wonder what it
is they feel in the gut about the rifles at the windows of their
worlds, about the assassination of deer in soft oak woods and
the culling of Presidents in concrete plazas. The tourists do not
have an answer for me. Nor does the attendant of the lot where

I have parked my car, though he comes closer to it. The attendant has a curious manner of speaking; his voice, a fine rolling Texan drawl, seems to rise at the end of each statement in a looping question mark. I have asked of him directions to Fort Worth. Thinking, he runs a wrinkled hand over his white hair. Then he says, "Sharp right at the light, downhill, the way Kennedy went. When they got him?"

The modern history of firearms control in this country was opened in Dallas, at the Schoolbook Depository, on November 22, 1963. Everything before then is ancient, including John F. Kennedy's unsuccessful senatorial effort a few years earlier to pinch off the importation of surplus European military rifles as a measure of protection, not for Presidents in open limousines, but for gun manufacturers in Massachusetts and Connecticut. The 1960s were good years to feel bad—or mad—about guns. Three years after Dallas, young Charles Whitman dragged a footlocker to the observation desk of the University of Texas tower at Austin and took out a .357 Magnum revolver, a 9-mm. Luger, a 6-mm. bolt-action rifle with a four-power telescopic sight, a .30-caliber carbine, a 12-gauge shotgun, and 700 rounds of ammunition. Within an hour or so, fourteen people were dead or dying on the campus lawns below. Then the action moved out of Texas, mostly north. In 1967, ghetto people rioted in twenty tumbledown cities, and more than a few of the rioters had guns. In 1968, from a window in Memphis, James Earl Ray cut down Martin Luther King with a .30/06 rifle that the press would describe as of a kind made to kill deer. In Los Angeles later that year, Sirhan Sirhan put a pistol bullet into the brain of Robert F. Kennedy. Out of the reaction to these slaughters came the Gun Control Act of 1968, banning mail-order sales of firearms and ammunition, confining the purchase of guns and ammunition to the buyer's state of residence, requiring dealers to demand proof of each purchaser's identity, and forbidding dealers to sell handguns to persons under twenty-one and rifles and shotguns to persons under eighteen. The Gun Control Act did all of these things, but it did not stop the slaughter. The slaughter went on—on through all the years of congressional debate that so far has failed to yield an additional shred of meaningful gun-control legislation.

Lately the advocates of stronger control have focused their attention on handguns in general and on the so-called Saturday Night Special, the snub-nose revolver, in particular. They would have the federal government ban the manufacture and sale of the specials and require a criminal check of every pistol purchaser. The gun lobby, on the other hand, sees this effort as another attempt by the "bleeding hearts" to infringe the American people's right to keep and bear arms.

And what does all of this have to do with hunting? On the surface of it, not much. But it has plenty to do with hunting if you happen to subscribe to the Domino Theory as promulgated by the National Rifle Association of America, the troglodyte propagandists of the gunnery press, and U.S. Representative John D. Dingell of Michigan. In 1975, Congressman Dingell, a sometime director of the National Rifle Association and a persistent foe of gun control, advised the House crime subcommittee: "Any fool who can push a hacksaw can make a handgun out of a shotgun or rifle in ten minutes, and there is no way to 'regulate' that. The only way to eliminate handguns is to eliminate *all* guns, and it is foolish to make artificial distinctions. . . . If you are wondering why shotgun owners oppose the banning of handguns, that is the reason—they know they will be next on the chopping block."

John Dingell figures in a popular tale told along the corridors of the NRA's $5 million headquarters building in Washington, D.C. According to the story, the congressman was tending to his dying father when, from the deathbed, came the old man's parting words: "John, don't let the bastards get our guns." Told intensely, as it was to me by gun lobbyist John D. Aquilino, Jr., the story is perhaps less illuminating of the Dingell personality than it is of the far-out paranoia of the National Rifle Association of America.

·　·　·

It is one big country, Texas. For all I know, it could be nine or ten big countries. The South Texas plains are so different from the northeastern piney woods. There is honey mesquite and pencil cholla and wild lantana down this way, and coyotes are said to grow fat as hogs eating venison, though I suspect the song-dogs with teeth do no better on that score than thin people do, hunting with rifles. San Antonio sits squarely between the Brush Country of the southern plains and the Hill Country of the Edwards Plateau. It is an old and lovely city, but it is growing too fast for its own good, not to mention the good of the Brush and the Hill countries. Downtown, one finds the River Walk winding picturesquely along the San Antonio River, the HemisFair Plaza with its Tower of the Americas, and, at the very heart of the city, the Alamo. In December here there is Christmas and deer season. In April there is a nine-day fiesta, with many parades along Broadway. In May there is activity at the popular hotels. It is convention time. Among the conventions to be held are the 7th International Hunters' and Fishermen's Conference, sponsored by Game Coin, and closely preceding it, the 108th annual meeting of the National Rifle Association.

Texas is a splendid choice for the NRA, as it is a rifleman's state for certain. In some lonelier parts of the Lone Star, hardly a single pickup truck fails to display the prerequisite rifle racked upside down across the rear window of the cab. And San Antonio, with its Alamo, is surely a rifleman's town. Riflemen are not likely to forget the Alamo, where the old buck-skinned *posse comitatus* stood off Santa Ana's hordes and went down for the final count swinging, John Wayne style. The Alamo was a cradle of liberty, for ever afterward Texans were at liberty to keep and bear arms. For a while, they bore their arms with a vengeance. The author J. Frank Dobie recounts how, in the 1860s, the men of one Texas town vied with those of another to see who could kill the most game in a single day. Squirrels and rabbits counted for one point each, turkeys for five, and deer for ten. In one astonishing day's shoot-out, the total points scored by two competing hamlets was 3,470. I would be glad to say so much for the ancient history, except that the ancient history keeps hanging around. Here and there, in Texas and elsewhere, one can still see a faded bumper sticker proclaiming that "God, guns, and guts made America free."

By no great stretch of demographic coincidence, the top man in the NRA is a Texan named Harlon B. Carter. He grew up in Laredo, attended the University of Texas, served thirty-four years with the Border Patrol (and seven of those as its chief), and, during World War II, was in charge of what his official NRA biography describes as "several operations in alien enemy detention and prisoner programs." Carter was voted the "Outstanding American Handgunner of 1977," and he has a big bronze statue to prove it. He is a large, ruddy, bull-necked, blue-eyed man. During an interview with him shortly after his election to the NRA's executive vice-presidency, I noticed that Carter likes to preface statements of policy with the phrase "We law-abiding and decent people . . ." Which—since I was not then, am not now, and never shall be a member of the NRA—left me feeling a little indecent, if not downright illegal.

Harlon B. Carter believes in the Domino Theory, and he believes as well that the aim of the gun controllers is total confiscation of all privately owned firearms in America, of which there are believed to be no fewer than 150 million. Most of these weapons are not owned by hunters, or even by members of the Mafia. They are owned by people who are frightened by what they perceive through the windows of their worlds.

About half of the NRA's members are hunters, but hunting is not always the primary motive when a hunter joins the NRA. An opinion survey of 130,000 members found that "the most important single reason I first joined NRA" was not "Hunting" (at 14.7 percent, the second-highest of ten responses), but "Protecting My Gun Rights."

Having paid my respects to the Alamo, and left muted regrets at Game Coin to the effect that I shall be able to attend neither their convention nor the NRA's, I split for Brush and Hill Country feeling truly regretful only that I shall miss the April fiesta with its parades along Broadway. But maybe it is just as well, as things turn out, for I shall miss something else. I shall not be there when the former truck driver Ira Attebery, in his mobile home near the starting point of the biggest parade, pokes a rifle out of his window or doorway and, in forty-five minutes of shooting, kills two spectators and wounds at least thirty-one others before putting a bullet through his own head. The parade commemorates the Battle of San Jacinto in 1836, at which time Sam Houston's Texas troopers shouted "Remember the Alamo" as they put the Mexican army to rout. Attebery, probably remembering nothing, will almost rout the San Antonio police department. In his trailer, police will find an arsenal of rifles and pistols, but the killing weapon will turn out to be a U.S. military M-16, the rifle that lost a war in Vietnam. No doubt some cub reporter or crusty historian along the way will want to identify it as a deer rifle.

Cottage Industry

Texas is big, all right, but insofar as hunting is concerned, it is big enough only if you own a huntable piece of it or, if not, have a friend who does; and barring either of those eventualities, you had better have *muy grande* disposable income to purchase your lease on a stranger's land. If you want to hunt. For all its robust girth, Texas probably has less public land, proportionately, than any state west of the Mississippi River. Posted signs dominate the landscape of East Texas. In the center are wire fences. And in the west are riflemen not uneasy about using armed trespassers for target practice. Except for its harder edges, Texas represents the way it is going to be for many hunters across America in the years ahead. Increasingly, they will have to pay for their sport, the free hunt having gone out of style shortly after the nickel beer. In a sense, hunters always did pay, if not in money, then surely in time and effort. "The huntin' must have been mighty fine here in the 1870s," an old-time Texan near Hondo told me one afternoon. "No wire, no sign, no license, no limit. Exceptin' you still hadda pay the price. Prob'ly to the Comanches, who was huntin' *you.*"

While limited hunting—and not the best of it at that—is available on fewer than two million acres of federal and state lands, mostly in timbered East Texas, more than thirty million acres of private land are under day or seasonal lease to those who can afford the going rates. The day rates run anywhere from a low of twenty-five dollars per hunter in scratchier parts of the Hill Country to fifty dollars or so in the Brush, where the deer tend to grow bigger. Then there are the seasonal leases to groups or corporations that will take over an entire ranch at rates of up to four dollars an acre. I am told that one Louisiana corporation pays four dollars an acre for the exclusive right to hunt dove and quail on a Brush Country ranch, near Cotulla, owned by former Texas governor Dolph Briscoe. The ranch is 38,000 acres. On some leases, the lessee pays extra for his game. A ranch near Kerrville in the Hill Country advertises only in the *Wall Street Journal* and charges, in addition to its stiff day rate, a fee of five hundred dollars for a "trophy" buck. State big-game biologist Bob Cook says he once asked an East Coast visitor to that ranch why he came so far to shoot a deer.

The hunter replied, "Where else can I see a hundred of them, pick the one I want, and get wined and dined?"

Cook glanced at the man's trophy, a scrawny buck of barely a hundred pounds. "But look at what you got," said Cook.

"But where else can I have a guaranteed kill?" said the hunter.

Easy-does-it seems to be the main attraction. There are hunting-lease classifieds in every major newspaper. A phone number in Hondo offers "heated, elevated, corn-fed blinds" (meaning corn-fed deer). Other ads promise "jeep shuttle" or "meals served." A gun-shop owner outside of Fort Worth says to me, "You want to kill a deer down in Webb County, all you have to do is call the chamber of commerce. They'll send you to where you can do it." Bob Cook says to me, "You ought to see the rigs some of these fellas have, all set up for the African safari. One man can have a thousand dollars tied up in equipment. So the price of the lease, though high, is really next to nothing." More than 2,500 Texas hunters have paid $1,100 each to join the American Sportsman's Club. The club claims to have—for "have," read "lease"—a half million acres in Texas and an additional half million in Colorado, Wyoming, and Utah.

Some Texas outdoor writers, many Texas politicians and bureaucrats, most Texas hunters with personal incomes getting on toward $40,000 a year, and absolutely all of the lessors are delighted with the Texas hunting system. In Kerrville, I spoke on the telephone with veteran shooting scribe Byron Dalrymple, a refugee from northern Michigan. "I came down here twenty-five years ago and railed against the system," said Dalrymple. "But I have come to believe that it is the best system for the age we live in. It is the system of tomorrow. It is safer, and it is more likely to produce what the hunter wants. You hear men say that they want to get out into the country. Hell. Ninety-nine and nine tenths are out there to kill a deer."

In Austin, state wildlife director Ted Clark said he was concerned about the spiraling cost of hunting leases, yet added that the free-enterprise system seemed to be working. "Nobody can come close to our success rate," he said. "On that count, we lead the country in deer, turkey, mourning dove, and probably quail. Why? Because the game is treated as an asset when the landowner begins to see it as a cash crop." One member of the Texas Parks and Wildlife Commission is reported to have felt so strongly in favor of cash crops for the private sector that at one time he would have had the state get out of the public hunting business altogether. "There isn't a rancher in Texas today who can make as much money growing cows as he can with turkey and deer," a wildlife agency employee told me somewhere between Brush and Hill. "In total revenues, leasing as a cottage industry in Texas just might beat prostitution."

The Edwards Plateau rises north of San Antonio, along the Balcones Escarpment, and rolls upstate from there almost to San Angelo. It is a land of bubbling limestone springs and turquoise rivers, of cedar thickets and hackberry hillsides, cypress bottoms and shoulders of side oats grama and winter grass. The plateau embraces some twenty million acres in more than twenty counties. Six of the southernmost, including Kerr, are known collectively as the Hill Country, and it is very good country indeed for people who like their scenery sunny and out-of-doors. The country's climate is so healthy there is a saying that a person has to leave the Hills for distant precincts to discover if the time has come at last for him to die.

A white-tailed deer does not have that problem, though the physical climate is almost as salubrious for *Odocoileus virginianus* as it is for *Homo sapiens.* Thirty inches of rain on the plateau's loamy soils produces a spring abundance of forbs and woody plants, and the precipitation under live oaks is of acorns in the fall. Of an estimated 3.1 million whitetails statewide, half that number range across the Edwards Plateau. Statewide, the annual harvest is 350,000 animals; one in three is killed in the Hill Country. In the three counties surrounding the Hill city of Llano, fifty thousand deer are taken each year—more deer than are taken in most states. Yet, according to Texas biologists, for all the killing, the Hill Country harvest is not what it should be. And for all its presumed good marks as the wave of the future, the hunting-lease system is not the solution to the shortage of deerslayers. In the Hill Country, it turns out that leasing is part of the problem.

Bob Cook of the Department of Parks and Wildlife, in Kerrville, probably knows more about what may or may not be good for whitetails as a game species than any other person in Texas. We sat in his office one drizzling December morning and talked about the drift of circumstance that, as he saw it, was threatening the greatest concentration of deer in North America.

For openers, there was habitat. And there was the lack of habitat. "It used to be superb habitat," said Cook, "but it's in poor condition from overgrazing. The mouths that trim habitat on the Edwards Plateau are domestic, mostly sheep and goats, *and* deer. And we are losing more deer to starvation than to hunting."

"What's the solution?"

Cook said, "Reduce the grazing pressure by both the domestics and the deer."

"And you reduce the deer pressure by bringing in more hunters?"

"There aren't enough of them," Cook said. "Not enough to sustain the maximum harvest. Hunters should be taking half a million deer in Texas. But they can't. There are only half a million hunters, and there's just no way you're going to get a hundred percent success rate. The other problem is access to where deer are. The ranchers control that. Some don't want hunters coming in. Others who do, who lease, restrict the numbers. Add to that the fact that the cost to hunt in Texas is higher than anywhere else in the South, and you've got a bigger problem."

I asked Cook what he figured the net result might be, on deer.

"The size of the individual animal goes down as the number in the herd goes up." Cook then described one Hill Country experiment that showed a close relationship between herd density and animal size. At a controlled density of one deer per five acres, he said, adult bucks had been averaging eighty pounds, field dressed, but with the herd reduced to one deer for every fourteen acres, field-dressed weight increased to one hundred and twenty pounds. "The density in the Hill Country now is about one deer for every seven or eight acres," he said. "Deer can't get much smaller and go on living."

Another part of the problem is the hunter's ingrained suspicion that taking anything less than the biggest buck is not only un-American but unmasculine. Throughout Texas, as elsewhere, hunters are praised and rewarded in direct proportion to the weight of the carcass and the number of points on its antlers. A hunter coming home with a doe or even a spikehorn buck is regarded in some communities as a loser.

"The selection of the bigger buck is a selection against the species," Cook said.

I asked him, then, what other problems the whitetail herd of the Edwards Plateau might be facing. "Exotics," he said.

"Dozens of species have been introduced, for the most part for hunting, and they pose a very serious threat to our native game."

By most accounts, the first exotic ungulate imported to Texan soil outside of zoos was the nilgai antelope, an Indian creature which arrived at the King Ranch in 1924. Exactly one half century later, the Department of Parks and Wildlife conducted a statewide survey of alien critters and counted some fifty thousand of them, representing thirty-six species. Among the foreigners were eland, oryx, impala, greater kudu, ibex, springbok, European boar, and tahr in scant numbers and, in sizable herds scattered throughout central and southern Texas but most prominently upon the Edwards Plateau, axis, sika, and fallow deer, aoudad and mouflon sheep, and black-buck antelope. Except for a state-managed population of aoudads in the Palo Duro Canyon region, and axis deer in two counties, all of these animals are regarded under state law as if they were no more or less than domestic livestock. It is a view not generally shared by hunters who pay dearly for the privilege of hanging the animals' heads on their trophy-room walls.

The most numerous of the exotics—or Texotics, as some good ole boys prefer to call them—is the axis deer, a native of India and Ceylon. Of some 19,500 counted in the 1974 survey, about 6,000 were believed then to be ranging freely in the southwestern corner of the Edwards Plateau. Researcher Charles K. Winkler noted in a report to the state wildlife agency that the axis's size (20 percent larger than whitetail), its "massive, elk-like antlers, and reddish-brown coat with white spots" make it "very attractive" to hunters. The going rate for an axis buck taken at an exotic game ranch starts at about $750. The mouflon, somewhat tainted genetically through interbreeding with domesticated Barbados sheep, is the second most numerous of the aliens and goes for $350 or more. Black-buck antelope are third in numbers and are regarded as top trophy of all the hunted Texotics. Most black bucks are concentrated on the Edwards Plateau. Fallow and sika deer and aoudad round out the Big Six, or did at last count.

Biologist Bob Cook believes that the figures in the 1974 survey are conservative in that they may not reflect all of the free-ranging animals outside fenced pastures. In one staff report, he warns that the principal exotic species are competitors with native deer for their preferred forage. Food-habit studies at the Kerr Wildlife Management Area, he notes, indicate that the exotic ungulates for the most part prefer the same green forbs and browse that whitetails do. During periods of drought or under grazing pressure, the exotics shift to grasses, yet whitetails won't. "The end result," Cook reports, is that "while native deer are in extremely poor body condition or even dying due to starvation, exotic deer on the same range are observed to be in fair to good body condition." One Kerr Area experiment placed two male and four female whitetails in the same ninety-six-acre, deer-proof enclosure with two male and four female sika deer. Three years later, the whitetails numbered sixteen; the sika, fifteen. But three years after that, the sika had increased to thirty-one animals while the whitetails had plummeted to six.

"We can warn ranchers about these things," Cook was saying that December morning in Kerrville, "but we can't regulate what they do with their private property. And the way the law has it, that's all the exotics are. Property."

Before leaving Texas, I had hoped to pay a visit to one or two of the larger exotic game ranches in the Hill Country, possibly to such a ranch as Charles Schreiner's Y.O. at Mountain Home. But my requests for admission were turned aside with Hill Country graciousness, partly, I suspect, because many of the game ranches thereabouts had lately been cudgeled in the anti-hunting press. Still, I managed to find one rancher who would let me in. "Sure, and just come on out," said T. D. Hall on the phone. So I did that.

Hall owns a 1,300-acre ranch about thirty miles west of Kerrville, just off State Highway 41. On it range fifty fallow deer, fifty mouflon, fifty sika deer, thirty axis deer, and fifteen aoudads, as well as a herd of about one hundred whitetails.

The whole spread is enclosed by a deer-proof fence, meaning nothing gets in or out unless somebody cuts the wire. For a while, Hall ran black bucks on his place, but they had trouble with winter weather. He does not take his hunters afield after whitetail, but rather leases the right to hunt that native species exclusively to a corporation. For the exotics, he offers a guaranteed kill. "No kill, no pay," the saying goes. Almost all of his clients pay—and the rates are a bargain compared with those of some of his more commercial competitors, such as the Y.O., where Hall guided for seven years before going into exotics on his own. "It's our responsibility to furnish you with a good trophy head," he was saying in the living room of his ranch house. "If it takes us two days to do that, well, that's part of the deal. And I guess it pays off, because we get a lot of repeaters."

"What do they keep coming back for?" I asked.

Hall was staring out through a picture window at four axis deer grazing in his yard. "I suppose they keep coming back for other trophies," he replied. "To fill out their life list."

Book Three

GALLATIN DIVIDE

Going In

A cold wind came down Big Creek Canyon, crossed the valley of the Yellowstone, and flailed the grass where we were sitting with our backs to the Absarokas. The wind promised snow. Already, the ridgelines of the Gallatin Divide, across the valley, were powdered white down to eight thousand feet. Tom Davis said he figured the snow would be better for us than for elk. "It'll bring those bulls off the high ground," he said. "We'll be eating their livers for supper tomorrow night." I said, "If you score that fast, what will you do for the rest of the week?" Davis squinted at the mountains where the snow would be waiting for us in the morning. He said, "I've got a better idea. We'll eat liver for our last supper, coming out."

In the morning we would be going to camp, up Big Creek toward the divide—seven hunters, three wranglers, the outfitter, the cook, the dude with pencil and notebook, and about twice as many horses and mules as there were human fannies to set upon them. Always this time of year, October turning November, the hunters went in on Sunday and came out the following Saturday, so that each man and woman of them could put in a full five-day week, not counting commutation time, at the job of trying to kill an elk. And always this time of year, snow helped; though too much of it, too soon, could work against the hunters. Too much and horses would founder in drifts. Too much and some unlucky nonresident would drift in over his head, obliging the hometown mortician to defer interment until after spring thaw. But too little and the elk would stay high and dispersed on the ridgetops, and nothing to shoot at, and no wild liver for supper, and no horn for the trophy-room wall.

We sat in the grass on a steep slope above the inn at Chico Hot Springs. Davis was one of the hunters. He held an 8-mm. Mauser in the crook of his arm; and from time to time, as his eye ran along the edge of the timber above us, he snapped the rifle to his shoulder and used its telescopic sight for a spyglass. It was a strong-looking rifle. It showed much use. Years ago he had found it between the wallboards of a house his grandfather leased to seasonal tenants in Michigan. The Mauser was a war souvenir. Then, it had a scope with a broken lens and a very long barrel, and Davis supposed that once upon a time, somewhere in North Africa or Europe, it had belonged to a jack-booted sniper whose allegiance ran more or less toward the Third Reich. Davis took six inches off the barrel and had the entire action refitted with a sporter stock. Almost every year after that, he had taken a white-tailed deer in Michigan with the Mauser. And with it, too, he had taken antelope, elk, goat, moose, and mule deer out here in the big-sky, big-game West.

This Montana, in bygone times, was North America's Serengeti—game enough to bury any swaggering tenderfoot under tons of hides and antlers and boned-out meat; then, the time and place of beaver and bison, and of grizzlies scattered wide and saucy on the plains rather than bunched and skulking in parks in the mountains. Yet for all the shrinkage of wild populations and habitats, Montana still offers the widest variety of big-game hunting experiences available in the Lower Forty-eight, though Wyoming might give its neighbor a good fast run for that kind of money. Montana over the years has been able to claim with notable consistency that it is visited by more nonresident hunters than any other state. And, with one of the nation's most alert fish and game agencies manipulating the management tools, the Big Sky State has become known as the kind of place where, almost as often as not, a hunter can find—and kill—what he is hunting for.

Some examples. The success rate among deer hunters is 45 percent; in most states, success is rarely half as frequent. In better than three out of four cases, the antelope hunter is successful. Among holders of limited permits, drawn by lottery, for moose, the kill score is 68 percent; among those holding permits for mountain goat, 56 percent. At this point, odds begin to run statistically in favor of the game. Seekers of the wary bighorn sheep (numbering only some five hundred permitees) are successful but 20 percent of the time. Only one other kind of hunter runs a greater risk of getting skunked in Montana. It is the elk hunter, this Tom Davis cradling his Mauser as if it were a frontier Sharps on the buckskin fringes of plenty. As an elk hunter, Davis has a 17 percent chance of succeeding; thus, the odds against him are greater than five to one. Actually, they are not that bad, for Davis is a nonresident. Nonresident elk hunters are several percentage points more successful than residents. Nonresidents usually go after elk a week at a time, get deeper into the backcountry where most of the elk are, and are guided by professional outfitters. Still, the odds are in favor of skunking rather than success.

"Now, places down in Wyoming," Davis was saying, "elk are so easy they're practically giving them away. That's not for me. I'll take my chances up here, the hard way."

I had already guessed that hard is how Tom Davis would want the hunting to be. He is a wiry man, strong-looking like his rifle, just thirty-six that fall, showing some thinning out of the topknot, with faraway eyes the color of a mountain tarn. In Michigan, he is the proprietor of a concession offering sites for camping, horses for riding, and canoes for paddling. For fifteen dollars, one may paddle a canoe seventeen miles through a chain of lakes in the state-owned Pinckney Recreation Area northwest of Ann Arbor and wind up at Hell Creek Ranch, which is Davis's place. "It's a good living," Davis said. "Not rich, but good enough so that I can afford this."

"Why *Hell* Creek Ranch?"

"Why not?" Davis replied. "It's near Hell, Michigan."

"So, why Hell, Michigan?"

"Because there used to be some hellish mills along the river and because there was a helluva fire."

There were never hellish mills along this stretch of river,

this Yellowstone, and probably never will be. But there have been worse plans for it. North, up the valley toward Livingston, shoulders of the Gallatins and Absarokas drop to within a half mile of each other, in such a fashion that only a dummy could fail to see the potential for damming the river there. Development-minded folk may sometimes be scoundrels but they are not often dummies, especially in dry country desperate for water to develop eastern Montana's deposits of strippable coal. So, inevitably, it was proposed that a dam be raised between the almost-touching shoulders of the mountains—a dam that would create a thirty-one-mile-long reservoir, drown fifty-six miles of one of America's finest trout streams, and flood 32,000 acres of the most beautiful pastoral valley I have ever seen. Thanks in large part to opposition led by the Montana Department of Fish and Game, the dam proposal is currently more or less dead; but one must remember that in the business of dams, there is no such thing as death, only back burners.

"What do they call this valley?" Davis asked. "I've been here once before, but I'm not good with names."

I told him I wasn't good with names either, but that according to all the maps, the place where the Yellowstone flows is known as Paradise Valley, and that if he was truly from Hell, he'd better tread lightly.

"And what's the name of that little town up the road where we'll meet Neal in the morning?" Davis asked. Duane Neal was our outfitter.

"Pray," I said.

"Why Pray?"

"Why not Pray?" I said, and let it go at that.

There is an uncommonly large appreciation for natural country among big-game mountain hunters. I do not mean by this to belittle the relative importance of landscape to flatland gunners of critters with low profiles. I know waterfowlers who are filled with joy to behold no ducks against a horizon of unbroken spartina grass, and squirrelers who would measure paradise not by its capacity to grow bushy tails but rather oak, beech, and hickory along the same creek bottom. I suspect country gets under the skin of most hunters, whatever the quarry or the angle of the slope. But I suspect, too, that mountains somehow hone the appreciation a little sharper. In however large or small a hunter's measure of caring for country may be, there one can probably size up the worth of the hunter himself, and know why it is he hunts, and possibly begin to understand what he is seeking beyond the treasured horn or the tender flesh.

Sitting with Tom Davis in the grass above Chico, I was struck immediately by the man's involvement with the physical environment—the intense way he stared appraisingly at the snow-dusted mountains across the valley; the occasional quiver of his nostrils, testing the wind like a dog's; the persistence with which his perception of country kept cropping out like bedrock from accounts of other hunts and other places. "I just love those mountains," Davis at one point was saying of the Montana-Idaho Bitterroots, where he had killed a mountain goat several years earlier. "You feel like you're on top of the world. There's no way you can't love it." It was as though he were speaking of a woman. I knew then Tom Davis had already fallen head over heels for country.

Not all hunters are so enamored. There are some who stare appraisingly at nothing but the bolts of their rifles, whose noses quiver only for blood. They have no perception of country. Once, in Davis's home state of Michigan, I talked with a deer hunter who had gone north with a group from a downstate town on Opening Day. I asked him where they had hunted, Upper or Lower Peninsula. "I don't remember," he said. "I slept in the back seat going and coming and *where* we was didn't seem to matter when we got there." Then I asked him what the country looked like. He said he couldn't remember that either, though he did recall seeing, briefly, the white flag of one runaway deer. And that was *all* he remembered.

So I was glad to have run into Davis, here at Chico before the hunt, knowing he had the Mauser with him now only for balance, as some hikers carry staffs more for reason of personal style than need, and the Weaver 2X7 scope only to use as a spyglass. Davis said the scope was sighted in at one hundred yards. "Now, at four hundred yards," he explained, as though contemplating an actual shot, "I'd lay the horizontal cross hair across the elk's back. At four hundred yards, the bullet—it's a hundred seventy-five grains, Remington—the bullet drops about eight, nine inches. That would put it under and behind the shoulder, into the heart."

For a while, then, we talked about the one aspect of hunting with which most hunters do not often care to grapple—the kill, and to what extent it might figure as the essential goal of the whole hunting experience. Neither of us arrived at any profound conclusion. I found my own mind wandering in and out of the philosophies of the Spaniard José Ortega y Gasset, whose views of the blood sport had struck me as somewhat romantic, if not slightly askew, when I first read them in his classic treatise, *Meditations on Hunting.* Though now, having met Tom Davis, I wasn't all *that* sure that the old philosopher was off the mark. "To the sportsman," according to Ortega y Gasset, "the death of the game is not what interests him; that is not his purpose. What interests him is everything he had to do to achieve that death—that is, the hunt. . . . Death is essential because without it there is no authentic hunting: the killing of the animal is the natural end of the hunt and the goal of hunting itself, *not* of the hunter. . . . To sum up, one does not hunt in order to kill; on the contrary, one kills in order to have hunted."

I told Davis that I had heard a number of variations on this theme, and that possibly the most interesting had come my way from the mouth of a neurologist in New York City named Mortimer Shapiro, who hunts big game wherever he can, but mostly in Africa. Shapiro had said that for him, after all of the other things that go into a hunt, pulling the trigger has no more significance than putting a period at the end of a sentence.

"Maybe there are times when you don't need a period," Davis said. "You don't have to kill every time. Sometimes you can't kill because you don't get the chance. But still you have hunted."

And sometimes, I supposed, there were times when the hunter faced doubts. Ortega y Gasset had an opinion on that, too. "Every good hunter," he wrote, "is uneasy in the depths of his conscience when faced with the death he is about to inflict on the enchanting animal. He does not have the final and firm conviction that his conduct is correct. But neither, it should be understood, is he certain of the opposite."

Davis said, "I didn't have those doubts when I was younger. I think they grow on you the more you hunt."

"That, or you're slowing down. And besides, you've already taken every kind of animal worth taking in these mountains."

"No, I haven't," said Davis. "There's still the bighorn. I don't have a sheep yet."

"Does that bother you?"

"Not really," he said. "Maybe if I draw a permit someday. Or maybe not. It really doesn't matter much one way or another. But I sure would like to get up there and see where they're at."

What had started as sleet as we rode away from the trailhead, Sunday morning, was snow by the time we arrived in camp. It was a wet clumping snow that settled heavily on the lodgepole pine, Douglas fir, and Engelmann spruce, and there was much slipping of hooves on the trail going in. The camp was set up on a natural bench at the confluence of Big and Bark Cabin creeks, at about 6,500 feet of elevation, with plenty of open meadow round about for the pasturing stock. On the bench were five wall tents, a makeshift corral, and one latrine. The first tent on the left was reserved for occasional visitors and surplus gear. Our occasional visitor was Joe Gaab of Livingston, recently retired as supervisor of outfitters for the Montana Department of Fish and Game. In the second tent on the left was the boss, Duane Neal, and his three wranglers, Stan Broughtan, Perry Frost, and Lynn Simon. Next, in the middle, was the cook tent. In addition to the obvious culinary things, it was occupied by Juli Kane, the cook, from a suburb of Washington, D.C. The hunters took the two tents on the right. There was the Midwest tent, occupied by Tom Davis, his hunting partner from Hillman, Michigan, Earle Duffy, and the two gentlemen from Fond du Lac, Wisconsin, Louis H. Lange, Jr., and Daniel Edgarton. And, finally, there was the tent of the East, sheltering Jim Hare, Ed Sahrle, and Sid Wiedrick, all of Rochester, New York, and the dude with the notebook, from Connecticut.

Big Creek itself was not all that big—a cobbled brook by Montana standards, easily forded by the horses, running icily through a narrow valley to gather the tributary waters of Mist, Smokey, Bear, Bark Cabin, and Cottonwood creeks, all hell-bent for the Yellowstone. It was a clear, fast cutthroat-trout stream, and, looking at it, I was gravely sorry that amid all the rifles no one had thought to pack in a fly rod. Trout fishing is part of the nonresident elk hunter's bonus. For the same $225 license fee that entitles him to kill an elk, the nonresident may also kill cutthroat trout and upland game birds; and, if he wishes, he may take a mule deer and a black bear as well, and at no extra charge. Each year, Montana offers for sale up to 17,000 of these licenses. The annual revenues exceed $3 million and represent about 40 percent of the Department of Fish and Game's total income from hunting-license sales. Big-game hunting of this kind also primes the local economy, through the outfitter. There are about two hundred pack-horse outfitters licensed throughout the state. In our case, each hunter was priming the local money pump, through Duane Neal's Black Otter Guide Service, with about $800. Multiply that by seven or eight hunters, and multiply again by five for the number of weeklong hunts in the elk season, and in Neal's case alone one is speaking of an annual cash crop of more than $40,000, harvested by the state of Montana and the merchants of Paradise Valley, but grown right here among wall tents at the confluence of Big and Bark Cabin creeks.

When I first met Duane Neal, at Chico Hot Springs, I thought that here surely was a man to match these mountains—tall and craggy and tough. He had come out from Nebraska, maybe twenty years ago, had tried his luck with cattle and sheep, and then had bought Black Otter from his brother. This was his eleventh season outfitting elk hunters. By arrangement with the U.S. Forest Service, he maintained two separate camps in Gallatin National Forest—the one here at Big Creek, the other across the Yellowstone Valley in the Absarokas, at Hellroaring Creek. Neal traditionally packed two ten-day hunts into Hellroaring each September, with some hunters having an optional crack at mountain goat should they be so lucky as to have drawn the necessary permits; and then he crossed over to the Gallatin Range for five weeks of hunting here. Here, Neal had set up spike camps—one or two tents only—at the heads of Bear and Bark Cabin creeks, high up near the divide; and some hunters, weather permitting, used these to avoid a long ride up from base camp in the morning. Between Bear and Bark Cabin, the other drainages had good trails leading up through stands of lodgepole and spruce to un-timbered heights at nine to ten thousand feet. From the van-tage of the divide, as I would presently discover, one could see twenty miles south into Yellowstone National Park, north al-most to Bozeman, and west across the Gallatin River to the wilder shores of the Spanish Peaks. All of it from Big Creek to the divide was roadless, much of it had never been touched by an ax, and some of it, at the time, was being reviewed for possi-ble addition to the National Wilderness Preservation System.

"I guess I like it better over at Hellroaring," Duane Neal was saying that first afternoon in camp. "The Absarokas are wilder and they're diverse and the fishing's better, and maybe the scenery's better, too. But for elk I'd rather be here."

Sid Wiedrick asked how, for elk, the Gallatins could be that different from the Absarokas, and Neal replied, "Lot of elk over there come out of Yellowstone Park tame. Ones over here run wild and native. You get an elk over here, you've really *done* something."

Wiedrick slung his .300 Magnum over his shoulder and said he was going to test his legs on the slopes across the creek. It was midafternoon, too late to go far, two hours until supper. I joined him. Except for Duffy, Wiedrick at fifty-three was the oldest hunter. He had thirty-five years behind him at Eastman Kodak Company in Rochester, and five more to go before early retirement. He had two grown daughters. One was a disc jockey in Albany. The other was married to Jim Hare. Wiedrick went up the slope with short bursts of energy, resting frequently but not once breathing hard. Our feet slipped in the snow. After a while, I said, "Wiedrick, you are some kind of mountain goat. I figure we've already climbed eight hundred vertical feet, and back East there are hunters who won't go eight feet level from their cars."

"I run to keep in shape," Wiedrick said. "At home I run two miles every other day and then I run two miles *every* day for a month before coming out. Anyone who doesn't shape up for this kind of hunt is asking for trouble. Some of the western boys complain that us easterners are taking all the game. And I'll tell you why we're taking the game. We work for it."

At the top of the slope was a bench of grassland bordered by tall Engelmann spruce. Many of the spruce had been girdled by porcupines and were dead or dying. Wiedrick walked along the edge of the trees until he came to a place where the snow had been trampled by hooves. About four feet above the heaviest tracks, he placed his gloved hand against a spruce where the bark was worn thin, not as in a girdling, but as if it had been massaged by the side of a large animal.

"Elk rubbing," said Wiedrick. "Sure is good to know they're here."

As the Parthenon was to ancient Athens, so is the cook tent to the camp of the elk hunter. It is the place of wisdom and inspiration. It sustains the soul as well as the stomach. A man may carry his rifle with him to the latrine, but not to the cook tent. No guns allowed. The cook tent is sanctum sanctorum.

That first night Juli Kane fed us sausage and mashed potatoes and peas and lemon cake, and we sat under butane lanterns at a long table which accommodated all but the final one or two stragglers. After dinner, Duane Neal hunkered down on a chopping block near the wood stove and piled on the fresh logs. The temperature outside was dropping down through the bottom of the teens. At the far end of the tent, Joe Gaab stretched out across two bales of hay and, in his soft and slow western way, told how outfitting had changed a great deal over the past ten years. "Used to be," said Gaab, "when the kill was everything. Some outfitters even did the shooting for their clients. But now, it's different. It's not the kill, it's the outing. That's what you're selling. Huh, Duane?"

"That's what we're selling," Neal said. "I had forty-three hunters in here a few years back, after a hot summer, and the fall was warm, too, with no snow, and no one got a damn thing, not one elk, but every last one of those hunters re-booked."

Someone asked for a show of hands. How many of the hunters had been out with Neal at least once before? Everyone but Jim Hare raised his hand. And how many had got an elk? Only three raised their hands. "And that's not counting Tommie's moose," said Earle Duffy. Tom Davis had got a moose the year before, on Big Creek.

"When I first started in this business," Neal said, "I felt bad about clients going home without an animal. Now, a man calls me up, asking if I can guarantee him an elk or a moose and—well—that's when I tell him I'm booked full. I don't want to take that kind of man into this kind of country."

There is one animal that no honest outfitter in Montana would dare guarantee, and that is the grizzly. Inevitably that first night, the talk in the cook tent turned to the grizzer, and it was said that there were some big ones around, up toward the divide.

"I hope we see one," said Dan Edgarton.

"I hope we don't," said Jim Hare.

"I don't think I'd want to kill one, anyway," Tom Davis said.

"I think I would," Louie Lange said. "And I think the grizz would want to kill me."

By ruling of the U.S. Interior Department, the grizzly in Montana is listed as a threatened species, mainly because Montana encompasses most of the animal's shrinking range in the Lower Forty-eight. Still, the big bear's numbers are such that the rule book permits sport hunters to kill a few every year. The year before, Montana had issued about six hundred grizzly permits to residents and nonresidents, but only seven bears were killed. According to the regulations, if in a given year the total number of grizzlies killed under any circumstances—road kills, ranch kills (to end predation on livestock), plus hunting kills—hits twenty-five, the Department of Fish and Game is obligated to close the season, statewide, on forty-eight-hour notice. (Because of its proximity to Yellowstone National Park, hunting grizzly is prohibited in the Big Creek watershed.)

And inevitably, too, after grizz tales, the cook tent palaver turned to rifles. *No guns allowed* didn't mean a hunter couldn't talk about them.

In my own mind, there is something singularly American about the rifle. It seems to belong to us culturally, whether we like it or not. Whether we need it or not. At least the rifle seems to have been born in America, home-grown and star-spangled, although it wasn't; German and Austrian huntsmen were carrying rifles by 1600, at which time the idea of cutting a spiral groove inside the gun barrel, to put a spin on the bullet and thereby give it greater distance and accuracy than the projectile from a smoothbore musket, was already a hundred years old. In my mind, too, I see the rifle more as the hunter's tool than the soldier's, though for a while in America the hunter and soldier were one and the same. Our first and perhaps finest contribution to the world of arms, the graceful, sharpshooting Kentucky long rifle, was so named not because of the place of its manufacture, which happened to be Pennsylvania, but because it was the preferred weapon of the Kentucky hunters who helped Andrew Jackson whip the British in 1815 at New Orleans.

For the way West, for liver-eating roustabouts who poled the wide Missouri to beaver valleys below the shining mountains, for Kit Carson and for Jim Bridger, the rifle of choice was the Hawken. With its percussion-cap action replacing the old flintlock of the Kentucky rifle, its octagonal barrel shortened for horseback convenience and fast scabbard draw to the moving target, the Hawken was deadly in a .50 caliber, as good for Montana grizzly and elk as for galloping Flatheads and Blackfeet.

By the end of the Civil War, the muzzle-loaders were almost artifacts. Among the best of the new breech-loaders was Remington's "rolling-block" rifle (one rolled the breech block open and shut with his fingertips). This, too, came in a bore of .50 caliber. And this, too, was a rifle for the big-sky West. Men still tell the tale of headstrong Nelson Story, who, in 1866, rode north from Fort Leavenworth, Kansas, with three thousand head of Texas steers. Riding with Story were thirty cowpokes with Remington rolling-blocks in their saddle scabbards. At Fort Phil Kearney, in Wyoming, Story was warned not to go on. The Sioux up north were on the warpath. At Fort Phil Kearney were three hundred soldiers armed with Civil War muzzle-loaders. The soldiers were afraid to leave the fort. Yet Story rode on.

Somewhere near the Montana country, Crazy Horse surrounded the cowboys with five hundred braves. Story pulled his wagons into a circle while the boys eased their Remingtons out of their scabbards. And waited. Crazy Horse sat upon his pony at such a distance he could not see that those rifles pointing out between the wagons were different from the muzzle-loaders of the blue-eyes from Fort Phil Kearney. Fighting the blue-eyes, Crazy Horse had learned that the best way to deal with muzzle-loaders was to draw their fire with a feint—send in the most expendable braves, lose a few, and then, in the crucial defenseless lull while the enemy soldiers were laboriously reloading, charge down on them for-hell-and-leather. Which is exactly the tactic Crazy Horse employed against Nelson Story and his thirty rolling-blocks. But this time, something went wrong. The blue-eyes' rifles kept spitting lead after the first feint, and no lull, and each time Crazy Horse sent in a new wave of riders, many of the ponies returned with empty backs. Finally, Crazy Horse shook his head and rode away, vowing to settle the score even if it took him a decade. Nelson Story moseyed proudly on to Montana, where he founded that territory's cattle kingdom. As it turned out, cows were good news for neither Indians nor elk.

Meanwhile, George Armstrong Custer, the brevet of the flowing hair, cantered west from the Black Hills, boasting of buffalo slain with his own cherished Remington rolling-block. In June of 1876, the rifle went with him to the Little Bighorn, which flows to the Yellowstone on the far sunrise side of the Absarokas. Custer's troopers were armed, for the most part, with wretched little Springfield carbines, and defective ammunition. Crazy Horse had his revenge. Afterwards, soldiers from the relief column searched in vain for Custer's rolling-block. Possibly it had been taken by a departing warrior and presented to Crazy Horse. I like to think so. No one deserved a good rifle more.

The other great first-generation breech-loader was the Sharps, a ponderous thing of some eighteen pounds, and of .50 caliber. Hide hunters called it "the Big Fifty." It was curtains on bison at long range, and on Indians. At Adobe Walls, in the Texas Panhandle, the buffalo hunter William Dixon picked a skulking Comanche off a bluff at a range of 1,300 yards. The bullet probably had a good tail wind.

Even before the hide hunters began in earnest to decimate the bison herds with their Big Fifties, the first truly modern hunting firearm, the lever-action repeating rifle, made its debut at the Connecticut armory of Oliver Winchester. The earliest model was called the Henry rifle, after Benjamin Tyler Henry, its designer. It held sixteen .44-caliber rimfire cartridges in a tube under the barrel. It was, someone noted (though possibly in reference to the competing seven-shot Spencer rifle), the kind of gun one loaded on Sunday and shot all week. With certain design changes to speed up the loading process, Henry's repeater begat the famous Winchester Model 1866, which, in time, begat the even more widely acclaimed Model 1873 ("the gun that won the West"), and which begat the Model 1894, the surviving sire of Winchester's best-selling lever-action line. Teddy Roosevelt carried a Winchester on his western hunting trips, and later to Africa, and declared it to be the best rifle he ever had.

Nowadays, big-game hunters have such a wide variety of manufacturers, calibers, and models to choose from that only the most arrogant would dare pronounce any one rifle the best. In eastern whitetail country, the lever-action is still probably the most popular, especially in the .30/30 caliber. There are pump-action and semiautomatic models in the woods, too. But overall, for deer and bigger game, the most common is the bolt-action, perfected in Europe before the turn of the century by such gunsmiths as Mauser and Krag. Winchester and Remington and other U.S. sporting arms manufacturers turn out bolt-action models tooled for loads as light as the .222 and as large as the .375 Magnum. For big game in the West, most hunters prefer loads in the popular .30/06 category, meaning just about anything between the fast .270 and the powerful .300 Magnum. In our own group, though I counted only two .30/06s (Neal's and Sid Wiedrick's number-two gun), the chosen calibers tended to stick fairly close to one side or another of the .30/06 median.

On the heavy side were Wiedrick, Lange, and Duffy, with .300 Magnums, and Edgarton with a Browning automatic .308. And Davis, with his 8-mm. On the lighter side were Ed Sahrle and Stan Broughtan, who declared for the 7-mm., though Sahrle confessed he was not all *that* particular. "It doesn't matter much," he said, "whether it's two-seventy, seven millimeter, or thirty-thirty. It's where you put the bullet."

"There are people who believe, and maybe I'm one of 'em," said Joe Gaab from the hay bales at the end of the cook tent, "that nothing should have been invented after the thirty-thirty scabbard rifle." Gaab did not have a .30/30 with him, though he did have a .270 Winchester at home. "I never took anything at over a hundred yards," he said. "I used to run the hundred-yard dash, and that's a long way."

Duane Neal fed another log into the wood stove and said he figured he was ready for some shut-eye.

"What's lined up for tomorrow?" Tom Davis asked.

"Oh, I don't know," said Neal. "Go huntin'. I guess."

The Biggest Game

During the night the snow stopped, and in the tent of the East Jim Hare kept waking to feed the stove. Stan Broughtan barked "Let's go!" through the flaps of the tent at six o'clock. Sid Wiedrick lighted a Coleman lantern and, shivering out of our sleeping bags, we dressed quickly. Ed Sahrle said, if no one minded, he would stay *in* his bag and wear it to breakfast. The men from the Midwest were already up. They stood outside the cook tent waiting for Juli Kane to summon them in. And she did that, telling the hunters "Let's eat!" with a bark as authoritative as Broughtan's.

On the stove were eggs and bacon and thick slices of French toast, and there was Duane Neal saying, between sips of coffee, that Perry Frost would be riding up Mist Creek with Louie Lange and Dan Edgarton, that Broughtan and Lynn Simon would be herding the three New Yorkers up Smokey, and that he would be going with Davis and Duffy to the Triangle, a big swatch of meadow high on the mountain in back of camp. Meanwhile, Joe Gaab, Juli Kane, and I—the three noncombatants—would ride up Bark Cabin Creek to see what kind of sign had been left in the fresh snow. "Now remember," I said to Tom Davis as he swung into his saddle, "don't spoil it by getting your elk on the first day."

According to the record books, some mighty big elk had been taken in this mountain country over the years. I mean in the generous sense of a day or two's ride from Pray. And by "big elk" I mean big enough to rate a listing by the Boone and Crockett Club, the official judge of big-game trophy pecking orders in North America. Certainly, these would be animals larger than the seven-hundred-pound live-weight average for Rocky Mountain bull elk. And as I watched Tom Davis ride away that morning, I was startled to find myself wishing him the kind of luck that would bring down a truly big one, even at the risk of leaving the hunter spoiled and sedentary for the rest of the week.

One can learn much from the record books. I suspect more people buy and use them as tip sheets on where to go for the biggest game than for any other reason. If, indeed, there *is* any other reason to wallow through pages of names and measurements. One runs the eye down the long columns and soon discovers, for example, that if it's a trophy grizzly you want, then your best bet is out of Bella Coola, British Columbia. Or was, when the big ones were toppling round about. An Alaskan brown? Taxonomically, grizz and brown are the same critter. But Boone and Crockett types are not slavishly concerned with taxonomy. They play it by size as conditioned by geography, placing the browns along the robust shores of Alaska, where the bears grow tall and fat feasting on salmon; while the grizz is held to the interior, where size diminishes as a factor of sparser diet. Overall, the books list thirty-one categories of North American big game. These include three kinds of moose, though, biologically, there is only one species. A dead moose in Ontario may therefore vie with one from Maine for the honor of being listed as the biggest "Canada moose," but not with a moose from Wyoming, which is a category unto itself, nor with a moose from the Yukon-Alaska region, which is likewise gerrymandered as the range of a separate "subspecies."

Someone was mentioning browns. Want a big one? Get thee to Kodiak Island. Want a polar bear? Can't have one. Not now in Alaska. But when you could have had one, you would have safaried north from Kotzebue along the frozen shore of the Chukchi Sea. Can't have a jaguar now, either. At least, you can't bring the skin or head into this country; so why bother? But when you could have bothered, you would have headed for Nayarit, Mexico, probably. Want an elk? They grow big in Colorado and Utah, scattered all over the mountains. But they grow big here, too, in Park and Gallatin counties, Montana. And the tracks look huge in fresh snow when one leans out from the saddle to scan them.

It is a small world, for this Montana country is more or less where North American big-game scoring began, or at least where the Boone and Crockett Club may have begun in the mind of a man named George Bird Grinnell. In the annals of conservation, the self-effacing Grinnell is perhaps the most neglected of the early heroes. But here in Montana, his shadow looms large.

They say he came out of Yale in 1870 with Horace Greeley's advice to go West ringing loud in his ears. Four years later he was there, riding with Custer in the Black Hills; five years and he was reconnoitering the Yellowstone, as expeditionary naturalist, with the engineer William Ludlow. The ink was already three years drying on the documents making Yellowstone the first national park, yet what Grinnell saw at the interface of Wyoming and Montana was anything but parklike. The Yellowstone was crawling with hide hunters. Here was the last refuge of the American bison, and here they were being slaughtered for currency. The market gunners were taking everything. Not only bison, but elk and deer and moose and goat and sheep.

Grinnell was saddened and angered by what he had seen on the Ludlow expedition, but soon he would be able to channel that anger into constructive criticism of the park's management. After 1876, he was no mere tag-along naturalist. He was editor of the influential New York magazine *Forest and Stream*, and he used its pages effectively over the years to lead the nation's first crusade for wildlife. He purchased a ranch in Wyoming (the same year, 1883, that Teddy Roosevelt purchased one in Dakota) and prowled the mountains with a rifle (while Teddy prowled the plains). And in the summer of 1885—the same summer he discovered the glacier in northwest Montana that now bears his name—George Grinnell sat down at his desk in New York and wrote, for *Forest and Stream*, a patronizing review of Teddy Roosevelt's new book *Hunting Trips of a Ranchman.* "Mr. Roosevelt is not well known as a sportsman," Grinnell observed, "and his experience of the Western country is quite limited, but this very fact in one way lends an added charm to his book."

Charm be damned. No one was going to call Teddy Roosevelt an eastern dude. Whereupon the plainsman-politician called upon the mountaineer-editor to demand an explanation, which, apparently, he did get in such a straightforward way that the two became fast friends. They met frequently, discussing the West and the Indians and the game, and in particular the need to protect wildlife in order that, as Grinnell put it, "there might still be good hunting which should last for generations."

Grinnell was concerned about protecting birds as well as big game. In 1886, he founded in New York the first Audubon Society. Formation of other societies, modeled after Grinnell's, would lead in 1905 to an association later known as the National Audubon Society. Grinnell wondered then why there should not be a society of sportsmen who would speak up for big game as the Audubon people championed birds. It was a bully idea, and Roosevelt ran with it. In 1887, he invited to a dinner party such sporting New York bluebloods as John J. Pierrepont and Rutherford Stuyvesant, among others, and placed the proposition of a new club before them. The ayes had it. They would call it the Boone and Crockett Club, after those worthy scouts, and they would accept into membership one hundred men who had killed with a rifle, in "fair chase," at least one individual of three of various kinds of American big game. The purposes of the club would be to "promote manly sport with the rifle," to encourage exploration of wild country, to lobby for game laws, and to foster inquiry into the natural history of game animals. Roosevelt himself would later define "fair chase" to mean a kind of hunting that would—even before there were laws against such practices—eschew "killing bear, wolf, or cougar in traps," driving game with brush fires, chasing moose, elk, or deer in deep crusted snow, and "killing game from a boat while it is swimming in the water." In time, the club would fill out its membership rolls with the elite of Boston and Philadelphia and Washington, as well as New York. The eye would run down the long column and see such names as Gifford Pinchot, Henry Cabot Lodge, Owen Wister, and Elihu Root.

At first there was not much interest in keeping score of the record trophies. Grinnell and the Boone and Crockett Club were too busy trying to outlaw the jacklighting and hounding of deer in the Adirondacks of New York, to protect the game and the timber of Yellowstone Park in the West. But the hunter's life was full of changes after the First World War, and more so after the Second. Bluebloods began to die of old age. Since gentility was no longer a prerequisite afield, their sons took up golf. Democracy replaced them with men of sharp elbows and fast bucks. More and more of them roamed the mountains with rifles, but there were fewer and fewer animals large enough to massage their egos. Some men began to feel competitive about the game. The killing became a contest.

The Boone and Crockett Club published the first records of North American big-game trophies in 1932. Over the years there have been recurring disagreements over how the scorecards should be shuffled. Bears, for example, are graded by skull size. One scholar, believing the skull of a bear to be unrepresentative of its proportional overall size, insisted that the only fair way to grade a bruin was to measure the length of its femur. A more practical mind dissuaded the club from adopting such a method on the ground that most hunters don't know what a femur is. The loudest disagreement of recent years was over whether the club should keep score at all. Some members sensitive to the public disdain for trophies urged that the scoring be stopped. Others argued that to abandon the records would be to surrender them to sponsors unconcerned with the principles of fair chase. Rogues and Johnny-come-latelies would take over the awards program and pass out silver cups to men who stalk animals from aircraft. So the club continued its records program after all. Since 1973, it has been administered jointly with the National Rifle Association of America.

Having seen fresh tracks along Bark Cabin Creek and said goodbye for a day or two to Joe Gaab, who had to get back to Livingston to attend to cows, and left Juli Kane to her culinary duties at the cook tent, I went out from camp across a meadow to a large lichened rock from which all traces of snow had vanished in the afternoon sun. And waited there for the echo of a gunshot to roll down the mountains. It never came. Only the hunters came on horseback, one by one, slumped in their saddles, showing fatigue and, it seemed to me, a measure of surprise that all had shared this smallest of humiliations—being skunked the first day. Except for Tom Davis. Duffy had come down early from the Triangle to rest, and Neal had moseyed off to join the hunters on the slopes above Smokey, and come in with them. So Davis, now, was the last man out. And the last chance left for liver, to bring them all better luck the next morning.

Whatever Davis's own luck this day or tomorrow, he was not in the record-book league, and I supposed he never would be. Not that there weren't any number of regular-Joe-and-Josephine hunters in the record books, men and women who had just lucked into the big one without really trying. But as I was ruminating not long ago, one can learn much reading the scores; and it is downright surprising how often a few names keep turning up on the lists in a way that suggests that they really *were* trying. I mean names such as Otis Chandler and Elgin Gates and Basil Bradbury and George Glass and Bill Foster and C. J. McElroy and Herb Klein and Bert Klineburger. I know none of these men personally, know some by reputation only, and others not at all. Otis Chandler is head of the Times-Mirror Company of Los Angeles, publisher of newspapers, magazines, and books. Elgin Gates raced motorboats and retired from the big hunt when he took up trap shooting. Messrs. Glass and Bradbury, I know not. Bill Foster opened a restaurant in California (Foster's Bighorn) where the heads of his assembled trophies loom above the heads of the diners. C. J. McElroy presides in Tucson over Safari Club International. The late Herb Klein came out of Dallas with money in oil and Weatherby rifles. Bert Klineburger for many years was proprietor of Jonas Brothers, the Seattle taxidermy emporium with sideline safari service to exotic places. None of these men was or is a member of the exclusive Boone and Crockett Club. It is their names only that are admitted to the lists of the club's North American big-game trophy program.

For many years, too, it might have appeared to anyone studying the records that Herb Klein and Bert Klineburger were in some kind of fierce contest to see who could get his name more often into the lists and at a higher level of achievement. I do not mean to suggest here that either man threw a gauntlet to the boot of the other. I guess only that each knew the other was trying to excel at hunting and killing and mounting the largest specimens of game animals on this continent, and that the presence of one runaway performer must certainly have put the spur to the other's quest. Both did most of their high-score shooting in the 1960s, though one of Klein's standing records, for goat, goes back to 1934.

I cannot begin to call the winner of this contest. Klein had 41 recognized entries spread over 21 categories of game in the 1976 record book; Klineburger had 14 spread over 10—an entry being any individual specimen exceeding the minimum size set by the Boone and Crockett Club for each of the 31 game categories. So, in terms of trophy numbers only, Klein had it. And Klein got it through dogged persistence, as in the case of the Barren Ground caribou. In 1955 Klein entered the lists by killing a Barren Ground caribou that would qualify for the rank of 299th; that is, as of publication of the 1976 records, there were only 298 sets of caribou antlers recognized officially as being superior to Klein's 1955 entry. In 1960, Klein killed another Barren Ground caribou—ranked 286th— and thereby moved 13 places closer to *numero uno*. But that wasn't good enough for Klein. In 1964, he killed two more Barren Ground caribou, moving to 170th place with one animal and to 61st with the other. And in 1967, he killed three more, losing considerable ground with two of these animals, but progressing to 41st place with the third. Yet when Klein arrived proudly at 41st place, who do you suppose was already 20 steps ahead of him, in 21st place? None other than Bert Klineburger.

That was Klineburger's style—not so many animals as good ones almost every time, or at least ones that might often be better than Klein's. Running down the 1976 lists, one sees that, for grizzly, Klein and Klineburger were tied in 33rd place; for brown bear, Klein's 48th topped Klineburger's 118th; for polar bear, Klein's 81st beat Klineburger's 95th; but that Klineburger then turned the tables on Klein in six other categories, beating him at Pacific walrus (37th to 54th), at mountain caribou (28th to 36th), at Barren Ground caribou, at bison (9th to 72nd), at musk-ox (12th to 79th), and at Alaska-Yukon moose (1st to 66th). A counterattack by Klein in the Canada moose category managed to edge out Klineburger, 18th to 19th. So, counting rank as well as numbers, who knows? Having the biggest Alaska-Yukon moose is an impressive accomplishment (for Klineburger). But so is having the 9th largest desert sheep, the 10th largest Stone's sheep, and the 13th largest bighorn sheep (for Klein). Not that it matters at all to me. Nor much, I'd guess, to the elk hunter from Hell, Tom Davis.

They were waiting for Davis in the Midwest tent with a bottle of Irish Mist. Duffy was pouring. Duffy was the sartorial prince of the lot of them. He wore red plaid wool trousers with suspenders, a red chamois-cloth shirt, and a bush hat with the brim pinched flat against one side of the crown in the rakish fashion of the Australian outbacker. This was his tenth elk hunt in Montana. The last time out, and the time before, he had not taken an elk. This time, by lottery, he had drawn a special permit that entitled him to take a cow elk, while the rest of the hunters were restricted to bulls only. Duffy was in his seventies. In Hillman, Michigan, he had retired from his plumbing business and now served on the city council, supervising the town's sewer and water facilities. As a sideline, he also managed the affairs of a hunting camp nearby in the cedar-swamp woods. Originally, Duffy was from Ypsilanti, near Ann Arbor. He was a close friend of Tom Davis's father. The way Duffy told it, by the time Tom Davis was a teen-ager, his father wasn't going out to hunt much any more. But Duffy was. Duffy couldn't get enough of hunting. And after a while, neither could Tom. Duffy said, "We've been hunting together twenty years, Tommie and me. We've been some wonderful places and we've had some wonderful times." He passed the Irish Mist to his left and asked if anyone had the time. Someone had ten minutes to five. "Tommie's running late," said Duffy, looking out through a slit in the tent flaps. "It'll be dark soon."

If Duffy was the most outlandishly fashionable of these hunters, then Louie Lange was perhaps the most elegantly equipped. At the far end of the tent, his gear was stashed in ditty bags beside a well-lofted Eddie Bauer Polarguard sleeping bag rated for comfort at zero degrees, and the bag itself rested upon a cot with a folding aluminum frame. None of the other men had a cot; they slept on foam pads, on the ground. Lange explained his meticulous ways by praising the virtues of order and cleanliness. "Why be a bum?" he said. "There was a dentist from Fond du Lac came hunting out here and lived for a week like a bum. At the end of the trip he went into a Livingston motel, dumped his gear on the floor, stripped naked, and called for room service. When the busboy arrived, the dentist pointed to the pile at his feet and said, 'Burn it.'" Someone noticed that Lange had a .44-caliber single-action revolver strapped, in a holster, to the tent pole next to the top of his sleeping bag. "What's the gat for, Louie?" "It's for Duffy," said Lange. "In case he snores again like he did last night."

"You mean to say," said Ed Sahrle, "that was *Duffy* I heard all the way up in our tent? All this time I've been blaming poor Sid."

Then Sahrle spoke about hunting in northern Pennsylvania, near Osceola, where he had lived before moving to Rochester. "Everyone down there hunts," he said. "It's a way of life and people don't question it. But Rochester, that's something else. That's city. My son—he's thirteen, but he won't know hunting and fishing the way I did. There are so many other things to do in the city. There's Scouts and lessons for this and that and ball games and sports, and what with the other kids, my wife and I are playing chauffeur six nights a week and both days weekends. You don't have that in the country."

"Does the boy hunt?" I asked.

"Just last Saturday," Sahrle said, "the day I got out here, some friends back home in Osceola took him out after turkey. I guess I won't know till next Saturday if he got one."

"What do people in Rochester think about your coming out here to kill an elk?"

"Oh, brother," he said. "What do they *think?* These two girls at Kodak found out what I was up to and they said to me, 'How can you go all the way to Montana to shoot at a beautiful animal?' How do you answer that? They just don't understand. They *can't* understand."

The other men nodded in sympathy, for there is always this burden on hunters who move among people appalled by the hunt. It is safe enough to hang the head of an elk on a wall in Osceola, Pennsylvania, but in Rochester, New York, one risks the loss of good friends. In city places I have seen more trophies sequestered behind lock and key in basement workshops than on open display upstairs in dens and living rooms.

Dan Edgarton was about to put in about the way folks feel about hunting in Fond du Lac when the tent flaps snapped open and there, silhouetted against the dusky sky, stood Davis, cradling his Mauser.

"Where you been, Tommie?" said Duffy.

"In the wrong place at the wrong time," Davis replied. "Came off the ridge above the Triangle and saw where they had bedded down in the meadow. Two bulls and four cows. They crossed over Bear Creek and went up the other side and that's where I scoped them. Big bulls."

"What the hell good is that?" someone said. "Why didn't you shoot one?"

Davis was under the light from the Coleman now, and he looked tired. "Shoot one?" he said softly. "At over a thousand yards?"

In the morning we rode up the ridge between Big and Bear creeks and, looking from a switchback across the valley at the great open scar of the Triangle, saw eight elk grazing there. "That figures," said Davis. "Now they're over there, where I scoped them from yesterday, and we're over here, where they ought to have stayed. And there's a mile between us." It was the second day of the hunt. For supper that evening we ate beefsteaks and boiled potatoes. And no liver.

Spike Camp

Wednesday morning—two days down and three to go—Tom Davis and I watched the others ride out to give the Triangle another working over, then pointed our own horses up the winding trail to the spike camp at the head of Bark Cabin Creek. It was a pleasant ride through lodgepole forest first; past a couple of meadow ponds looking productive of moose, but no sign of any; past the bleached, slivered ruins of a trapper's cabin, but no sign of any wolfskins, no more the rendezvous of mountain men with Hawken rifles; and at last, steeply, through spruce into open parkland with islands of whitebark pine and alpine fir at 8,500 feet. We had come out onto the floor of a bowl. West a scant mile, the final upthrust of the Gallatin Divide rose sharply another 1,300 feet to the dome-shaped prominence of the Sentinel, where the divide trail swung in from Windy Pass. North and south, rimrock ledges ran out from the main divide and tumbled into talus slopes, while to the east, the canyon of the creek we had ascended opened just wide enough to frame the smoky-blue maze of the Absarokas beyond the Yellowstone. Smiling, Davis turned slowly in his saddle and said that this was where he would take his trophy elk.

Two hunters, not of our party but friends of Neal's, were already ensconced in the one-tent spike camp when we arrived. They appeared at the open flaps in blaze orange jackets and introduced themselves as Dexter and Lee. We unsaddled, tied up the horses, stashed our meager gear, drank some coffee, asked about elk, heard there were fresh tracks just below the divide. The four of us walked then across the bowl with loud crunching underfoot in the crusted snow. "We better split up here," Lee said. Lee was a retired Air Force major and some-time rodeo cowboy. His home was in Livingston. He said, "Just poke along nice and easy and remember to look behind you as often as in front. I learned that cowboying. Same as cows, elk'll pussyfoot out behind you after you've passed."

For an hour or so, we tried to pussyfoot ourselves, poking around the edges of conifer islands, Davis with the Mauser un-slung, at the ready, and I staying a fair distance behind so as not to be in the way. Presently we came to an old upended fir and stopped to lean against its trunk, and we talked for a while about the good feeling one gets being high in the mountains, away from the road hunters and the constant crackle of gunfire one hears so often at hunting times in eastern woods. Davis said he figured it was getting awfully crowded for hunters in Michi-gan, and that next year he might put the Mauser aside during the regular deer season and try hunting instead with a bow. He said with the earlier bow season falling in October, the woods were prettier then, and with fewer hunters, less busy, too. Davis didn't like busy places. The country around Hell Creek Ranch was going that way. Most of southern Michigan had gone that way long ago. Near Gunnison, Colorado, he had bought a small piece of land some years ago, figuring one day it might be a place to retire. Now, he might not wait that long. Maybe he would move out to Colorado and start outfitting for hunters, like Duane Neal here in Montana. Or maybe he would run summer pack trips just for people who liked going high and wild. Neal did that here, too. "One of these years," he said. "But then, I don't know. Even Colorado's getting crowded. Seems everyone in Texas wants to go to the mountains."

I asked Davis how long he figured it would be before the mountains here got so busy there would be only one place left, called Alaska. Davis said, "Country like this should last forever, but nothing ever does. I've got two boys at home, both under ten. I like to think a place like this will still be here for them. I don't know if they'll ever hunt. But if they do, there's sure got to be something a whole lot better than Big Louie's." Big

Louie's is an outdoor shooting gallery in southern Michigan—game animals are the targets—and not unlike some of the exotic game ranches in Texas. "It's not hunting," Davis added, "if you and the animal are inside a wire fence."

We saw good elk sign later that day. One cleft print in the snow was the size of my fist, and Davis said that its maker might be pushing nine hundred pounds. But we saw no elk, heard none bugling. Nor did Dexter and Lee. As we headed back across the bowl toward the spike camp, I kept watching Davis for some signal that his confidence might at last be eroding. We were three days down and two to go, the weather was warming up, and new snow was nowhere in prospect. Conditions were running to favor the elk. Yet here was Davis as jauntily full of great expectations as a country boy on Opening Day of his first hunting season.

In the tent, after supper, Lee told us about his cowboying years in the West, Dexter spoke nostalgically of the wild hunting country that no longer abides in his homeland of southern California, and Davis said that he hoped someday to hunt in Alaska. It occurred to me as we were turning in for the night that no one had mentioned Africa. I expect the omission struck me because I had packed along with my gear a copy of Ernest Hemingway's *Green Hills of Africa,* a dog-eared schoolboy edition of Papa's 1935 epic of a safari through Masai country. In the tent now, with the others zipped into their sleeping bags, and the lantern dying, and a flashlight to carry on, I read through the first chapter to the part in which Hemingway described his own expectations as a hunter. They had been seeking greater kudu for ten days, had not yet seen a mature bull, and had only three days more before heavy rains moving north from Rhodesia would spoil it all. So Hemingway wrote:

"Now it is pleasant to hunt something that you want very much over a long period of time, being outwitted, out-maneuvered, and failing at the end of each day, but having the hunt and knowing every time you are out that, sooner or later, your luck will change and that you will get the chance that you are seeking. But it is not pleasant to have a time limit by which you must get your kudu or perhaps never get it, or even see one. It is not the way hunting should be."

I closed the book and lay in the dark, cold, hearing the wind and the occasional stomp and whinny of a tethered horse; and I thought how differently—how more gracious, though deprived—Tom Davis might have felt with ten days down and three to go, and no kudu, on the hot, dry plains beneath the snows of Kilimanjaro.

Beneath the star-spangled Gallatin Divide, somewhere in the dark insomniac tent of my mind, sheep jump over a wire fence. Here are a Dall and a Stone, a bighorn, an aoudad and a mouflon, and a Marco Polo from the mountains of Afghanistan. And here, too, out of Africa, by way of the trophy-room walls of Tom Goodnow's place in Connecticut, come a warthog and a ' Cape buffalo, a lechwe and a Grant's gazelle, impala and reed buck, hartebeest and kudu, waterbuck and eland, oryx and roan antelope, and a great burnt-orange bongo from the forests of the southern Sudan. A damn fine bongo it is at that, well up in the record books, though unlisted. Tom Goodnow disdains the idea that some men would make a contest of the hunt.

Next over the fence, I am running these hunters with the masks of death in Africa hanging on their walls. Here come the macho types, the arcane ones of hairy chests and bald libidos and subscriptions to *Guns and Ammo* magazine. They are so alike, so stuffed themselves, so woolly around the edges that I suspect I may fall asleep. They bore me, for they have nothing to say, except to each other, competitively. But now I see the other kind. I see Tom Goodnow in his African trophy room in Connecticut, and he is speaking modestly of his passion for rare editions of nineteenth-century ornithological books. Mr. Goodnow, I did not come here to speak of birds and books. I want to know about your bongo.

"It is the best head on the wall," he says. "A beautiful animal. I went to the Sudan and fired two cartridges. One for the bongo. The other for the lechwe. I use a thirty-aught-six. It is good for almost anything except the Cape buffalo."

It is good for the elephant? And the lion?

"I don't shoot elephant or lion. The lion should be protected. Too many are being poisoned. The cattle business, you see. Besides, the lion doesn't look like much when it's dead. And the elephant? What do you do with the head? To mount one, you'd need St. Paul's Cathedral."

What are you missing here? I ask. What heads do you lack?

"I wouldn't mind getting a better Cape buffalo someday. Maybe a giant eland, but that's getting far back into the bush. Possibly a lesser kudu. But I'd never shoot another bongo. Don't need to. With one or two exceptions, I've done all the shooting I'd want to do."

Why Africa?

"Africa spoils you. There's nothing like it. It's the country. It's being in the animal's habitat on its own terms. Some people say to me, 'Why go to Africa? Why don't you go down to Texas? It's closer. They've got oryx there, too.' Well—" and he laughs. "If Texas was across the driveway, I wouldn't walk there to kill an oryx under those circumstances. Do you understand what I mean? It's the memory of the hunt and the country. That's what you appreciate later. That's what you hang on the wall."

There are memories, too, on the walls of Mortimer Shapiro's study in New York City. He is the neurologist who tells me that squeezing the trigger is like putting a period at the end of a sentence, that what counts is not so much the death of the animal as everything that comes before. "There is a wild romanticism about Africa," he is saying. "Almost always you see game around you and the panorama is superb. Hunting, there, you are living with the moving finger of time. There is only the present. You see the tracks. You see the animal and it becomes a love object. There is tremendous sexuality in this. I don't mean the parlor sexuality of the psychoanalyst who sees the gun as a phallic symbol, but sexuality in the sense of wanting something deeply, in the sense of eros. All quests, all desires are ultimately the same, don't you think? And as you close in on the animal, all the cold fat of your being is cut away. All the wheels are turning and greased. And as the animal moves into your sights, you are most thoroughly alive. Of course, there must be handicaps. All games depend on handicaps. In tennis, it's the net. In shooting elephant, it's getting close enough— mere yards away—to place the bullet into its brain. One shot. You lessen your odds considerably doing that, because at that range the elephant can kill you."

In the cold, dark tent, now, I see a bull elephant with flared ears and bright tusks bearing down on my fence. The tusks bring sleep.

Tom Davis did not get his elk the next day in the bowl at the head of Bark Cabin Creek. In fact, after an hour of scouting, we decided to climb out of it up the steep side ridge that stood like a wall between us and the drainage of Cottonwood Creek. Elk have a tendency to feed moving uphill in the morning, and, with nothing to lose but the wind in our lungs, we figured we might as well tend more or less in that direction ourselves. Which, as things turned out, brought us across the track of the grizzly.

I have a special fascination with, and fondness for, the grizzer. And much respect. I suppose it is because, since the demise of dire wolves and saber-toothed cats, North America has been singularly deficient in the production and distribution of four-legged man-killers. The cougar might be capable of killing an adult human, but probably never has in historic times, for it is only the shyest miniature shadow of Asian and African cats; and the bison never charged with anything like the fierce horn-tossing determination to kill that is the hallmark of the fabled Cape buffalo. Unfortunately, it is a relatively safe place for people, this North America; and would be more so—to a distressing degree—were it not for the presence, here and there from Montana north to Alaska's Arctic Slope, of this great silvertip bear, this *Ursus horribilis* with claws as sure and deadly as .50-caliber bullets. God bless grizzer. Like it or not, grizzer keeps the western wilderness honest. Keeps *us* honest, too, as hard as we may try to forget that bears once hung human skulls against the walls of their own dens. No doubt in tribute to memorable dinners.

The print of the bear's paw seemed huge in the wet snow. Davis, in size-nine clodhoppers, placed his boot beside the print, and for length, we almost had a match, give or take a couple of inches in the boot's favor. The bear was angling up-hill, following a game trail. Davis squatted over one of the tracks, took off his gloves, and touched his fingers to the compacted snow. "Couldn't be more than a few hours old," he said. "Let's see where he goes." We followed the tracks to a ledge at the foot of a talus slope, where the spoor of another bear, smaller and unmistakably a black, with angular claw marks, came in from our left. The grizzer, encountering these tracks, had made several widening circles around them and then taken off on the same course with them along the ledge. So the grizzly was following the black. Even as we followed the grizzly.

For my own part, I would not have wanted to be in that black bear's place. Not that the grizzly was up to any specific inter-ursine mischief, though silvertips have been known on occasion to feast on blacks, or at least to attack them out of some haughty sense of territorial imperative. There are those who say that no critter extant anywhere is a match for an angry grizzly. The nineteenth-century historian Horace Bell told of one captive grizz, chained to a post in a pit in Old California, that managed to kill two fighting bulls before a third got its horn close enough to render a fatal goring and then died in the bear's embrace. Bell also told of a staged encounter in Monterrey, Mexico, between another California grizzly and an African lion named Parnell. The way Bell had it, the "great Californian handled the African king as a cat would a rat."

"Maybe we'd better cool it here," I said to Davis. "If we surprise it and it runs the wrong way, our way, you sure as hell don't want to have to shoot it."

Davis said, "It's probably sitting up on top right now laughing at us. But I'll tell you what. Right now I guess I'd rather see that bear than shoot an elk."

We saw no bear, nor elk either, though we heard one bugling late that morning across the bowl. In the afternoon we rode up to the Sentinel with Lee, and down again, and Davis said he'd stay another night at spike, and I said I wouldn't, and everyone said goodbye as I headed down the trail to the main camp at Big Creek. I was past the ruined trapper's cabin, watching dusk come on and wondering where our friend with the big sharp claws might be, when I heard a horseman coming down behind me. It was Davis.

"I thought you were staying up there."

"I changed my mind," he said. "Tomorrow's the last day. I want to see how Duffy's making out, and in the morning I've got a date with an elk at the Triangle."

At the edge of a meadow near camp, a great horned owl watched us approach from its perch high on a branch of a skeleton spruce. Silhouetted against the sky, its head swiveled slowly as we passed. A small animal, a rodent of a kind we could not identify in the half-light, hung slack from the owl's talons. Saluting the owl with a tip of his hat, Davis said, "Some guys have all the luck."

Coming Out

Four down and one to go. And the air space under the meat pole was empty when we rode into camp. In the cook tent, after supper, Duane Neal took his stand beside the stove, and Joe Gaab, who had tended his cows near Livingston and returned in the afternoon, stretched out on the bales of hay behind the mess table. Louie Lange said, "Tomorrow's Plan X. After the artillery barrage, we jump off at three a.m. for the frontal assault on the Triangle."

"Well, some do," said Neal. "What if Stan here takes Ed and Tom up to the Triangle, and Jim and Sid, you go on up to the Horse Pasture." The Horse Pasture was the high bench across the creek where Sid and I had seen the elk rubbing first day in. "And Dan and Louie, you get along up Mist and Smokey." Duffy was resting in the Midwest tent and would probably stick closer to camp in the morning. Suddenly a sound of hammering came from Duffy's direction. Davis hollered through the tent flaps, "Hey, Duff! Haven't you finished that elk trap yet?" Then everyone retired, a bit earlier than usual and, it seemed to me, with a curious lack of interest in snooze-off palaver. One to go.

There was little talk, too, in the morning at breakfast, and less as the hunters saddled up and rode out toward their appointed beats. Davis turned in his saddle and tipped his hat, going down to the creek, and I guessed from the faraway look on his face that he already knew how the day might be ending. I watched his horse splash across the creek, and the mist rising from the water. In the meadow beyond, wet grass glistened between patches of melting snow. And I thought, then, that possibly Papa Hemingway had a point after all about time limits and the way that hunting should not be, for I had many times felt the hollowness of being skunked myself, fishing. Now, perhaps fishing is not quite the same as hunting, though surely the only difference is the vehicle of death and the phylum and environment of your prey species. Yet in the rushing waters of northern trout streams, after three or four days of no luck, there had always been this feeling the day before leaving, this sense of incompleteness attached to the empty creel, this shameful, puerile embarrassment in defeat. And all of it gilded over by the joy of being in good clean country with robust companions, and always the cultured necessity of wearing the mask of a damn fine sport.

In recent years, forest and wildlife management researchers have delved into the expectations of hunters, especially insofar as hunting success is related to hunter satisfaction. One study, applied to deer and elk hunters in the Sapphire Mountains south of Missoula, Montana, by George Stankey, Robert Lucas, and Robert Ream, sought to discover the meaning to an individual of "quality big-game hunting." Two thirds of the hunters—there were some four hundred respondents—replied that *quality* predominantly meant either getting an animal or knowing that animals were there to be had. The other third, however, cited reasons related to general outdoor enjoyment, a closeness to nature, and appreciation of the country in which they had hunted. Among elk hunters specifically, one in four mentioned "non-mechanized access" as one of the most positive amenities. And in a similar study of hunters in Washington State, Forest Service researchers Dale Potter, John Hendee, and Roger Clark reported: "The expectation of success is necessary, but by itself, it is insufficient to produce quality hunting experiences." Yet the management agencies, in their obdurate traditional ways, continue to measure quality as though it were a correlative of days afield, animals harvested, and licenses sold.

Joe Gaab and I were talking about such things later in the day on our way back from Windy Pass. With Juli Kane, we had gone up Big Creek in the morning, after the hunters departed, and zigzagged then to the top of the divide. Even at 9,000 feet, the snow lay in patches, melting; and the sky was a clean blue slate. From the pass, we could see Electric Peak down in Yellowstone National Park, and across to the Spanish Peaks Primitive Area, and north up the Gallatin Valley toward Bozeman. Downhill on the Gallatin side were a number of large clear-cuts, over which Juli Kane voiced a mournful lament and Joe Gaab articulated his own dark fears that logging might yet be the ruination of western Montana. Then we turned our horses away from the clear-cuts and rode back through the tall timber on the Big Creek side, where "non-mechanized access" must surely be counted among the watershed's positive amenities.

"To survive hunting pressure," Joe Gaab was saying, "the elk up here need cover, not clear-cuts. The loggers' claim that clear-cuts benefit elk is more of that same old book learning. It's bunk."

I had heard down below, from Neal, that Gaab probably knew this country north of the Yellowstone, and its wildlife, better than anyone else. Gaab had been prowling it for more than thirty years, first as a game biologist, next as a warden, and finally as supervisor of outfitters, and he believed that the best way to manage game was to forsake the desk for the mountains, and the pickup truck for a horse.

"Twenty years ago," he was saying on the way back to camp, "you could ride all through this country and see plenty of moose. Well, you've been riding through here all week, and how much moose sign did you see? Not much, huh? They just sold too many licenses. Moose season here should have been shut down five years ago. And goat? I don't see how the state of Montana can justify a season on goat anywhere. Why, there aren't even fifty goat left in the Crazy Mountains. One of the things that has brought this on is the Pittman-Robertson Act. The way it works, the more licenses you sell, the more money you get from the federal government. That kind of thing just turns a conservation agency into a money-making bureaucracy."

"What about elk?" I asked.

"The state's supporting about as many elk as it can," Gaab said. "We need the hunter for balance."

I asked Gaab if he would be going after an elk himself this season.

"I don't hunt anymore," he said. "I've spent so much time protecting animals, and seen so many species going downhill, mostly from loss of habitat, I guess I just don't want to kill anything wild. Not anymore."

The hunters sat in silence at the table in the cook tent, waiting for Ed Sahrle to return. He was the last man out and it was already after six, and dark. Sahrle had gone off to circle the Triangle, solo; and Davis had waited for him a half hour and then come in, thinking that Sahrle had misunderstood about a rendezvous and soloed to camp instead. But Sahrle was still up on the mountain somewhere. Our last hope.

Stan Broughtan said at last, "I can't understand it. I was in elk all afternoon, but all I could see were cows and calves."

"I say the elk ran it up on us," said Louie Lange.

"And it wasn't even fair," said Dan Edgarton. "They had *all* the advantages."

"I've been trying to figure every possible thing my wife is

going to say to me when I come home after a week empty-handed," Lange confessed.

"I've been trying to figure every possible thing *my* wife is going to say when I tell her the deer season back home starts in ten days," said Edgarton.

From the hay bales, Joe Gaab put in, "Come on down through Livingston, boys, and I'll sell you a couple of fine steers."

Then Sahrle burst through the tent flaps. His face was flushed. For a moment, he looked along the two rows of hunters until his eyes fixed on Davis. "You *turkey!*" he shouted. "I've been busting down through the blowdowns feeling guilty for leaving you up there alone in the dark."

"I thought you'd already come in," Davis said evenly. "Welcome to the last supper."

We packed our gear, cinched up the duffels and panniers, and rode out in the morning with a warm wind blowing down on our backs from the Gallatin Divide. At a stream crossing along the way, Davis stopped for a while to water his horse. I reined in beside him.

"Was it a good hunt?" I asked. "I mean, for you."

Davis looked back over his shoulder in the direction of camp. "Good?" he said. "You better believe it was good. We almost caught up with that big grizzly." Then he twisted around in the saddle and tipped his hat toward the unseen divide. "There's still next year," he said, staring up the riderless trail. "And there's still that big bull elk up there at the Triangle, waiting for *me.*"

Next year? Yes, and the year after that, I supposed. And all the years after, for as long as there would ever be country like this, and men like Davis with ancient yearnings to prowl high and wild. Or at least until such time as there might be, one way or another, an end to the game.

Book Four

YUNGNAQUAGUQ

War in the Woods

No one can be certain of the figures, for it is difficult to count what one cannot readily see, and Alaska is so huge, wall to wall, some people measure it by time zones instead of miles. In such a land, and in its waters, the state of the art of taking census of wildlife populations cannot be far removed from the science of counting fingers. Still, people try. One of the latest attempts came up with thirteen million waterfowl, two hundred thousand caribou, one hundred fifty thousand moose, ditto the walrus, forty thousand Dall sheep, ditto the Sitka black-tailed deer, and three million seal of several species. On a statewide basis, no one much bothers keeping track of snowshoe hare, porcupine, beaver, and ptarmigan, which are likewise edible and generally plentiful. And only Saint Peter knows how many millions of char, grayling, halibut, lake trout, pike, chinook, coho, sockeye, and sheefish are swimming around in the Great Land's lakes and rivers and bays. By any measure, it is a movable feast—seemingly enough to sustain the expectations of Alaska's licensed hunters and fishermen, their household kin, and a visiting corps of sportsmen from Outside; enough, too, to feed some thirty thousand bush Alaskans for whom the rifle, the snare, and the net are the primary tools of daily life. Yet for all the bountiful appearances, some of Alaska's game species are stretched against the hard thin line of human demand. And the numbers are such that not a few of the resource users may have to do without in the years ahead. It has already come to that, swiftly and surprisingly, in this last great wild hunting ground of the United States.

When shortages come, hard decisions cannot be far behind. When a renewable resource is pressed to the line, how does one decide who is to get the so-called surplus? To whom goes the moose of Nowitna? To the poverty-level Athapaskan Indian who lives out there, or to the dentist from Fairbanks who arrives by chartered plane? Who gets the salmon off Angoon? The villagers, or the trawlers from Sitka and Seattle? Where and when should the migratory geese of the Kuskokwim fall? In the spring, on the subsistence hunter from Eek? Or in the autumn, on the blind of the sport hunter at Lake Berryassa, California?

In Alaska, the word "subsistence" goes by a hundred different definitions, depending on the definer and whether he is white and rich and asphalted in the city or red and poor in the bush, or vice versa, and to what degree he may or may not believe that the old ways are now compromised by gasoline engines, nylon nets, and telescopic sights. "I guess the word 'subsistence' does not yield to a consensus definition," says David Johnson, a game biologist in Kotzebue. "If it doesn't yield, I wonder if it even exists as such."

"Subsistence is bullshit," says Darrell Farmen, an Anchorage taxidermist and member of the State Board of Game.

Tom Lonner is chief of the Department of Fish and Game's Subsistence Division. He says, "Complexity is something most people cannot deal with. So they simplify in favor of bias and they say, 'Subsistence does not exist.'"

"Please try to fathom our great desire to survive in a way somewhat different from yours," say the Eskimo elders of Nightmute, "and thus see why the hunters will continue to go out."

"Subsistence is based on need," says John Schaeffer, the executive director of the Northeast Alaska Native Corporation. "Who needs the resource more? Who is going to starve if the resources are made available to the subsistence hunter before they are made available to some trophy hunter? That is the whole point of the game. It is not just food for the stomach. It is food for the soul."

"There was an Eskimo in Togiak," says Ohio congressman John Seiberling. "He summed it up in one sentence. He said, 'We must hunt or die.'"

The Yupik Eskimos have their own special word: *Yungnaquaguq,* the means to perpetuate life. And they ask, "Does one way of life have to die so another can live?" The answer from the hunter's gun has always been *yes.* One life must end to nourish another. It could be different with people and their traditional life styles, if only the clock will allow it.

There was a time in Alaska, and a recent time at that, when the questions and answers came a little easier. Then, according to the state constitution, fish and game were to be "reserved to the people for common use," and all regulations governing disposal of natural resources were to "apply equally to all persons." Then, state game laws could define subsistence hunting as "the taking of game animals by a state resident for food or clothing for personal or immediate family use." Which was simplicity itself, for under that definition, everyone in Alaska—rich or poor, urban or rural, red or white—could consider himself a subsistence hunter. And almost everyone did; or did until the mid-1970s, when the U.S. Congress began redefining "subsistence" in the process of drafting legislation for the National Interest d-2 Lands of Alaska (the approximately 100 million acres to be set aside as parks and refuges under Section d-2 of the Alaska Native Claims Settlement Act of 1971); and when, simultaneously, the once great numbers of the Western Arctic caribou herd came tumbling down.

The crash of the Western caribou herd, from 250,000 animals in 1970 to barely 50,000 six years later, left many Alaskans with a feeling of déjà vu. They had been here before: the Nelchina herd, northeast of Anchorage, falling from 70,000 to 8,000 in ten years; the Fortymile herd on the Klondike Plateau, down from 50,000 to 6,000; and the 12,000 moose of the Tanana Flats south of Fairbanks quartered to 3,000 in less than a decade. After those earlier crashes, they had listened to the game managers speak of calf losses due to severe winters and "too many" wolves. Yet hardly anyone spoke of too many hunters. Hardly anyone noticed—in the context of available game—that Anchorage was now the third-fastest-growing city in the nation, or that Fairbanks was fairly brimming with thousands of oil workers newly arrived from the hunting grounds of Texas and Oklahoma. And when the moose biologists went to the Game Board to ask that the season be closed in the over-harvested Tanana Flats, the Game Board refused.

But the disaster in the Western Arctic was something else. Out in the bush of that region, sourdough loners and Native villagers depended on caribou meat for their tables. True, a trapper could mush down the Wulik River to the little store at Kivalina and trade in his food stamps for beefsteak. But at six dollars a pound, or more, after air freight? And the villagers could simply eat fish. But for how long?

Seeing a clear need for some kind of preferential regulation, the Game Board decided to issue permits for the taking of three thousand caribou bulls. Each bush village would receive a quota based on recommendations by Native corporations and village councils, and the councils in turn would issue the permits on the basis of need, considering such factors as family size, alternate food sources, and employment opportunities— the last consideration being somewhat moot, as jobs in the bush are rare. In any event, most of the Natives of the Northwest were willing to work with the new regulations. But not the Tanana Valley Sportsmen's Association of Fairbanks. On behalf of a white man who claimed he was denied a caribou permit at Nuiqsut, the sportsmen filed a suit in the state's Supreme Court seeking to overturn the new regulations on the issue of "common use" and constitutional rights. The court found in favor of the plaintiffs. The caribou permit hunt was closed in the Northwest. And sportsmen's hats sailed into the air at Fairbanks, where there are always alternate sources of food and some jobs for skilled workers, and usually cash rather than food stamps, and where beefsteak is not quite so dear as in Nuiqsut or Kivalina.

Federal policy for managing the d-2 lands in Alaska

brought further complexity to the subsistence puzzle. Most of the villagers living in the bush are Indians, Eskimos, and Aleuts, and there was much concern in Washington this time to do right by them after more than a century of broken treaties and abrogated rights for aboriginal Americans in the Lower Forty-eight. There was also a huge disdain both Inside and Outside for Alaska's competency in managing fish and game on federal lands. Many Outsiders of the environmentalist persuasion felt it was bad enough that the game herds should collapse, but even worse that the state's response more often than not should be war on wolves. It was this same skeptical constituency which helped shape the first d-2 bill to reach the floor of the U.S. House of Representatives. Arizona congressman Morris Udall's H.R. 39 would have given subsistence users priority over other consumptive users on some 100 million acres of federal land, whenever harvest restrictions became necessary (as in the case of the Western Arctic herd). And in its original version, H.R. 39 would have taken from the state, and handed over to the Secretary of the Interior, sole authority for managing subsistence uses of those lands. Though the Udall measure died in the U.S. Senate in 1978, Washington's message to Juneau was loud and clear: Either protect subsistence on federal lands or lose what the state has viewed as its traditional right to manage resident fish and game on these lands.

This time Alaska responded with something more substantial than a war on wolves. Out of the state legislature came House Bill 960, amending the old inclusive definition of subsistence to mean "the customary and traditional uses in Alaska of wild, renewable resources for such direct personal or family consumption as food, shelter, fuel, clothing, tools, or transportation, for the making and selling of handicraft articles out of nonedible byproducts of fish and wildlife resources, . . . and for the customary trade, barter, or sharing for personal or family consumption." Within the Department of Fish and Game, the measure established a Subsistence Division with special advisory responsibilities; and it further authorized the boards of fish and game to make subsistence "the priority use." In extreme cases, allocation of a resource could be restricted to local residents demonstrating "customary and direct dependence upon the resource as the mainstay of one's livelihood."

Not everyone was pleased with House Bill 960. Most of the villagers were, for the law staked out their prior right to local resources. And the feds were pleased, if only for the sake of the Eskimos and Indians. And there was satisfaction as well for some Outside environmentalists, although others with a certain anthropomorphic friendship for animals would continue to wonder why Eskimos couldn't eat food stamps instead of seals and caribou. But the urban sport hunters of Alaska were *not* happy. And the big-game guides with clients from Houston and Stockholm and Frankfurt am Main were definitely not happy. And some of the sourdough loners out in the bush were not happy either, remembering, however inappropriately to any clear understanding of the law, that there had been this white man who had gone in vain to Nuiqsut for a permit. And now it is getting ugly, out there in the woods.

Shots have been fired at floatplanes. One hunting party returned to its aircraft to find it demolished by an ax. An adventuresome Outsider, floating the Koyukuk, had his raft shot from under him and hid in the bush for two nights awaiting police rescue. Silent strangers glower at each other from passing canoes. Athapaskans radio the game warden to demand that he "check out" Eskimos coming upriver with rifles and moose tags. Eskimos on the coast complain that Indians net too many spawning-run salmon upstream. The Alaska Outdoor Association of Anchorage warns its sporting followers that their "rights" are being "given away to the Alaskan Natives and/or the so-called subsistence users." The Real Alaska Coalition, headed by guide Ken Fanning, calls for a "Monumental Trespass" by sport hunters on some fifty million acres of d-2 land designated national monuments under the Antiquities Act. National Park Service regulations allow only subsistence users to hunt within most of these monuments. Yet Fanning is telling all Alaskans to "go out into the monuments and do everything" they did in the past.

It could get even uglier. The hunting population of Alaska,

in the bush as well as in the cities and towns, keeps growing. Native youths are coming home to their villages from regional high schools and colleges, and from some jobs that no longer exist, to indulge a sense of place and cultural identity, and to await the disposition of awards—slim, on an individual basis— accruing from the Alaska Native Claims Settlement Act of 1971. Civilized ways will follow them home, to be sure; and, to some extent, an increasing dependence on the cash economy. There will have to be cash for subsistence. One cannot pour seal oil into a snow machine and expect the engine to start; nor stuff fox pelts into the breech of a .30/06 and have something come out the other end. But the sports in Fairbanks and Anchorage say: Baloney. If you want to subsist, go back to the dogsled and the bow and arrow.

One day, perhaps, after the Antiquities Act monuments have evolved by law into d-2 national parks, in a time of traditional life styles balanced even more precariously against the march of technology and urban ways, there may also be trouble between the subsistence hunter and his sometime ally, the preservationist from Outside. Half a dozen Alaskans of as many persuasions have shared with me this vision, and I subscribe to it. The vision is of this group of wilderness backpackers, all from Outside, topping a tundra rise in the Gates of the Arctic, at the foot of the Arrigetch Peaks. Suddenly they are brought up short by what is before them. But not by the sawtooth crags of the Arrigetch. By this Eskimo hunter kneeling over a head-shot caribou, and by the steam that is rising from the animal's body as the Eskimo's knife opens the gut to the autumn air. And the backpackers, as might be expected since they hail from such cities as Berkeley and Santa Barbara and Greenwich and Palm Beach, turn away with disgust and a vow to urge their congressmen to outlaw *all* hunting in Alaska's new national parks. For they each have this certain friendship for animals, and the conviction that food stamps and tourism and scenery should be more than enough to nourish an Eskimo's soul.

. . .

Bob Willard is a Tlingit Indian from Angoon. We have come to
the Viking Café in Juneau to speak of his people and subsistence. It is May. Salmon are moving again through the jade-
green Chatham Strait. They are schooling up for the spring
run. The open boats of the fishermen are trolling the shoals of
Admiralty Island, probing the fjords of Chichagof and the
coves of Kuiu. It is harvest time in the Southeast. Yet here at
dusk in Juneau is this Tlingit, talking politics in a white man's
café.

Politics have been a good part of Bob Willard's life away
from Angoon. For four years, by appointment of former Governor Keith Miller, he served as the state's human rights commissioner. He has worked with the Sealaska Corporation, one of
thirteen regional profit-seeking entities established by the
Alaska Native Claims Settlement Act. And he is chairman of
the legislative affairs committee of the Alaska Native Brother-
hood, an organization founded by Tlingits in 1912 to help Indians achieve citizenship and voting rights in the new territory.
At that time, the laws governing such things stipulated that Indians must first sever their tribal relationships. To obtain the
right to vote, a Tlingit was expected to adopt the civilized ways
of the whiskey-soaked white men who had plundered the land
of its gold, spoiled the salmon streams, and spread smallpox
and syphilis through the villages. Somehow the Tlingits survived all of it. Even the franchise.

"In 1890," Willard is saying, "twenty-two of the chiefs met
up near Haines to talk about driving the white men out. They
were very angry. The whites were ravaging the creeks and taking the timber and changing the life style of the people. But it
was September." And now Willard laughs. "It was harvest
time. It is almost always harvest time in the Southeast. The
Tlingits were too busy to fight. Otherwise we would have
thrown you all out." Willard looks at me closely and smiles.
"It's still not a bad idea, you know. We're just not that serious
about it. Yet."

Willard speaks cautiously of the new national monument
on Admiralty Island which would be designated as wilderness
under various d-2 scenarios. Angoon is likewise on Admiralty

Island, and Willard says its people are in favor of wilderness so long as it keeps out the big pulpwood operators from the mainland and protects the villagers' traditional use of deer and bear and berries and roots, and sawlogs for the winter stoves. "But we do not forget what happened at Glacier Bay," he adds. "We don't want Admiralty to be turned into another Glacier Bay. When that place was set up as a national monument, the government told the Tlingits they would have exclusive subsistence use. The government said the Tlingits could go in there and hunt. But later, somebody changed the rules. Later, the people had to check in their rifles before the rangers would let them go into the monument. We sure don't want that again."

Resource regulations are monumentally abhorrent to the Tlingits, as, indeed, they are to most Native peoples of Alaska. And most of the bad feeling is directed not at the federal government but at the state's Department of Fish and Game. As "IRS" spells trouble to many enterprisers of the cash economy, so does the bureaucratic "Fish 'n' Game" to the practitioner of bush subsistence. Let Juneau send a biologist to Angoon to catalogue the villagers' wild harvest, and it is as if King John had dispatched the sheriff of Nottingham into Sherwood Forest to audit the assets of Robin Hood. "We have it all catalogued," says Bob Willard. "But we won't give it up. The more you speak of numbers, the more you get regulated."

Once, in Kivalina on the Chukchi Sea, I sat by the shore with an Eskimo woman, awaiting the return of her husband from a seal hunt off Cape Krusenstern. And she told me this story of the state's Fish 'n' Game man coming from Nome to ask her for a list of the Kivalina hunters. "What is it you want of them?" the woman inquired of the stranger. He said he had come to discover how many caribou the hunters were taking. She gave him a list of names, and he went away, knocking at doors. Later, the woman met the stranger on his way to the airstrip. "Did you find what you came for?" she asked. The man had a sad look on his face and he shook his head no. "If I were a hunter," said the woman, "I wouldn't tell a game warden anything either." The man from Nome said, "But I'm not a game warden. I'm a wildlife biologist." And the woman said, "That doesn't make any difference. I'm not a fool. I'm an Eskimo."

Now, in the Viking Café in Juneau, Bob Willard suddenly remembers again that it is harvest time in the Southeast. "Wait a minute," he says. "I wonder what I'm doing here. This is May. There's no *r* in the month. I could be taking all the clams I can use. The abalone's ready. The seaweed, too. The table is set. What am I doing in here with you guys when I could be out *there?* The trend is to go home. We see our people coming back."

And what about Bob Willard?

"Next year," he says. "My job here is just about done. Next year, I'm going to hunt and fish and do what I was made to do. I'm going home to Angoon."

In the morning, a floatplane took me from Juneau to Angoon. We landed on a bay behind the village, taxied to a pier where half a dozen fishing boats were moored. Some of the boats, or rather their operators, are licensed to fish commercially; and because of the resulting cash income from salmon and shellfish, and the sharing ways of the people, who regard themselves as being all of one family, five hundred strong, Angoon is not altogether the sort of village that one might consider typically bush. Nor is it urban, for the old ways of setting the table with the fat of the land and the sea still prevail.

At a conference table in one of the public buildings, I spoke with some of Angoon's elders and the leaders of its village corporation, Kootznoowoo, Inc. Charlie Jim, Sr., said: "You people don't eat what we eat. What would you think if *we* made the rules and I said to you, 'Listen—we limit you people to one cow and three chickens.' Too many laws are made behind our backs. This thing hurts."

George Jim, Sr., who is seventy-seven and leader of the Tlingit's Shark Clan, said: "We use it all." Because someone had mentioned allegations of waste. "We use it all. We dry the fish and put it away for wintertime. And the eggs. We use it all. And seal, we use the skin for shoes. Bear, for wintertime. Deer, we dry it. Just the way we always been using it."

Daniel Johnson said: "In each region of Alaska, it's different. Each region will have to define its own needs, its own way of life. We've lost some of it. But we're still holding on to the most crucial parts of it. And we're being cut down by the regulations. On deer, before, there was no limit to what we could smoke or salt. Now, we are limited to the same as the sport hunters. Now, they are taking the happiness out of the people."

Jimmy George, who is ninety and leader of the Tlingit's Killer Whale Clan, said: "We try to obey the United States because they adopted us. But they treat us as foreigners. What's going to happen to us? They never listen to us. They do not hear what we have to say."

And Jimmy George's wife, Lydia, said: "My generation is lost between the two cultures. But the younger people—they will try to make our history work for us."

And Edweel John said: "The people who make the regulations—do they know what the word 'subsistence' means? Do you? We do. All our people do. Did the state define the word 'subsistence'? They can't. They don't know nothing. But you take *me* out, partner, out in the cold. I still know what to do. I know where I'm *at*. The old-timers taught me. Jimmy George. George Jim. My dad. They taught me how to get along. *Subsistence!* You can't define subsistence. It's *our* way of life."

Then Charlie Jim of Kootznoowoo put in again: "Our people, when they had nothing but their regular food—no false teeth, no eyeglasses, no sickness among them. All right. When the others came moving in on us, we began to eat white people's food. I remember one chief said our people began to live on cow's milk instead of their mother's and that's why they're crazy. Today, some of our children can't speak their own tongue. But we still remember. We're not eating up everything from Alaska. When we were living here—the Natives, alone—there was always enough food. Where did it all go? There is no man alive who can say we can't have what is here. This is our food. We were made to have it."

·   ·   ·

Tom Lonner holds the third-toughest job in Alaska, after those of the governor, Jay Hammond, and the Commissioner of Fish and Game, Ronald Skoog, who is Lonner's boss. Possibly it is just as tough to be a wildlife biologist from Nome on assignment to Kivalina, but I doubt it. For Lonner is a sociologist in a bureaucracy that plays by the rules of biopolitics. He is chief of the Subsistence Division of the Alaska Department of Fish and Game, and his job is to close the widening gap that prevails between the regulators in Juneau and what he refers to as "the unseen economy" of the bush.

As Lonner saw it when I spoke with him at his office in Juneau, the gap must be filled with information. What, he asked, is the true level of need in rural Alaska, in all of Alaska? How great is the harvest in pounds of food and cash equivalents? What is the level of human effort involved in subsistence? To what extent does subsistence offset the burden of welfare? These are difficult questions in Alaska—as difficult for the traditional Fish 'n' Game man lacking rapport with the villagers as for the Native hunter, who fears that sharing data with Fish 'n' Game will only lead to further regulation, and who, when asked why he needs more game than the law allows, simply replies that this is his food, and that he was made to have it.

Over the years, various Native, state, and federal researchers have attempted to piece together estimates of the subsistence harvest in pounds of food and cash equivalents. All of these studies were of a regional or local nature, and the figures were often drawn from calendar forms distributed to villagers who may or may not have been diligent in computing their harvest of wild foods. In any event, the ball-park figure appears to fall somewhere between 800 and 1,600 pounds per person per year. Which coincides, at the middle of that range, with Lonner's own estimate of 40 million pounds of wild edibles annually statewide.

A few examples. One household survey conducted by the University of Alaska in 1972 determined that a large majority of the people of Akiachak and Mountain Village, both in the Yukon-Kuskokwim Delta region, obtained more than three quarters of their meat and fish by hunting and fishing. Those who tended to rely on protein obtained from the village stores were generally older people incapable of hunting or fishing. In 1973, the U.S. Fish and Wildlife Service surveyed a number of Yukon-Kuskokwim villages. At Tuluksak, they found that 180 villagers, in an average year, harvested 10 moose, 6 bears, 500 beavers, 2,000 muskrats, 2,000 geese and ducks, 3,000 ptarmigans, 16,000 whitefish, 8,000 salmon, 3,000 smelt, 8,000 pounds of berries and wild rhubarb, as well as various pounds and numbers of other critters and plants. The per capita consumption of this food was computed at 1,619 pounds. Apprised of Tuluksak's prodigious appetite, the Alaska Department of Fish and Game scoffed, and said the figures were inflated. And perhaps they were, especially when one considers the fact that the average person in Anchorage annually consumes only about 260 pounds of store-bought fish and meat. On the other hand, one must remember that the person in Anchorage also eats great quantities of potatoes, rice, vegetables, and dairy products, while the Kuskokwim Eskimo generally does not. Moreover, much of the wild meat and fish is dried before it is eaten, and in the drying process loses up to three quarters of its original weight. And one must remember, too, that meat in the bush often spoils for lack of proper storage, and that even though snowmobiles have largely replaced the sled, sled dogs are still maintained—and fed—by some village families.

As for cash equivalents, the Fish and Wildlife Service figured that the Tuluksak villager's 1,619 pounds of wild food carried a value, if it had passed by the cash register of a market in Bethel (the regional center), of $2,146. That was in 1973 dollars. Today the value would be well over $3,000.

"If subsistence should ever collapse in this state," Lonner was saying, "the replacement food will have to come in by air and it will cost at least a hundred million dollars a year. Who's going to pay for it? From whose treasury will the dollars flow?"

I asked him how long he felt subsistence could last, given the growing demand from all quarters on a renewable but finite resource. And he said: "No one knows. Alaska is like a desert. The richness of life you see is only at the oases. A couple of bad winters and you can lose an oasis. Ecosystem management doesn't go on here. There's this vast system. You stick your fist in it and the ripples go out. But you never see where they end up. And we've only begun to try."

I worry for Lonner, as I worry for the economy of the bush, and for the wildlife which supports it. I worry for Lonner because I do not detect, among the rank and file of the Game Division of the Department of Fish and Game, much enthusiasm for what he believes in and for what he is charged by the legislature to do. For better or worse, game managers in Alaska, as elsewhere, still pay their dues to the sportsmen. Both manager and sport tend to be cut from the same bolt of cloth. They speak the same language. They mourn the diminishment of favors for the great middle class. Certainly there are sensitive and perceptive men at headquarters and in the field, but there are more who say, in effect, that subsistence hunters have neither the right nor the need to be treated preferentially in the allocation of scarce resources, and who openly proclaim that the issue of subsistence must surely fall somewhere between baloney and a sinister plot. Or so it would seem when Game Division Director Ron Somerville is quoted in the Anchorage *Times* as having told a gathering of the Alaska Outdoor Association that the subsistence issue is "a front to cover the deals and the unholy alliance between the Natives and preservationists." And so it would seem when Game Board member Jim Rearden is quoted in the Fairbanks *Daily News-Miner* as saying that subsistence would not be a real concern in the villages if it were not for the agitations of "full-time, paid employees" of such "special-interest groups" as the Rural Alaska Community Action Program (RurAL CAP) and the Alaska Federation of Natives. So the war goes on. And no end in sight.

Delta Springtime

The way the old Yupik Eskimos used to tell it, Raven created the earth and then raked the land with his talons, and that is how the great rivers of the Yukon and the Kuskokwim found their way to the Bering Sea. Raven did well, for otherwise there would never have been this vast plain built on the rivers' sediments, sprawling across western Alaska from Kuskokwim Bay to Norton Sound. There would never have been these winding sloughs and lakes and potholes by the thousands speckling the tundra from the Kilbuck Mountains north to the Nulato Hills. And probably, too, there would never have been this whirring of feathered wings in the springtime as Raven's multitudinous children—brant and scaup and eider and oldsquaw and pintail and teal, emperor and white-fronted and Canada geese—came down from the flyway to nest in the tussocks where the Yupik crouched, waiting with his *qilamitaaq.* For Raven had taught the Eskimo hunter how to catch a low-flying bird when his family was hungry for fresh red meat. Raven had shown how to make weights out of whalebone or walrus ivory. Each of five weights was tied to a braided sinew, and the sinews were fastened at their unweighted ends to a single grip made of wing feathers. When the hunter hurled his *qilamitaaq* aloft, the sinews cut through the air like whips, and woe to the duck or the goose that happened to get in their way. This is how Raven turned the Yupik people into waterfowlers. They were good at it, too; though not as good as they would be after Raven and the *qilamitaaq* were replaced by Remington and his shotgun.

It seems a place more splendid for birds than for people, the Yukon-Kuskokwim Delta. Fifty thousand square miles—an area the size of New York State—and half of it water, running to the sea or pooled in ponds and cutoff riverbeds running nowhere. Except for willow and alder, and spruce along the upland reaches of the two main rivers, trees eschew the Delta, leaving it instead to moss and lichens, to grass and sedge. As for mammals, apart from people, there are seals along the coast and furbearers inland. But moose and caribou are uncommon in the lowlands, and those that occasionally drift into the downstream country are regarded as migratory aberrations. Considering such circumstances, an Outsider might wonder why the ancient Yupiks selected this sparse country for their homeland, and why so many contemporary ones choose to remain. When the first whites—the *gussoks*—began to poke up the rivers in their whaleboats, ten thousand Eskimos were living on the Delta. Now they are seventeen thousand. They live in villages called Platinum and Pilot Station and Nightmute and Aniak and Russian Mission and Crooked Creek, and for the most part they subsist on salmon. The salmon are dried on racks in the sun. After a long winter of eating dried fish, the Yupiks are eager for spring. When spring comes to the Delta, the Yupiks know that fresh red meat cannot be far behind.

They say that the first birds arrive at their nesting grounds even while snow still covers the tundra and the ponds remain locked in ice. One hundred and seventy species have been sighted in the Delta, shore and water birds mostly, maybe as many as 100 million individuals in a given season. Of all swans winging the Pacific flyway, eight of ten are believed to nest in the Yukon-Kuskokwim Delta. And eight of ten of the continent's emperor geese nest here, too. During fall migration, some birds from the Delta set course for, and ultimately touch down on, most of the Canadian provinces, all of the contiguous United States, Mexico, Central and South America, many of the Pacific islands, and much of eastern Asia. The U.S. Fish and Wildlife Service guesses that nowhere else in the world is there an area of similar size "as critical to so many species."

Migratory game-bird hunting regulations for Alaska are promulgated by the Fish and Wildlife Service; and by Outside standards, they are fairly liberal. In the Delta region, the season for waterfowl runs from September 1 to December 16. The daily bag limits are ten to fifteen ducks, depending on the species; four white-fronted or Canada geese, singly or in aggregate; six emperor geese, four brant, and two cranes. Researchers figure that half of all the waterfowl harvested throughout Alaska in the course of a year are taken in the Yukon-Kuskokwim Delta, which half adds up to about 125,000 birds. Of these, most are shot out of season, in the spring. In a study of harvest patterns in the mid-1960s, David R. Klein of the University of Alaska figured that the typical Yupik hunter probably killed about seventy-eight ducks and geese each year, and that more than half of these were taken during the illegal spring season. Nowadays, the individual harvest may be even higher. And the total harvest most certainly is. Since 1964, the human population of the Delta has doubled, and some demographers expect it to top forty thousand by the year 2000. If it should, and if the harvest should increase proportionately, Delta hunters could be taking more birds than the resource can safely afford to lose.

For certain champions of the subsistence life style, it is difficult to place much stock in the dour projections when ducks and geese seem to rise like thick clouds of smoke across the Delta horizon. Once, in Washington, D.C., I raised the question of numbers with a lobbyist for one of the Alaskan Native organizations, and he said to me: "It can't happen. To make a dent in those birds, you'd need a battery of Gatling guns in every village." And yet in some villages, there are hunters who fear that it *can* happen; that, in fact, a great diminishment of numbers has already begun. Not necessarily because of shotguns on the Delta; because of what is happening to the birds Outside. At the Delta village of Hooper Bay, Raphael Murran said to me: "According to the older men, each spring fewer and fewer of the birds come back from where they have wintered. There is much stress on the birds in the south. Look at California. All chemicals and pollution, and they fill the marshes with cement. And down there are many sport hunters. They outnumber us. They take more birds. What use do they have for the birds? They don't *need* them. They take them for fun."

There is considerable misunderstanding between the subsistence waterfowlers of Alaska and the sportsmen Outside. Oregonians and Californians, camouflaged in their October duck blinds, also note a diminishment of numbers, and they curse bush Alaskans for shooting "their" birds out of season in May. The sports wonder why the hunters of the Delta cannot hold their fire until the first of September. Yet when the hunters of the Delta hear this complaint, they are incensed. I'd be incensed, too. By the first of September, many of the birds are not only out of range but out of Alaska, already on their way toward the blinds of California. There is also a matter of feathers. Outside, the sports have this theory that Eskimos waste honkers in order to market the goosedown to Eddie Bauer and L. L. Bean. In the Yupik villages, elders note youths returning from

Anchorage with parkas and sleeping bags lofted with down, and, knowing it is not they who supply the material, suspect it must be those white-face hunters at the other end of the flyway. (In fact, most of the down used commercially for garments and sleeping bags comes from domestic geese in Canada, Germany, and the People's Republic of China.)

And finally it would seem that the bird in the bush gets the can of worms, for there is confusion and misunderstanding as well in the matter of international treaties. An accord signed in 1916 by the United States and Canada prohibited the hunting of most species from March 10 to September 1. A 1936 treaty with Mexico outlawed the taking of ducks during the same period, but said nothing of geese or swans, or of subsistence, for that matter. In Alaska, federal fish and wildlife agents were thoroughly bewildered. One year there was token enforcement, the next year there wasn't. At Barrow, in 1960, they arrested an Eskimo for shooting ducks out of season. Two days later, 138 other Eskimos shot ducks, then presented themselves for arrest. After some legal maneuvering, charges against all of them were dropped. The feds warned that further violations would be prosecuted. But they were not, for the game wardens turned the other way. And now there was another treaty, with Japan. It provided for subsistence use of migratory birds by Alaskan Indians and Eskimos, but not by Aleuts or bush whites; and it further proscribed the taking of fowl during their principal nesting season. In effect, the treaty gave with one hand and took away with the other. Next came an agreement with the Soviet Union, which sanctioned the taking of migratory birds and their eggs, under U.S. Department of the Interior regulation, by indigenous Alaskans for their own nutritional and other needs in remote villages. And which also inspired the United States and Canada to amend their old 1916 accord with similar language. But before the Secretary of the Interior can issue subsistence regulations legalizing a spring-summer hunt by bush Alaskans—thereby gaining some measure of control over the harvest—the Japanese and Mexican treaties must likewise be amended. Toward that end, negotiations proceed slowly at the bargaining table. No doubt the diplomats involved might act more expeditiously were they to spend a winter in a Delta village, dining on dried salmon, dreaming of meat.

Chevak is a Delta village located halfway between the mouths of the Yukon and Kuskokwim rivers. It sits on a low bluff above its own meandering river, nameless on most maps, about six miles inland from the mud flats of Hooper Bay. The population is three hundred, more or less. Most of the people eat salmon and whitefish and seal and berries, and birds in the spring. And there is always some *gussok* food at the general store for those who can afford it. For those who, affording it, can stomach it.

The birds had come to Chevak ahead of me. Now they were out on the tundra making their nests. Most of the shooting was over, at least for a while, for the first king salmon had just been taken near Hooper Bay and soon the fish would be making their run; and the people had put away their shotguns in order to ready their boats and nets for the crucial catch. We walked down from the airstrip into the village and straightaway saw some birds that would not be nesting. They hung from the drying racks upside down, plucked and brown, and wrinkled by the sun—the layaway surplus of a harvest of fresh meat. Then a cool wind came off the river, and the drying birds turned slowly under the racks, each like a small chicken charred on a roasting spit.

Chevak is a relatively new village, dating to 1951. Old-timers still think of themselves as the *Qemirmuiit*, the people from the hills, and they remember the place called Kashunuk, to the south, where there were houses made of driftwood and tundra sod, and everyone went to fish camp after the birds came in May, and when it took all day to reach the ocean, going for seals, paddling first with the current and then against the tide, instead of an hour or two with the revved-up power of a hundred horses slung from the back of one's boat. Going back generations, there are stories of Russian traders who exchanged their rifles for the Eskimos' furs—how the bargain was struck when the *gussok* held the rifle straight up, butt on the ground, and the Yupik trapper piled his skins one upon another until the stack of furs was level with the rifle's muzzle. One stack for one rifle. It cost that much, even then.

It is different now, in Chevak, though not altogether. The houses are made of plywood and particle board and tar paper in the eclectic *gussok* style of poor man's Anchorage, or Albuquerque, or Appalachia. It is not an efficient way to live, warm, in the subarctic; but it is the way now nonetheless—sod insulation having been decreed unsuitable for civilized people according to the wisdom of missionaries and government meddlers over the years. And besides, there is oil for the stoves, though warmth may cost a small family two hundred dollars a month, and often more. And there is the big generator of the Alaska Village Electrical Cooperative, fired by Number One oil beside the general store, and the power lines in frostproof conduits running along the boardwalks and into the houses to light the lamps and service the freezers where some of the wild foods are stored.

There is television in Chevak. It comes by relay out of Bethel, though at the time of my visit it was not in operation. The translator device, the village's central receiver, was on the fritz and the village council had voted not to repair it, at least for the duration of the summer. I was informed that the decision was in the best interest of the children. True, there was much to be learned from television about the world Outside. But television was best for the winter, to keep the children quiet and out of mischief indoors. Now the days were long and warm, and it was better that the children learn a thing or two about their own outside while the Sonys and Sylvanias stood darkly silent in the corners of the thin frame houses. And as I strolled through the village that first evening, I watched the children in scattered groups chattering delightedly, each individual taking his or her turn, at whatever they happened to be playing, without the peevish competitive bawling I generally associate with prepubescents gaming in the backyards of my own experience. "Hi!" they called in English when they spied me watching. "What's *your* name?" Dark eyes and ruddy cheeks turning my way. Tummies full of bird meat, probably. Too young yet to wonder about treaties and regulations, or about the forces that would soon be pulling them, one way or another, between the old and the new. The gentle people, I remembered someone saying of the Yupiks. The gentlest in the harshest of all possible worlds.

"My father saw the ocean as a plate." It was mealtime, and Leo Moses sat at the kitchen table of his home in Chevak. With the tips of his fingers, he lightly touched the edge of a plastic dinner plate set before him. Resting in the center of the plate were a bowl of fish soup and the breast and thighs of a dried ptarmigan. The fingers tiptoed across the plastic to the food. "The ocean was a plate," he said, "and you always took the first bite from the edge that was closest to you." The fingers took hold of a piece of the bird and held it up for his inspection. "We were told never to finish all the food that was in the plate," he went on. "The big one, out there. The ocean. We were told not to do that so there would always be something left for tomorrow." Leo Moses stared for a long time at the piece of meat, and then he said, "Excuse me," and ate it. Watching, I wondered if the apology was being offered to us. Or to the bird.

Moses is an uncommon Eskimo in that he has tasted not only of the white man's world, both Inside and Out, but also of the bitter sauce of making regulations. For a time, by appointment of former Governor William Egan, he sat as a member of the then joint Board of Fish and Game. It was a painful experience. "There were laws then that we were violating and are still violating," he said. "Like barter." I interrupted to explain that it was my understanding that trade and barter of wildlife was now permissible under the new legal definition of subsistence, but he dismissed the information. Perhaps he felt that while the language of the law might have changed, the intent in Juneau, still, was to restrict the Eskimo's bartering custom. As if nothing had changed, he said, "The law says you cannot barter subsistence food. But it is our way. What is the difference? Salmon or money. They are the same."

"Except that you can eat the salmon," I said.

"But first you must buy the net," he replied. "With money."

Was there no need, then, for any regulations? Should the people be allowed to take whatever, whenever they wanted?

"Of course not," said Moses. "There *must* be regulations, but they must make sense. It's not like it used to be in the old days. There is no longer plenty of everything left out there. You hear of wanton waste. Sure, but we're not wasting. You have more than you need, you share it. Of course—birds. Some are just killing off too many. I know damn well they're not *that* hungry. Good thing shotgun shells are rising in cost." He laughed, then came out of it, suddenly, with a frown. "Why are the geese depleting so fast? In my time, when I was young, there used to be *lots*. *Geese!* Right now, you go out hunting and you see a few flying around. What is there going to be twenty, thirty years from now? It's a joy to kill those animals, to eat them, but how do you preserve enough so that everybody will be satisfied? And cranes. Cranes are going down, too. Man, there used to be cranes just like music." Moses lifted his face toward the ceiling, mimicked the crane with a guttural cry. And was silent for a while before saying, "We're in a race with a dying world. Not here so much. There's a lot you can see flying from here to Bethel, and from Bethel to Anchorage, and Anchorage to Juneau. There's a lot of land here in Alaska no one has ever set foot on. No one. But when I flew from Tacoma to D.C., I look down there and the whole earth is just like a checkerboard. I get lost out there. Sure. We're taking a lot more than we used to. Before the shotgun time, we were told, 'Do not rejoice that the birds are flying, for they aren't going to come falling down on you.' Now, because of the equipment, the shotguns and the outboard motors, when the geese molt the boats go out there and get all they want. And there's a lot more families than we had years ago, too. The problem is, what will we eat if we don't watch out what we're doing? Some people don't think. They're alive, but just day to day. They don't know how to look to the future."

Village elders share Leo Moses's concern for the future, as well as his reverence for the past. The oldest among them is Joe Friday, who was seventy-seven the spring I spoke with him in Chevak, one of the last of the Kashunuk people. David Friday, his son, turned the English into Yupik, and back again, as we sat by the stove. I had a feeling of redundancy sitting there, as all Outsiders who come to Chevak to learn of subsistence eventually wind up beside the Friday stove. Congressman Morris Udall, the d-2 architect, had lowered his six-foot-four frame through this same doorway to speak with Joe Friday, and, forgetting the scale of an Eskimo's house, cracked his head on the doorjamb going out. Members of the entourage were amused, for across the obstruction a bumper sticker proclaimed the Fridays' allegiance: "Save Alaska's Wilderness." As Udall went out, he said he was grateful for the reminder.

I learned this about Joe Friday. When school is in session in Chevak, twice each week he leaves the side of his stove and goes down the boardwalk to the classrooms to tell the children about the old times at Kashunuk, about the traders and the piles of fur, the whales on the beach, the journeys by dogsled and kayak, the adventures of Raven, and the way it was when the stoves burned driftwood, the lamps were filled with seal oil, and walls were made of tundra sod to turn back the winds of December. I learned that Joe Friday does not tell the children that this is the way it can be again, or even ought to be, only that they should know this was the way their grandparents had come, and that the things of the land and the sea—of the air, too—were the Eskimo's strength, and always would be, until they were Eskimo no more. Should it ever come to that. And sometimes, when schoolboys are of a certain age, Joe Friday invites them to join him and the elders at the *qasgiq*, the fire bathhouse that is sunk in the ground, with a deep pit for the willow logs, the hot smoky air flushing the senses, the hunters imparting the wisdom of their accumulated years. They would speak of the birds, and how each hunter had to be careful to dress himself in the colors of the tundra, then crouching and using only one's voice to bring the birds into range. Then, on the tundra, when the birds were on their nests with eggs, it was said that "the whole world is food." But now such a thing is said only in the *qasgiq*. Now, with shotguns and baskets on the tundra, to say such a thing would not only be foolish. It would make people sad.

Alaska, as anyone who isn't a Texan might already have guessed, is a state of superlatives. Among other distinctions, it has the highest per capita income in the nation, a fast two thousand bucks beyond the U.S. average. And it used to be higher, proportionately, when pointy-toe boots were taking a shine off the pipeline between Prudhoe Bay and Valdez. The bucks come and the bucks go, also with distinction, for Alaska matches its blue-ribbon incomes with a cost of living higher than that of any other state in the Union. Shelf prices on some items in Anchorage are 60 percent higher than in Seattle; in Bethel, 40 percent higher than in Anchorage. By the time a box of cereal or a gallon of gasoline reaches Chevak, the value of the Seattle dollar may have deflated 130 percent. Which might be acceptable if there were adequate income in Chevak. But there isn't. For more than half of the Native families of the Yukon-Kuskokwim Delta, incomes fall below the national bottom line, otherwise known as the Poverty Level. The figure for Native poverty statewide, as measured by family dollars, is nearly 40 percent. So here in this great wealthy state are these gaping holes into which government sticks its welfare and food stamp programs. And Raven only knows how much more it might cost—Tom Lonner guessed $100 million—if most of the poor ones did not already prefer to help plug the holes with their shotguns and rifles and nets.

Some of the sports in Fairbanks and Anchorage do not like to dwell intellectually on this side of the bush economy. They seem to prefer to traffic in tales of Eskimos at Barrow riding in taxicabs, full-fare, to the sea to shoot at ducks; of hunters from Anaktuvuk flying in chartered planes, courtesy of the Bureau of Indian Affairs, to shoot at caribou; and of Tlingit fishermen on holiday in Hawaii, surfing on a surfeit of cash from the salmon of Alaska's Southeast. The sports like to see it that way. There are sports who drive taxis in New York City. The way they tell it, the people of Harlem have rocking chairs on Easy Street. Because once or twice there was this black man in a Cadillac outside the Plaza Hotel, and the sun just happened to sparkle on the rings on his fingers when the cabbie cruised by. I suppose some people see only what they want to see.

In the bush, nothing is easy. Not now. For if one takes a job for cash wages, then he has scant time for the hunting. And if one does *not* have a job, or income from furs or fish, then he may have all the time in the world, but not enough cash to hunt. Consider the facts as assembled by Michael Nowak, a researcher who spent five summers on Nunivak Island, southwest of Hooper Bay, appraising the hunters of Mekoryuk. At the time of his observations, about three quarters of the men were employed, full- or part-time, mostly in small public works projects. Nowak's objective was to ascertain the cost to these men of acquiring (on holidays and weekends for the fully employed) about 2,000 pounds per family of traditional Eskimo foods. In his computations, equipment expense was amortized over a "primary life-span" of four years (at 1975 prices). The checklist included a .222 rifle at $190, a 12-gauge shotgun at $230, and a 20-gauge at $180; one boat, with two outboards and fuel tanks, at about $2,200, plus maintenance; a snowmobile at $1,800; a fishnet at $120, and assorted lines and lures for taking tomcod through the ice in winter. Ammunition for the three weapons was calculated at the rate of about $28 for sixty shells, and fuel for the engines at $1.10 a gallon. Nowak then shuffled these expenses into five separate decks of subsistence activity: the taking of seal, reindeer (harvested by permit from a managed herd on Nunivak Island), salmon, tomcod, and birds, and came up with the following results.

To kill five seals for 620 pounds of dressed meat and oil, the Mekoryuk hunter had to spend $812. The cost per pound: $1.31. To kill four reindeer, total weight 400 pounds, $450. And cost per pound: $1.13. To net 375 pounds of salmon, dried weight, $525. Cost per pound: $1.40. To catch 250 pounds of tomcod, $150. Cost per pound: $0.60. And to take 25 geese, 60 ducks, and 25 ptarmigan, $688. Cost per pound: $1.91. Nowak figured all this hunting and fishing added up to about 76 days afield per hunter-fisher. But the value of man-hours was not fed into the computations.

So, what did it all mean? To Nowak it meant that while subsistence was costly, it was far less costly than the supermarket shelf. While the price of fresh, frozen, and canned *gussok* meats and fish averaged out at $2.19 a pound, the Mekoryuk hunter's game averaged $1.30. And Nowak observed: "In parts of southwestern Alaska where income levels are lower, the economic significance of traditional subsistence activities is even greater. There a family with an income of $4,500, obtaining 2,000 pounds of traditional game, could save a little over 39 percent of that income." There was, however, a certain grim prospect in this, for Nowak also found that inflation was affecting major equipment costs to a greater extent than groceries. If the trend should accelerate, he warned, "the present savings realized through pursuit of traditional foods will continue to diminish until at such time in the future they may cease to exist at all." In which case, should it come to that, the cost-benefit ratios might have to take something else into account—namely, nutrition.

It is a lopsided contest, game vs. *gussok* food. Seal meat has ten times more iron than beef does. A ptarmigan has twice the vitamin B of a chicken. Stack a steer against a moose, and Old Bossie turns out to have twelve times the saturated fats of the wilder ungulate, and only one third the protein, gram for gram. Stack the steer against a caribou and the point spread is even greater.

Nutritionists have been fascinated and awed by the high-protein, low-carbohydrate diet of traditional northern peoples ever since the early Arctic explorers faltered on scurvy while their Eskimo guides remained healthy and strong. Possibly the Native stomach had evolved but little, biochemically, from glacial times when there were few greens to eat. Whatever the adaptive reason, fish and meat have always brought vigor to Arctic people. But some of the old strength is going out of them because of the white flour, the sugared breakfast cereals, the soda pop and candy so many are now bringing home from the *gussok*'s shelf. There are better items to choose from, but not better by much. Problems of transportation and winter supply are such in the North that many of the foodstuffs must come to the bush in cans, and half of the contents are either water or additives. "In rural Alaska," says Michael Holloway, an Anchorage physician who works on Native health problems, "there's only one word to describe the imported food. It's junk."

The effects of junk are beginning to show among the young—in anemia, in dental cavities, in otitus media (the ear disease said to be triggered, in part, by high sugar intake), in vitamin deficiency. A survey conducted for the Yukon-Kuskokwim Health Corporation by nutritionist Barbara Knapp of Bethel found that the dietary compositions of five Delta villages, including Hooper Bay, have changed drastically over the past two decades. Comparing her own findings with those of a similar survey in 1961, Knapp discovered that protein intake had decreased overall by 50 percent, only to be replaced by "low nutrient" carbohydrates. Intake of calcium and iron was well below the recommended daily allowance, and dangerously so for women of child-bearing age. And this was occurring even among families in which at least half the food eaten was obtained from the subsistence harvest.

The effects of junk are beginning to show, too, in rural Alaska's rising rate of alcoholism. Not that eating canned tuna makes one any more disposed to the bottle than caribou does. It is just that the switch in the supply systems—the substitution of food stamps for foraging—leaves some of the people with nothing to do. At a hearing in Anchorage on Morris Udall's House Bill 39, the d-2 icebreaker, one of those giving statements was Don Mitchell, an attorney for the Alaska Federation of Natives. Mitchell spoke of the subsistence resource, and what it might cost to replace that if the resource were lost. Maryland congressman Goodloe Byron listened to Mitchell, then wondered aloud about food stamps. "We are talking," said Byron, "about a free food stamp program for all Americans who make less than four thousand dollars a year. You don't have to buy anything any more. It's given to you. Wouldn't that draw in the food industry?"

Mitchell replied: "I doubt that very much when you are talking about villages of two or three hundred people way out on the end of the economic food chain. More important, even if it did, I think the fundamental issue about subsistence—and why Native people are so upset about it, and they are not upset about it because of our statistics about dollars—[is that] the only reason those villages exist, the only purpose they have, is to allow a convenient staging area for a group of people who have lived together over hundreds of years to get game in their area. If you take away that function, there is no reason to be there. The severe alcohol abuse problems in rural Alaska are ungodly. I wouldn't want to sit around all day reading paperback books and waiting for someone to bring me something to eat. I'd go nuts."

"I think," said Ohio congressman John Seiberling, "it is very difficult for a person who has never lived in a Native village to comprehend that the subsistence life style is the foundation of the Native culture. If we substitute food stamps, even if they are free, even if they are adequate, even if we can get the food up there, we have destroyed their culture."

Apropos of going nuts, a story is told of an Eskimo village on a northern river where the elders would as soon turn back the clock as watch their people be wasted by too much leisure. I cannot vouch for the tale's accuracy, and since I do not wish to slander the place I shall leave it unnamed. In any event, I am told that some years ago the village council decided to take a giant step forward into the Age of Petroleum by installing tanks for the storage of heating oil. The oil would replace firewood in the villagers' stoves, after conversion of the hardware, and those who could afford the oil seemed delighted, for now they would not have to forage by snow machine or sled for the logs that had warmed them through the cold in traditional times. The first winter came and went, and the second and third. Then the village council members began to brood. Something had taken the happiness out of the people. It wasn't a shortage of money; some of the men had jobs on the pipeline. It was a surge of drinking and drugs and divorce. The councillors went about knocking on doors, asking the people why it had come down to this. Then they pooled the responses. And were stunned to learn that some of the people were troubled because, in the fall and winter, there was nothing to do. Before the oil tanks, some of the people had spent as much as half of their cold-weather time gathering wood. After the tanks, they sat inside their houses, looking at calendars. Or bottles.

"What's the solution?" a council elder asked of his colleagues.

The youngest replied, "Simple. We blow up the tanks and tell the people to go out and get wood."

Going for Uguruk

It is June in Kivalina on the shore of the Chukchi Sea, in the land of the saltwater people. It is the time when the sun is high above the drifting ice and the air is warm; a time, too, for the sky to play tricks on a stranger. Beyond the lead of open water and the edge of the ice, a great white wall looms above the horizon, as though it were cantilevered on a cushion of air. Landward, over the barren hills between Kivalina and Cape Krusenstern, tall mountains hover like faraway clouds. This is a puzzlement for the stranger, to see things that he knows cannot possibly be, for the mountains in reality and substance are sixty miles beyond the limit of human vision, screened by the curve of the earth. What is it, then, that makes such a liar of the sky? The Eskimo·hunters smile. It is *innipkak,* they say in Inupiat, the tongue of the North, which is different from Yupik. It is the mirage that occurs when the wind is from the west and sunlight refraction causes an image beyond the horizon to hover above it. *Innipkak,* now, is a very good sign. It means that the succulent, red-bellied Arctic char will be running again down the Wulik River; that the leads will be widening in the rotting sea ice; and that the time has come at last for the hunters to be out in their boats, as we are, going for *uguruk.*

Uguruk—the bearded seal in *gussok* words, *Erignathus barbatus* in the taxonomist's—commands a place of honor on the

Eskimo's list of wild foods. It is the fatted pig of the North, both staple and *pièce de résistance* at the saltwater people's table. Custom, taste, and the availability of species vary somewhat, place to place, so that among the gifts of the sea, it is not always the *uguruk* that scores the highest. Some villages place greater merit with the beluga whale, others with the choice parts of the walrus. But in Kivalina, the *uguruk* is all things to all people, though landward the Barren Ground caribou is also important, when circumstance and game laws allow it to be had.

In June, the seals begin to follow the ice as it recedes to the north. They bask in the sun at the edge of the floes, each adult weighing four to seven hundred pounds (the largest of all the hair seals); and yielding, when taken, a great store of flavorful meat, enough blubber to fill a barrel, and a tough yet pliable hide from which the Eskimos fashion their snug *mukluk* boots— *mukluk* being the Yupik word for the bearded seal. In earlier times, the hide was also used to cover the ribs of the *umiak*, the old skin boat that has now been replaced, for the most part, by the long, double-hulled wood dory with the engine of many horses and the spoor of unburned hydrocarbons awash in its wake.

We are cruising south, now, through the jagged leads two or three miles offshore. Ray Hawley is at the wheel. His son, Abner, sits next to him, with binoculars. In the bow, in a white parka and rubber hip boots, head turning slowly from side to side as he scans the ice, is James Hawley. And David Swan is there, too. The elder Hawleys are brothers, members of one of Kivalina's oldest and largest families. It is said in the village that all of the Hawleys are great hunters, though possibly James is the greatest when the *uguruks* are taking the sun on the ice and his fast, flat-shooting .25/06 is close at hand under the covered prow of the boat. There is no doubt who is in charge here, yet no one speaks in tones of deference or command. In fact, no one speaks. James points with his hand, the boat follows. The hand reaches back, fingers spread wide above the open palm, and the engine stops. The boat drifts through the water. There is a sound as from a thousand fountains, slowly dripping. In shining droplets, the ice returns itself to the glass-smooth sea.

Hawley and Swan crouch low in the bow of the boat. Now I can see the *uguruk,* a hundred yards out from the edge of the ice, sleeping. It is a big one, probably a bull. Hawley takes his rifle from under the prow and locks a cartridge into the chamber. The drifting boat grinds lightly against the ice. The animal raises its head. Hawley leans forward and rests his elbows on the prow for support. Steady. Steady now. Taking his time to make sure the *uguruk* has not been alarmed. Knowing he cannot afford to miss this time. Not after the pup, the little one a few miles back, shot clean but then lost in the water, sunk. If it was the best of times to be going for *uguruk,* it was also the worst, for the ice-floe fountains render the seawater fresh to a depth of twenty feet, and what goes down into it, deprived of saline buoyancy, does not soon come up. We tried to retrieve the pup, using a barbed, weighted *niksik* like a grappling hook in the water, to no avail. So many seals are lost, and few recovered, when they go like this, flopping head-shot into the unbuoyant sea. The critics of subsistence call it wanton waste, as if the loss were intentional. The hunters call it bad luck. And mourn the loss, not only for themselves but for the animal, believing, as I am told they do, that the life of an animal taken will somehow flow on through the people who use it, as long as they use it well.

The recoil from the .25/06 kicks a puff of dust out of the shoulder of Hawley's parka. The head of the *uguruk* falls to the ice. There is the briefest silence after the shot, except for the water, dripping, and then the echo comes back at us, bouncing like a pinball off the *innipkak* walls of the Chukchi Sea. Hawley snaps the bolt of his rifle open and shut, leans forward across the prow—steady, steady now—and squeezes off one more, for insurance. Now the seal is surely dead. Even so, no one speaks.

There is a certain rhythm to subsistence in the North that is scored by the cycle of the seasons. In Kivalina and in scattered camps along the Chukchi coast toward Kotzebue, each month or two seems to offer a special harvest or, if not, at least a time to prepare for the next. The Hawley brothers tell of this, as does David Swan; and there is also the splendid monograph prepared by William and Carrie Uhl for the Cooperative Park Studies Unit at the University of Alaska, a work that examines the subsistence patterns of the beach dwellers of the Cape Krusenstern area. Piecing these written and oral reports together, one might construct a calendar running on from *uguruk* time somewhat like this:

July and August, in the old days, were the months for trade, chiefly with the people of the Noatak Valley, inland. Now, for those who can, the summer is a time of harvesting cash. Sometimes there are jobs in the commercial salmon fishery at Kotzebue, or with the U.S. Bureau of Land Management, fighting fires in the interior. One summer, seventeen of the men of Kivalina went off to the fire lines, and that was a lot, in wages, even for a village of two hundred and fifty people. Summer, too, is for harvesting sour dock and berries. The sour dock, a rhubarb-like plant, is ready for picking in July, and some families will put away as much as one hundred pounds of it, for cooking, or will store it in barrels and sealskin pokes. Raw, sour dock ferments and is used for pickling certain fishes and meats. No sooner has this been done than it is time to harvest blueberries and *akpik*, the cherished salmonberry with its citrus flavor. Inupiat Eskimos are so fond of *akpik* they will travel far afield, and at great expense of time and energy, to gather it. Groups of women will go off for ten days, camping and picking *akpik*, while the men, the hunters, stay at home minding children. A hunter will do even that, for *akpik*.

In the fall, September and October, char return from the sea to the Wulik and Kivalina rivers, and the people take them with lures and nets. There are a few late-flying geese and ducks also, though not as many as in the spring; and offshore, new ice brings *natchiq*, the ringed seal, the little cousin of *uguruk*. Now *tuttu*, the caribou, are coming down from the passes of the Brooks Range, and it is good to take them at this time of year when they are still fat and the meat is not yet too strong from the rut. And down in the lagoons of Cape Krusenstern are whitefish that, in aggregate, can only be measured in tons.

According to the Uhls—and to Robert Belous, a National Parks Service specialist who flew charter with me one day over the Krusenstern lagoons—the saltwater people have developed an ingenious method of exploiting these whitefish. And nature does most of the work. The whitefish come to the lagoons in the spring, flushed from the mouths of the Kobuk and Noatak rivers by the crest of the runoff and carried by it to the cape across Kotzebue Sound. Here, the fish enter the lagoons through open sloughs, and spend the summer subsisting on insects. And what the whitefish don't know will ultimately hurt them, for some lagoons in the summer soon become traps.

It happens like this. When the fish find the open sloughs in the spring, there is still enough ice offshore to block the sea's natural urge to hurl swells at the shore. The inshore water is therefore glass-smooth. But after the ice recedes, the sea becomes its old bitchy self, scratching the face of the shore and redistributing loose sand and gravel in such a way as to plug up the outlets of the whitefish lagoons.

Now come the Eskimos with shovels and sacks in September. They dig a ditch. They start on the beach and dig inland toward the lagoon. The ditch is wide and shallow near the sea, then becomes progressively narrower as it approaches the lip of the plugged-up lagoon. When the final break is made with the shovels, the water of the lagoon rushes toward the sea. But never quite gets there; the porous gravel of the beach sops it up. The whitefish in the lagoon feel the pull of the water, and perceiving a way to the sea, follow the flow—only to be left, flopping, high and dry on the beach. Where the Eskimos sack them.

The days grow shorter, the ice is almost fast once again at the shore. Now, in November and December, some of the men turn to trapping, running their lines up the rivers and creeks. In Kotzebue, the skin of a wolf will fetch $250; a good wolverine, more than $300. A white fox brings $50. And sometimes, with luck, there is lynx. Its fur is considered by some the best for the insides of parkas, and the meat is good, too—like the breast of a turkey, some *gussoks* say. Short days also bring snowshoe hare and ptarmigan to the hunter's pot, and the large Arctic hare, *ukallisugruk*. Then the midday sun hangs low on the southern horizon, the snow piles high, and the people wait. For February.

With increasing daylight in late winter, and generally good conditions for snow-machine travel, the men go out from the village after ringed seal in one direction, and caribou in the other. And some of the women jig through holes in the ice for whitefish and Bering cisco. Then April comes, and May and June with the birds nesting, the sky playing tricks, the hunters in white parkas going out in their boats, the hand of James Hawley reaching back, stopping the engine, now drifting, the bolt of the rifle snapping in place, the elbows braced, and once again, between the shot and the echo, a sound as of fountains, slowly dripping.

Our boat rides low in the water. It is late in the day, and we are returning to Kivalina with a ton and a half of *uguruks,* five of them side by side under the tarps. The last killed is my cushion, I can feel its lingering warmth through the canvas. When the boat swerves to starboard to avoid an ice floe, the yielding blubber beneath me rolls the same way. I move to the floor.

James Hawley, my windbreak, still sits in the bow, scanning the ice. I admire his skill with the rifle. Besides the first pup, only one other seal was lost in the water. So it is five for seven, and Hawley has taken them all. That is the uncommon thing about subsistence hunters. It seems not to matter at all who gets the shot, so long as the shooting is clean and effective. There is no taking of turns, no prize for the first or the biggest. It is not a game they are playing. True, Abner did take one shot, but only because it is part of his education to learn to kill seals. Ray Hawley and David Swan did not fire once. They did not have to. They already know how to kill seals, though not as well as James Hawley does.

The boat grinds against the gravel shore. Village boys, fishing nearby with handlines for char, pull in their lures and run down the beach to see what the boat brings. Village men stroll our way, waving. The hunters attach ropes through slits in each *uguruk*'s jaw and flippers, and the people heave and pull, laughing when someone slips on the gravel; and one by one the great silver animals slide reluctantly over the gunwale and up the wide beach to a bench of grass where the women are waiting with their sharpened *ulus*, the meat cleavers of the North.

Now the *uguruk* is rolled on its back. The knife moves swiftly along the belly, from chin to the anus. Then the skin is pulled off with the blubber attached. The abdomen flesh is cut away. Out come the internal organs. The ribs are sectioned and removed. The animal is reduced to smaller and smaller pieces. A young woman with a cup scoops blood from the carcass and pours it into a barrel that is sunk in the ground. Two others begin to slice the blubber into small strips the length of store-bought bacon. The strips will be stored in sealskin pokes, where fermentation renders the blubber into an oil that is used not only as preservative of other foods but as condiment for almost every meal. The head of the seal will be boiled for four hours and come out of the pot as a head cheese to be shared with neighbors. The shoulder meat will be hung to dry for a few days before pot-roasting. The flippers will be buried with oil in a grass-lined hole until the hair slips off, then savored as *uguruk*'s most succulent gift. The ribs will be hung on racks, drying for wintertime. The outer layers of the small intestines will be pinched from the inners and minced with blubber to make the delicacy called *qaiq*. And the blood in the barrel? The blood will be saved for broth, or mixed with wood ashes to coat the outside of a sealskin poke. So who is to say that the Eskimos are wrong? I mean about life after death, and the way in which animals live again in the viscera of the people who use them.

Still, there is a suspicion among city folk, inside and outside Alaska, that the corollary of subsistence is waste, in terms of both absolute animal numbers and the utilization of individual animal parts. Perhaps it is not enough that the outer layer of the *uguruk*'s intestine is eaten with blubber, and the inner part fed to the dogs; though the inners were once blown full of air and dried, for ditty bags, before some *gussok* invented plastic.

As for the absolute number of animals taken, sometimes there *is* waste. It has been documented, for example, that at the time of the crash of the Western Arctic caribou herd, some young Native men—not necessarily from Kivalina—did indeed kill more *tuttu* than their villages could possibly use, chasing the animals on snow machines and leaving the carcasses cached in the snow for ravens and wolves. Yet a white man at Kotzebue confessed to the same. Rotten apples in every barrel, I suppose; and besides, there was no legal limit then on how many *tuttu* a hunter might take. Now the trigger fingers are not quite so heavy throughout bush Alaska, for the people are warned.

"Let me lay it right on the table," said Congressman Morris Udall at a hearing in Shishmaref, speaking to Eskimos. "You want to cover thirty, forty miles a day, instead of the five or ten the way you used to. I think the motorboat is here to stay and the snow machine is here to stay. We will write this [d-2] bill so that subsistence use includes the right to use motorboats and snow machines. I think we ought to recognize, however, that subsistence is only going to be good if we can keep up the permanent level of the cache, if we can keep the walrus and seal populations coming back year after year.... To the extent that you have machines and modern equipment to go off after them, there is a danger you will deplete the species on which subsistence depends. You better bear that in mind."

On the bench of grass at Kivalina, the men stand apart, watching the women with *ulus* and talking among themselves of the hunt. The talk drifts to walrus. Many have been sighted on the ice to the north. Too many, maybe, a hunter says. And skinny—not enough clams for so many walrus. And these newspaper stories from Seattle and Anchorage, all about "head-hunting." Sure, there may be a few Eskimos here and there who take the walrus only for its tusks, ivory bringing the price that it does. But what about the walrus that die of natural causes, or the ones that are mournfully lost to the sea by a misplaced shot, and which later wash up on the beach, only to be de-tusked or beheaded by some *gussok* from a Cessna cruising the coast between Barrow and Nome? It happens both ways. Besides, when the too many walrus go the way of the caribou, crashing, then the federal and state Fish 'n' Game men will have to find scapegoats. And one Eskimo hunter says to another, "Hey, Scapegoat. Guess who?"

It is getting on toward midnight now, yet the sun still hangs in the sky, poised like an *innipkak* mirage over the coastal hills of the Brooks Range. I walk to the edge of the gravel beach and stare at the water. There is an iridescent film of petrol lapping at the shore, no doubt the smallest of spills from some outboard nearby. Or could it be a seep from the floor of the sea? Possibly, for geologists tell us that under the floor of the Chukchi is a mother lode of gases and oil. The same federal agency that would zealously protect the subsistence way of life in Alaska—the Department of the Interior—has published maps showing areas of the state's outer continental shelf that are under consideration for petroleum exploration and leasing. And drilling. One of these areas is identified as the Hope Basin. Across the lead of open water and the edge of the ice, I am looking at the Hope Basin now. And I recall a voice that I heard once in Washington, D.C., a voice concerned about walrus and *uguruk* and other creatures essential to the people who live on these shores. "Have you ever seen the rigs off Santa Barbara?" the voice is saying. "Well, that's the Hope Basin. When they get around to it, it's going to be full-tilt boogie."

Game on the Rivers

Alaskans are hugely partial to moose. No other big-game animal is distributed so widely across the Great Land, and none pursued with such fierce loving determination. Alaskans are in fact so determined to have their moose and eat them, too, that they kill about ten thousand every year, though fewer than half this number are officially tagged and reported to the authorities who keep score of the harvest. Moose steak is no less cherished in Anchorage than in Allakaket; it pleases the Euro-American to about the same high degree as the Athapaskan. Total consumption statewide runs to more than five million edible pounds each year, or about twelve and a half pounds per capita; which, though not a great deal, is still more than the national per capita ingestion of fish, and more than twice the consumption, per capita, of lamb and veal in the Lower Forty-eight. However you slice it, there is nothing quite like the prospect of moose, or of no moose at all, to bring out the feist in Alaskans. Men break laws to assure a fresh moose in the meat locker. Given the gap between supply and demand in the woods, men may soon be breaking each other.

Time used to be, say twenty years ago, a man could take his moose in his own backyard, or not far beyond it. At dawn, he could drive a few miles past the city limits of Anchorage, or go out of Fairbanks, across the Tanana River and into the willow flats, and, with luck, have his moose on the ground by noon. Time, too, when the Indian stalking a moose on the banks of the faraway Koyukuk River never saw white men on Opening Day. Times change. Now, because of increasing mobility and leisure, but mostly because of intolerable pressures on game near the cities, the hunters of Fairbanks and Anchorage are pushing into gamier places farther from home, into places the villagers view as their own.

Consider the Koyukuk, a remote watershed rolling from the Central Brooks Range to the Yukon River near Galena, some three hundred miles from Fairbanks. According to one estimate, about six thousand pounds of game meat was taken out of this area by airplane in 1975. By 1977, the airborne meat had quadrupled to nearly twenty-four thousand pounds, much of which went to Anchorage and Fairbanks. There could have been more. By the same estimate, for every four pounds of game flown out, six were left behind on the ground, at the site of the kill. And the sports speak of waste.

The prospect of meat left to rot on the ground and of moose antlers flying to faraway cities infuriates the people of bush Alaska. Their councillors write angry letters to the Board of Game. Their Native associations demand regulations to discourage the influx of alien guns. In response to these demands—in reluctant response, some would have it—the Board approved a number of changes in the rules. For critical areas here and there, the season for moose was drastically shortened, which turned away some of the urban hunters (but few of the rural ones, since much of the local harvest occurs out of season in any event). For some areas, too, the Board authorized "registration hunts," and these require each hunter to obtain, carry, and later surrender for the record a special permit bearing his home address. Not that this of itself is a deterrent to urban hunters; it simply gives the game managers a more accurate picture of where hunters are coming from and of what they are taking away.

The only real deterrent, so far, is what is known as a controlled use zone. The control is of transportation. In effect, you may walk in, or swim in—but fly into a controlled use zone you must not. Leaving is easier: You may fly *out*. Yet if you do, and have killed a moose, you can't take it with you. Controlled use zones are nice places to visit, but you wouldn't want to hunt there. The last I heard, only two had been approved by the Board, both on the Koyukuk River.

Under the state's new subsistence provisions, the ultimate step would be to declare an area off limits to all hunters from Outside, whatever their mode of travel. But the sports are certain to test this provision in court. They have promised as much. Tom Scarborough, a director of the Real Alaska Coalition and past president of the Tanana Valley Sportsmen's Association, told me in Fairbanks that attorneys are prepared to challenge subsistence zoning on constitutional grounds. "We'll stir up a lawsuit," he said, "to settle this issue of common use once and for all." Shades of the caribou permits at Nuiqsut.

So anger in the bush is matched by pique in the cities. Among hunting folk, the distemper seems to run strongest in Fairbanks, where sporting bias is curried by the hometown press, the *Daily News-Miner,* and by the newsletter of the Interior Wildlife Association of Alaska ("the voice of the hunter in the State of Alaska"), which holds that "hunting, fishing, and trapping as we have known it [*sic*] is practically wiped out" as a result of the Alaska Native Claims Settlement Act and President "Adolf Carter's Salt Agreement: *Steal Alaskans' Land Today*," otherwise known as the Antiquities Act. Fairbanks provides fertile ground for such palaver. Regardless of its voting profile, despite its university, I'd guess Fairbanks ranks among the most intrinsically conservative cities of America—a legacy, no doubt, of past or present affiliation with Big Oil, Big Military, and Regular Guys who believe that bigness is the best way to go. Except in government.

Poking into the woof and warp of hunting sentiment in Fairbanks, I found people more or less hanging to the ends of two threads. One led to the conclusion that those who pay should have the say; that whereas fish and game management in Alaska is financed through license fees and matching funds, and whereas most of these fees are paid by urban sportsmen and Outsiders on guided trips, and whereas many bush folk pay nothing at all, now therefore be it resolved that sportsmen, having paid their dues, should be entitled to take moose anywhere that moose are available for common-use taking, subject to reasonable biological, rather than socioeconomic, constraints. Moreover, the feeling goes, the Natives had better get flexible about subsistence. Otherwise the rug will come out from under them as legislative reapportionment deflates the Bush Caucus and restores power to the solons of Fairbanks and Anchorage, where more than half of Alaska's people already live.

The other thread leads back to the Alaska Native Claims Settlement Act (ANCSA) of 1971. The act extinguished all claims based on "aboriginal title" in exchange for the transfer to Native groups of 44 million acres of federal land and the payment, over time, of some $900 million. Sportsmen of a certain pique say this should have been more than enough to keep the Natives happy. They say that ANCSA effectively abolished for all Natives any preferential right to fish and game. Yet the final report of the House-Senate conference committee on ANCSA said otherwise. The committee said it believed that "all Native interest in subsistence resource lands can and will be protected by the Secretary [of the Interior] through the exercise of his existing withdrawal authority. The Secretary could, for example, withdraw appropriate lands and classify them in a manner which would protect Native subsistence needs and requirements ... when the subsistence resources of these lands are in short supply or otherwise threatened. The conference committee expects both the Secretary and the state to take any action necessary to protect subsistence needs of the Natives."

Pique and anger in moose country are heightened further by a good bit of confusion as to who may or may not qualify as a bona fide subsistence hunter. The intent of the language from Congress may be clear enough insofar as Indians and Eskimos are concerned, but what about the pale-skin sourdough loners who have come into the country with the dew of Boston or Birmingham behind their ears? Congressman John Seiberling wondered about this himself at a hearing in Anaktuvuk.

"Let me ask you the sixty-four-thousand-dollar question," he said to Rosita Worl, a Harvard anthropologist who was offering d-2 testimony on the strength of two years' work among the people of the Arctic Slope. "As a practical matter, how can the authorities, whether they are federal or state, know which are subsistence hunters and which are not? ... We can't just say Natives have the right because I think that would probably violate the federal constitution.... We are going to have to make it clear if a white man comes up here and starts to live Native-style and live on the land, that he is a subsistence user also. Do you agree with that?"

"No," Rosita Worl responded. "I said that subsistence is a right that has been achieved after three thousand years or ten thousand years."

Seiberling did not buy altogether the Worl criteria. Neither do those Indians and Eskimos who are married to bush whites, much less the sourdoughs themselves. "Damn it to hell," a boondock exile from Outside told me one day in a middle Yukon village. "My people were eating moose meat ten thousand years ago, too. The Pilgrims ate wild turkeys. And my great-great-grandpappy lived on deer. So because my own folks eat cows in Missouri, who's the dropout? Papa or me?"

. . .

The village hangs above the river where the rounded ridges of the Kuskokwim Mountains tumble down to the Yukon trench. Indians once called the place Melozikaket, after the Melozitna River, which comes out of the Ray Mountains and enters the Yukon two miles upstream, on the other side. That was before 1907, when white men discovered gold in the village creek. Afterwards, many of the Indians moved out, to a place called Kokrines, upriver, and many white men moved in. By 1912, there were one thousand whites in Melozikaket, only they didn't call it that any more.They called it Ruby. And in honor of their own cultural heritage and their individual expectations, they went about renaming almost everything; so that before long the maps showed Boston Dome and New York Creek, and Easy Money Creek, and down the trail a faraway piece, an outpost called Poorman, which proved in time to be the most appropriate name of all. Then the Indians came home again from Kokrines. When I flew into Ruby last time out, the census digits showed a population of 190 Indians and 30 whites. But the digits keep going up, for in addition to being a splendid place for Indians, Ruby is as likely a perch as any for those moose-hungry sourdough loners from Outside.

Moose and salmon are the mainstays of Ruby. The salmon come in seasonal waves, silvers and chums, the latter being known by Eskimos downstream as dog salmon, since these are the fish which they feed to their dogs. Indians do not especially care what Eskimo dogs eat. But to hear the word "dog"—applied to a salmon *they* eat—hurts. It is a small enough matter, inter-tribally, though it adds somewhat to the ancient territorial rancor.

The moose also come in waves; not seasonally, but decade to decade, depending on weather and wolves and browse, and more recently on the number of boats and floatplanes bringing urban hunters from far away. Ruby hunters, and their subsistence counterparts from Tanana upstream, have a special place that is generally better than others for moose. It is the taiga country of the Nowitna River, which joins the Yukon between the two villages. But now the Nowitna has become a special place for autumn travelers from Fairbanks and Anchorage, too. In the autumn of my own visit, the Game Board had imposed a ten-day season along the Nowitna, and ordered that the hunt be by registration, so that permits would show where the hunters were coming from and what they were taking away. "We wanted this four years ago," said Harold Esmailka, operator of Harold's Air Service, which is based in Galena, though Harold himself lives in Ruby. "But the urban votes on the Board were against it. Now we have it. The game is here for everyone. And God help us all if the moose should ever be shot out from under us."

Down a dirt road from Esmailka's place is the home of Albert and Dolly Yryana, the elders of Ruby's pale-skin tribe. Dolly's parents mined for gold near Dawson, in the Yukon Territory, then moved to Alaska in 1917. By the time she reached Ruby, most of the miners and grubstakers were gone, but new folk were moving in, including Albert Yryana, who arrived from a farm near Houghton, Michigan, by way of Southeast, in 1935. Houghton is in the iron and tall-timber precincts of Michigan's Upper Peninsula. It is a place of tough-minded Finns and irascible winters; and there was and is, probably, no better turf for seasoning those who would trade the Outside for the bush of Alaska. Albert Yryana, pushing seventy, hunts moose and traps marten and beaver and takes fish from the river, prospects a little for gold, and, with Dolly, tends to a summer garden where cabbages grow bigger than basketballs under round-the-clock sun. "It's the best place in the world to make a living," he said to me in his backyard, sweeping his arm from the cabbage patch toward the dark spruce forest beyond. "You fertilize the garden, throw down the seeds, and jump back—just in time to get out of the vegetables' way."

The prospect of agriculture in Alaska is intriguing to white-haired Albert Yryana, as it is to many whose ethnic roots lie behind them somewhere deep in the hardscrabble fields of Northern Europe. It seems an incongruity to hear them speaking of farming here on the edge of nowhere. Yet farming is what all pioneers have eventually wanted to do, after the moose

and beaver were gone, and the gold. Down the Alaska Highway from Fairbanks, near a place called Delta Junction, ten
thousand acres are in cultivation, mostly to barley, and agron-
omists already are speaking of seeding a half million more.
There are expectations of a market in Japan. And if that
doesn't work, then the grain will be used to support a domestic
meat industry. Barnyard sheep—grain-fed in winter, in summer grazing Granite Mountain and the Macomb Plateau. And
this greatly worries the wildlife people, who remember what
happened to the wild bighorns, Outside, when domestics were
unleashed on the Rocky Mountains. But Albert Yryana wasn't
speaking of the Delta project in his backyard at Ruby. He was
speaking of *Ruby,* and of Yukon River places round about, the
Flats upriver, possibly, and of fields of waving grain, and
barges, and draglines dredging a fifty-mile canal to spill the
Yukon's waters into the Kuskokwim at Bethel, the nearest sea-
port.

"What's wrong with *that* idea?" said Albert Yryana. I said
nothing, though I expect I should have, if only to inquire how
one could possibly hold agribusiness by one hand and salmon
and beaver and moose by the other.

We walked out in front of his place and stood on the dusty
road that goes down to the edge of the river, and then I did ask
Yryana to share with me his thoughts on subsistence in general,
and moose in particular. He addressed himself to both suc-
cinctly, and democratically. "Each man is entitled to the same
privileges," he said. "That is the American way. If a man wants
to hunt, *any* man, then let him hunt. But we must not forget
that people are increasing in Alaska, and so are wolves. One or
another is going to have to give up moose meat. Or there won't
be any left."

Jim and Betsy Hart are the proprietors of the Ruby Roadhouse, a homey hostel offering bed and board, downhill from
Albert Yryana's cabbage patch. The roadhouse dates to mining
days, when there was a little more traffic than there is today; although the roads, now as then, go nowhere, except to Poorman,

which is also nowhere in any event. Judged by the criteria of Harvard anthropologist Rosita Worl, the Harts, with their modest business and white skin, would not qualify as subsistence users, for they lack the uninterrupted ten-thousand-year continuum of scratching a living out of the woods. But under less rigid values, the Harts would seem to come about as close as village white folk can, for they do take fish from the river and game and fuel from the woods, and without these resources they would not in all likelihood be able to carry on. Nor would they want to.

Jim and Betsy Hart met in 1970 at a commune near Fort Collins, Colorado. He was a carpenter; she, a candlemaker. In the youthful, earthy spirit of that time, they longed to be off to wilder places, which, at least on this continent, are generally known to be found by following the compass north by northwest. Soon they were heading for Alaska, but got only as far as Washington State. In Washington, they encountered other young couples who had already tested their verve against the long Alaskan winters and, deciding that discretion was the better part of valor, had returned to the Outside. The Harts agreed they would put Alaska out of their minds. They bought a piece of land west of Spokane, miles from the nearest human settlement, erected a tent, and proceeded to build a log cabin, where they lived for nearly three years. But Jim kept dreaming of Alaska. "Forget it," said Betsy. "We're not going." Jim said they were. And they did. Fairbanks was booming in 1975. Good carpenters could count on good money. If the work slowed in one place, you simply moved to another. Still, there was this yearning for the bush, for living close to the land. For a while, they lived at Emmonak, a Yupik village near the mouth of the Yukon. And then Galena. And after four years in Alaska, they felt they were seasoned. Jim and Betsy Hart were ready for Ruby.

I stayed with the Harts at the Ruby Roadhouse for two days in early September, waiting for the moose season to open on the Nowitna, the "Novi," as everyone seemed to call it in town. We ate salmon hearts for breakfast and sheefish for supper—fresh, and no cardboard and cellophane for the trash. On the third day, Jim Hart took me to the Novi in his boat, about fifty miles the way the Yukon turns, two and a half hours by the clock, with the big outboard engine straining against the knotty current. And as the golden foliage of riverbank birches flicked by, we talked about city and country things, and hunting, and how bush people feel when strangers come into their woods, looking to take away moose.

"Even in Washington," Hart was saying, "it used to drive me nuts. You're living out there in the woods, making a huge payment on the land every month, and here come these guys in hunting season, who are living in town on hundred-foot lots, making huge payments on houses. Well, hell. It was *their* choice." He pointed to the left bank, where a cluster of tumbledown huts hunkered above the river. "Kokrines," he said. "The old village. Just ghosts, now." And then picked up the train of his thoughts. "I have these friends in Fairbanks," he said. "Nice guys. They live there, I live here. They have movies and fancy clothes. I do without. But I have moose and salmon. That's *my* choice. So why shouldn't they do without some of the things we have here?"

The river straightened out ahead of us like a lake. Hart lowered his head behind the windscreen, lit a cigarette, and said, "You know? So many people spend so much time getting ready to move to the country, they never quite get here."

"There're still a lot who do," I said.

"Nine out of ten won't stay."

"That still leaves one. Times how many?"

"Who knows?" he said.

No one knows how many young men and women from tamer places are moving to rural Alaska, and staying, as the Harts did. By some accounts, the rate of immigration has leveled off. By other estimates, it is growing yearly. In Juneau, Robert LeResche, the state's Commissioner of Natural Resources, told me: "Everyone's dream of Alaska is a little cabin out in the bush. The Natives are getting worried. And I don't blame them." In Kotzebue, John Schaeffer of the Northwest Alaska Native Association said: "The hippies—I don't mean that nastily, but that's what most of them were ten years ago—

the hippies bring the Western culture with them. When you have twenty of them moving into an Eskimo village of, say, a hundred people, then you are going to have disruption."

The state of Alaska no longer officially tolerates squatters in cabins on its own remote lands. Instead, it encourages a kind of pay-as-you-go homesteading, parochially known as "open to entry." After just one year's residency, for example, a *nouveau* Alaskan might purchase, near Circle Hot Springs northeast of Fairbanks, a 4.3-acre lot for as little as $2,600; or rent it, on a five-year lease, for $182 a year, with the right to build and an option either to buy or to renew the lease for another five years. Of, if a parcel is unsurveyed, one might stake out five acres himself and pay annual rental of only $150 for ten years, meanwhile living there in a homemade cabin, with an option to buy at the expiration of the lease. Or, with at least three years' residency under the belt, one might apply for a "home-site entry," also of five acres, and live and die on it at absolutely no cost other than the expense of filing the application, platting the land, and building the cabin. Given the price of housing Outside, where the most modest of homes on a hundred-foot lot starts somewhere around $40,000, I'd guess one hell of a lot of young folks in the years ahead will be spending less time getting ready to move to the country, and more of it living there. Which isn't good news for Robert LeResche or John Schaeffer. Or Jim Hart, for that matter.

"So what are you going to do," I asked him, "when it starts getting crowded around here?"

We had come to the mouth of the Novi, and now Hart swung the boat in a wide arc that carried us out of the silt-creamed Yukon into the tannin waters of the tributary stream. "I don't know what I'm going to do," he said. "Maybe I'll buy an old paddle-wheel steamboat and take the tourists up and down the river. And maybe I won't. Maybe Betsy and the kids and I—we'll go on down the river somewhere and build a cabin and fish and hunt and trap—goodbye, roadhouse—and just watch all the water roll by. Maybe."

· · ·

The two Indian men had pitched their tent on a point of land a mile up from the mouth of the Novi. With a chain saw, they laid in a good supply of spruce logs for the fire. Then they hung some salmon strips on the branch of a willow, set up a latrine back in the brush, and fashioned a sign out of two spruce stakes, an old poncho, and some paint. The sign addressed itself to the river and to whoever might be passing by. It said, though not in so many words, that this was where, if you didn't have one already, you could pick up a Fish 'n' Game permit to go up the Novi with rifles, for moose. Having done all of this, the two men, Fred Jordan of Tanana and Jim Honea of Ruby, sat down on a couple of stumps and waited for Roland Quimby.

September is a splendid time to be on the Novi. Warm days and cool nights, mosquitoes in full retreat, hardwood foliage bright against the Gothic spruce. It is a flat, muskeggy kind of country upstream, with ponds and bogs enough to wet the fetlocks of a fair number of moose, and browse enough to give the bulls a head start toward trophy antlers. Probably, the Novi has always been a pretty good place for browsers, though, going back far enough, of a different kind. Upriver a way, years ago, earlier travelers found mastodon bones exposed in the side of an undercut bank; and ever since, there has been speculation as to whether these great Pleistocene elephants were ever hunted here by men, and if so, whether the hunters were settled-down residents of the country or outsiders trespassing through, on their way to Nowhere from Asia.

Roland Quimby was coming to the Novi more or less from that direction though he had started a good bit closer, in Galena. Quimby is the state's wildlife biologist for the middle Yukon region. Into this turf of his, you could drop the entire state of Kentucky and still have room for Maryland, if you spread it around the edges. In Louisville or Annapolis, a biologist gets in his car and is out of bounds in an hour. In Galena, Quimby gets in his putt-putt to make the rounds and has to count days to make sure he'll get home before freeze-up. And now he was up beyond Ruby and Kokrines, turning at the Novi to Jordan and Honea's camp on the eve of Opening Day.

All through the afternoon before Quimby's arrival, and my own, Jordan and Honea had sat on the point of land counting boats. Eighteen had come by since noon, mostly small boats with two or three hunters in each, but some with groups much larger. Altogether, Jordan figured, there were probably sixty rifles upriver, not counting those coming in by floatplane. The traffic let up for a while and then, just before dark, four more boats came by, including a cabin cruiser and a larger vessel of a kind that once might have been used for commercial fishing. I counted eight faces on the fishing boat, but there might have been more hidden among the crates and duffels and coolers and tarps and tents, and oil drums, cluttering the deck.

Two of the men needed permits and came ashore. They were from Fairbanks. They said they had put into the Yukon off the Haul Road, 230 miles upriver. They hoped to rendezvous in the morning with another boat that had put in at Manley Hot Springs, on the Tanana River. They wanted to know how many hunters were already checked through, ahead of them. "Lots," said Fred Jordan. Honea and Jordan were filling out the permits. They were not regular employees of the Department of Fish and Game; just temporaries, salaried under a grant to the state from the Bureau of Indian Affairs. One of the Fairbanks hunters kept looking at Quimby and me as Jordan asked him some routine questions for the permit. The hunter seemed to be wondering what an Indian was doing here on white man's business. I wanted to say to him, but didn't: What are *you* doing here on *Indian* business? Then the two went away with their permits, and Quimby called after them, "Take 'er easy." The hunters turned and waved. "Don't know what they'll do if they get a moose," said Quimby, watching the boat pull away with its gunwales scant inches out of the water. "If they try to take one out of here, they'll sink."

After supper, we sat by the fire, roasting our boots. Fred Jordan told us of the people's resentment in Tanana when the boat hunters come through. Jim Honea said it was probably not as bad in Ruby since the boat hunters rarely went that far, though a few went even beyond, past Galena and then up the Koyukuk.

"Most of the hunters are from Fairbanks," I said. "Where are the local people?"

"Busy with other things," Jim Hart put in. He had decided to spend the night and go back to Ruby in the morning. "Commercial fishing just ended here the other day. People are getting in their firewood now. And the weather's still warm. Lot of the people don't have the freezer capacity for a moose. They'll wait until the end of the month. Then it'll be cold enough to hang the meat in a shed."

"So a ten-day season in September doesn't have much value for the local people."

"Let's just say," said Jim Hart, "that it's not used."

Quimby dropped another spruce log into the fire. The log flared, and light flickered softly across his face. After a while, he said, "If there's anything that's really impacting the boreal ecosystem up here, it's not mineral development and it's not the pipeline. It's the BLM [Bureau of Land Management] and its policy of putting out fires." Around the campfire, heads nodded agreement. "I don't know," he went on. "If it keeps going like this—I mean as far as moose are concerned—only thing to do is drop back and punt."

Forest fires seem to be the key to moose survival in interior Alaska. A fire will sweep away the spruce cover, fertilize the earth with its ashes, and bring on a bloom of rich browse. Studies show a big difference between moose densities in old-growth forests and those on burnt-over lands some five years, say, after the fire. Yet the BLM, for the most part, still subscribes to the gospel according to Smokey the Bear. And so does the state of Alaska, which, for all its official obeisance to hunting, seems more intent on growing mortgages than moose.

In the morning, Hart went back to Ruby, to put away fish for the winter, while Quimby and I moseyed along the Novi, checking out sloughs for moose. And it wasn't long before we saw one, a cow, about a hundred yards off at the dry end of a meander. Quimby throttled down the outboard, stilled it, and we drifted. "I guess this beats going to meetings," he said.

"It ought to," I said. "You must take a lot of heat."

"They never prepared me for it at Syracuse. Few years ago, the forestry school sent letters to alumni asking how well we felt the curriculum prepared us for our work. I wrote back saying everything was fine, but that I sure could have used some learning in the politics of wildlife."

"The Natives don't think very highly of you guys."

"So I've discovered. But we're not trying to win a popularity contest. We're trying to manage a— There she goes." I looked down the slough in time to see the cow pussyfoot into a line of willows. Quimby went on. "I see RurAL CAP people and sport hunting people come into these meetings and shout, *'Hey! How about us?'* But I've never seen a moose come to any meeting. I kind of feel *someone's* got to speak for the moose."

Onion Portage

Before it was over, there was another river, another golden autumn morning looking for game. This river was the Kobuk, two hundred miles from Ruby, north by northwest; the morning, at a place known as Onion Portage, where Kobuk people used to shortcut a riverine oxbow before aft-slung motors and fossil fuel made portaging silly. Bob Belous of the National Park Service was with us, and David Cline of the National Audubon Society, and Nelson and Edna Greist, an Eskimo couple from Ambler, upstream. Proof of the pudding that State Game Director Ron Somerville was right on the target: an "unholy alliance between the Natives and preservationists." What more could you ask?

The previous afternoon, we had come downriver from Ambler in Greist's boat. We passed some fish camps, a few other boats with berry pickers chugging upstream, passed the Portage and Greist's own camp nearby, and pulled in at the homestead of Howard and Erna Kantner on a hill overlooking a broad valley near the Kobuk's confluence with the Hunt River. Beyond the hill were the Baird Mountains, and unseen beyond them, the Noatak Valley and the main stem of the Brooks Range. Beyond that, the Arctic Slope, north by northwest. And then, nothing. Not even Nowhere.

Howard and Erna Kantner—he from Toledo, she from Cleveland—have lived on the Kobuk River for sixteen years. They have two sons. Their home is a log igloo built into the side of the hill, sod-roofed, one room with alcoves, and windows on one side only, facing the river. There is a wood stove, made from an oil drum; a small windmill with generator, for light in the winter; a garden with zucchini, for the summer; an outhouse, a sauna also built into the hillside, and a meat shack on stilts. For a month in the summer, the family goes to Kotzebue to work in the commercial fishery. In the winter, Kantner traps lynx. They eat the lynx meat; also berries, fish, and caribou, and sometimes moose. In good years, the caribou come south out of the mountains along the Hunt River in the fall, and Kantner takes them on the tundra plain behind his hill, as the ancient people may have done when they, too, lived in igloos of logs at Onion Portage.

We climbed the hill and sat with the Kantners, drinking coffee and talking about the country. Their place, and the Portage, lie just inside the eastern boundary of Kobuk National Monument. The Kantners are uneasy about living inside a park, especially since it happens they don't own the land. They simply moved onto it, sixteen years ago, and no one in the federal government seemed to care much, one way or the other. But suddenly the government does care, for Bob Belous of the Park Service was here in their home now, speaking of options, of leases or conveyances. There would surely be some accommodation. And the Kantners listened closely, nodding their heads; wondering, possibly, how different it might be with the Smokey the Bear hats cruising back and forth on their street, the river.

Dave Cline and Belous wrestled with that idea far into the night, after we left the Kantners, in a candlelit cabin not far from the Greists' fish camp. The cabin was built by the late J. L. Giddings, the Brown University scientist whose trowel first uncovered the middens and house pits of the long-ago caribou hunters of Onion Portage. And Giddings had lived here through all the summers of his painstaking dig.

In the morning, while Nelson Greist loaded the boat with turnips from his garden, and Cline scouted the shoreline for wild onions, Belous and I walked up through the site of the main dig to a knoll overlooking the river on one side, and, on the other, tundra rolling off to the barren slopes of the Bairds and the notch where the Hunt River comes out of the mountains.

Belous said: "From here you can see forever. From here, people for ten thousand years have been looking up at that pass, and at this time of year, too. There weren't any spruce or birch here then, along the river. The trees didn't come in until about seven thousand years ago. But the people were here then. Imagine it. The men with their spears, coming up here to wait for the caribou. The herd coming down from the mountains, piling up at the edge of the river, then plunging across. That's probably where the people took most of them. In the water, from boats. All those years. My God, what a resource."

Giddings himself had pictured the early hunts in much the same fashion. In his book *Ancient Men of the Arctic,* he wrote of the caribou streaming "determinedly by the thousands down past the slopes of Jade Mountain onto the high ground leading to Onion Portage." And there, he guessed, the Kobuk people had built "diverting fences to lead the caribou down slopes and into the water where they might be slaughtered with spears from one-man bark canoes. As soon as the animals began to appear," Giddings went on, "men, women, and children all took part, urging the caribou along until they plunged into the stream where the spearsmen waited. I could visualize the brown-gray herds pouring rhythmically over the bare slopes between the mouth of Jade Creek and Onion Portage, the splashing of paddles in the boats, the plunging of spears and knives into the demoralized swimmers, the spurts of blood mingling with the rush of the blue Kobuk water, and the dead and dying animals, held aloft by their buoyant coats, drifting with the current to the gravel beach at Onion Portage."

The caribou would be coming soon. We had seen the leaders the day before, from the air, survivors of the herd that had crashed and was on its way back, building strength in numbers. The lead bulls were out on the plain below Jade Mountain, breasts showing white against the purpled heath. Already the word had gone out in Ambler and Kiana and Noorvik. The men in their boats would be on their way any day now. With rifles.

Belous had been watching the pass with his hand at an angle against the temple, shading his eyes. Suddenly the hand came down, the wrist flicked out of the cuff of his jacket, the edge of a watch flashed in the sunlight. Belous seemed surprised, and maybe a little bit sorry, that the watch was there.

"Time we were getting back?" I asked.

Belous nodded, but his eyes were still fixed on that notch in the mountains.

Book Five

COUNTRY MATTERS

Home

I was born and raised and I first hunted in Cincinnati, Ohio. When I left it, about 1950, it was the sixteenth-largest city in the United States. Now, there are twice as many cities ahead of Cincinnati in the statistical pecking order, and people no longer hunt game in any one of them, though they sometimes hunt each other.

My own game-hunting years fell into the forties. Even then, it was probably unlawful to discharge a firearm within the city limits of Cincinnati, but I do not recall any great fear of pursuit and arrest. There seemed to be little enforcement in my precincts, possibly because the excitable spinster sisters who lived next door were hard of hearing, and because the war sharply limited the availability of sporting ammunition and imposed on youthful wastrels a certain single-shot thrift. My other advantage was space. A great wooded hollow ran beside our place, with oak and maple and beech on its slopes and sumac and sycamore along the bottom. There was a grassy swale, too, always good for rabbit, and sometimes quail, too, though I was parentally forbidden to shoot the latter, bobwhites being a protected species in Ohio in those days.

If I have places to blame for my lingering inclination toward the out-of-doors, I suspect that the hollow of home should rank high among them. From the beginning of memory, it was a delicious place in every season, and it stirred my imagination hugely. Going back to a time before I was old enough to be entrusted with an air rifle, while death was still make-believe, the hollow with very little effort could be induced to assume the qualities of Cumberland Gap or Dodge City or the Little Bighorn or the Western Front, depending on what I might be reading at the time, or what I had seen at the picture show the previous Sunday at Hyde Park Square. I prowled the sumac thicket with a sumac stick snugged in the crook of my arm, stalking the Big Indian. And before that, I went to the hollow stalking the biggest of game. The mangamoonga.

There was not a great deal known about the mangamoonga. Descriptions were sketchy and, as time went on, contradictory. My older brother was largely responsible for the confusion. At first it was said that the beast resembled a panther somewhat, though not very closely. Then came reports that it was not like a panther at all, but rather of the sort one might possibly mistake for a rhino, not armor-plated but longhaired in the shaggy fashion of the Pleistocene. In one version, it had fangs; in the next, flaring tusks. Its breath smelled of corned beef and boiled cabbage, which I detested. There were traces of smoke about its nostrils. Its paws were enormous, yet they left no tracks. It hadn't eaten since that Irish boy had vanished from O'Brienville in 1937. The reports grew more terrible each year. My brother and sister insisted that they had seen the mangamoonga on many occasions. Was something the matter with me? I tried harder and had not seen it once.

I suppose that trying was the best part of it. Day after day, with an astonishing lack of caution but no small measure of tingling dread, I slipped into the woods in hope of catching a glimpse of the surly beast, and possibly loosing a sumac shot at it. I kept watch on my belly in the darkest thickets. I climbed trees. I posted myself beside a rainwater pool, assuming that the mangamoonga must surely take a drink now and then in the heat of the day. I studied the rabbits and squirrels, the flickers and robins, seeking from their behavior some sign that the creature might be coming our way. And once, in a rage of imagined contempt, I stood at the edge of the hollow and shouted, "Moonga is *chicken!*" until the insult rolled back in echoes off a neighboring hill. If that doesn't bring him out, I thought, nothing will. And nothing did.

Exactly when or how it occurred to me that the manga-moonga and I were never to meet—all of that escapes remembrance. Possibly it was about the time I discovered that the hollow, after all, had limits; that there were streets and houses, and chain-link fences, on the other side. In any event, I do know that of the two discoveries, the more painful pertained to the creature I had sought in vain. It was as if all the rules of a wonderful game had suddenly been changed. However vast or truncated, the woods no longer seemed to crackle with excitement. Where there had been mystery, fantasy, danger, wildness, now there were solutions, facts, safety, domesticity. The effort to stay alert at all times was no longer essential. I grew languid and bored. But only for a while. Months or years later, a member of the family caught my eye at dinner and wanted to know if I had ever seen the mangamoonga. I replied that of course I had, and on many occasions. And what had become of the critter? I was asked. Dead, I said. Oh. And how had it perished? I replied that I did not know. Then, someone said, maybe the great beast simply curled up in its lair, gave a deep sigh, and died of old age. "Of *whose* old age?" said the wisest sibling.

I have been back to the hollow once or twice in recent years, if only to assure myself that it is still there. And it is. Most of it, anyway. Only the far northern end of it is a goner, all paved and buttressed under a cloverleaf interchange on I-71. We used to call that place Duck Creek. Now the creek runs through a sewer line and the old towering willows that furnished us switches are goners, too. There was one tree with a deep cavity in which we cached secret messages, and squirrels took the paper away for their nests. Now a public message hangs in steel above the expressway to inform the traveler, indirectly, that Columbus is less than two hours away.

The part of the hollow below our old place is as good a piece of country as it ever was. Maybe better. The sycamores are giants now; the swale, overgrown with brush and probably a lot better for songbirds than quail; the trail still winding through, on its way from what used to be Duck Creek to O'Brienville. Last time in there, I met a schoolboy on the trail.

He seemed in a great hurry. He was carrying a baseball bat and catcher's mitt, and looked to be on his late way to some sandlot game in Hyde Park. On a perverse impulse, I said to him as he passed, "Have you seen the mangamoonga?" He stopped and said, "The *what?*" I said, "The mangamoonga." The boy stared at me suspiciously for a while, shook his head, then resumed his way along the trail. "I haven't even heard of that one," he called back to me over his shoulder. "What channel—what night is it on?"

The other city place I hunted was Hinkel's Woods. It was a fair-sized piece of undeveloped country, probably thirty acres or more, with a brook running through it and a good hilltop view of the eastern suburbs, though this, too, was well within the city limits, about a mile from the hollow and only seven or eight from the heart of Downtown. I do not recall ever taking any game from Hinkel's Woods. There were at any one time too many of us, in threes or fours, first with air rifles and later with .22s, making too much noise together to be at all effective in the pursuit of rabbits or squirrels. In that sense, going to Hinkel's was like going to hunting camp—throwing up a lean-to and building a fire in front of it, and stacking the rifles against a tree, and roasting meat on sticks, and smelling wood smoke, and being away for a while from family and other friends. Other friends were not especially sympathetic to this kind of behavior. Other friends, then in Cincinnati, were of a kind who spent their Saturdays with footballs (as I later would myself) or baseball bats. To each his own. The others could have their sandlot talk of Knute Rockne and Bucky Walters, the Redleg hero of Crosley Field. We had our wet feet and smoky eyes and lean-to talk of Daniel Boone and Erroll Flynn, who had just died with his boots on in the last picture show at Hyde Park Square.

I have often wondered what might have made the difference between the two kinds of us, the jocks and the woodsboys. It surely could not have been heredity. There were Germans and Irish and English and Italians in both camps. Nor was it economic; for there were rich men's sons and sons of men who were not so rich in both camps. Nor was it parental guidance, in the sense of do-as-I-did, for the fathers of some of my Hinkel's Woods colleagues had probably never owned a gun, only golf clubs; while the fathers of some of the jocks had grown up in the country with animal blood on their hands. Among the latter cases, I suspect there may have been *some* gentle guidance toward the playing fields, for in those days there was a tendency for country folk to want to shed the rural heritage and citify themselves as fast as possible; and no doubt a few of the fathers must have felt somehow that it was more urbanely civilized to send their boys into violent bone-crunching gridiron battle than to encourage their participation in a desultory slaughter of squirrels. All of which is natural enough, and possibly appropriate. If humankind had not evolved as a hunting society, would we now have football? Of course not. In which case, Knute Rockne would never have invented the forward pass, the gridiron's longbow, though he might have become a heroic pitcher, like Bucky Walters.

Still, it is a puzzlement to understand what might have made the difference, turning some of us to Hinkel's Woods and others to the ball fields. No doubt a few of my woodsy fellows for a while were more or less motivated along malevolent lines, for there is no use denying the dark and scabrous bloodlust of the adolescent male in his earliest seasons of the hunt. He is insatiable. And some, burdened by a defect of mind or character, remain adolescent through the rest of their years, wondering why it is that so many people regard hunters in general as slobs. Not so, I think, with my own hometown hunters, though I have lost touch and can vouch for neither their current sanity nor their continued interest in hunting. Not so because, then, on autumn Saturdays in Hinkel's Woods, emerging from the trace of atavistic grit within each one of us, was something else that may have come close to the essence of hunting as it should be; if, indeed, it should be at all. I mean an appreciation of landscape, and an understanding of its parts in some small way approaching Aldo Leopold's perception. I hadn't heard of Leopold then, and wouldn't read his writing for another twenty years. But I guess I would have liked what he had to say about the autumn landscape in the north woods, and how it all added up to "the land, plus a red maple, plus a ruffed grouse." In terms of physics, Leopold advised, "the grouse represents only a millionth of either the mass or the energy of an acre. Yet subtract the grouse and the whole thing is dead." Of course, there were no grouse in Hinkel's Woods in those years. And now, not even quail.

Perhaps what made the difference was our own perception. Not brains, or vigor, or a degree of aggressiveness, or anything that might have made us better or worse than our ball-field peers. None of those, but simply a way of looking at the land, and noting where the acorns fell, and which side of a tree the moss grew on, and how the prickly buckeye fruits split open in October, and why the stirred-up leaves and wisp of rabbit fur probably meant there was an owl nearby, dozing on a full stomach. Yet if land sense was truly the thing that set us apart, then how did we come by it in the first place? Had there been mangamoongas in the other boys' hollows, too? It never occurred to me to ask. And now it is too late to ask in any expectation of honest answers.

I do not go to Hinkel's Woods when I return as visitor to Cincinnati, though my brother now lives but a half block away. Hinkel's Woods is gone. All of it. All streets and houses, now. All trimmed and tidy, safe and domestic. All the facts and solutions of the twenty-five-year mortgage rolling down from the hilltop in tiers. I turn the corner near my brother's place and look across the street at the boys who are bound homeward from school. And I wonder if it will make any difference whatsoever to them, or to the world, that the things we saw and felt and knew in that place have been subtracted from it. The land is still there, yet the *whole* is dead.

Though rabbits and squirrels were the standard victims of our boyhood gunning, for several Buckeye years I aspired to bagging a ring-necked pheasant. To my mind, it was the most elegant and desirable of the upland game birds, a status not so much richly deserved as earned by default, ringnecks then being the only uplanders present and accounted for, and legal for taking, in southwestern Ohio. Which has to say something about the bird's uncanny talent for coping, for here in quail country was this exotic from China, strutting about the corn stubble in sufficient numbers to sustain a season, while the bobwhite for a time could barely hold its own under the protectorate of no season at all.

The hollow of home was no fit place for pheasant, nor was Hinkel's Woods. To flush a ringneck, one had to get out into the real country, out Brown County way where the father of my friend, the neighbor boy, had a weekend farm on the East Fork of the Little Miami River. One summer we spent Saturdays hauling catfish from the Fork with cane poles; Sundays, busting clay pigeons with my 20-gauge over-and-under. And in October went into the corn stubble flushing pheasants, but busting nothing. Clay just came easier to me. I don't know why. Maybe because, under field conditions, I wasn't a very good wing shot after all, although the pheasant, among game birds, is surely the broadest side of a barn door. And maybe, too, because in flight the cock of the species raised some unconscious doubts as to whether its death would be as desirable to me after the fact as before. One afternoon, I managed to knock some feathers out of one cock's tail; for all I knew, may have caused more damage than that, though the bird kept flying. Afterwards, I went back to the farmhouse, exchanged my shotgun for a cane pole and a can of worms, and went down through the woods to the East Fork, where a lunker catfish, just as I was about to land it, broke my leader and swam away with a double-barbed hook impaled in its mouth.

The ring-necked pheasant was introduced in Ohio in 1897. It did not take to the country at first, as it had in Oregon, as it would before long in Nebraska and South Dakota. Perhaps the farms of Ohio were too prosperous and tidy in the early years of the new century. Still, the game people kept at it, with a planting here and a planting there until, by 1940, the bird's population began to explode in the abandoned fields of farmers cleaned out by the long Depression. Those were good years for bird shooters in Ohio and elsewhere, the forties and fifties; not only plenty of birds, but plenty of unposted land one could tramp without risking trespass. Then a prosperity of sorts returned to the land, such that bankers were making loans on Caterpillar tractors, agrichemists were dispensing their chlorinated hydrocarbons and organophosphates, row crops were marching across coverts to the borrow pits of the county roads, and ringnecks were in trouble. By all accounts, they are still in trouble, though the game people are doing their damnedest to hold the line.

Holding the line may be about all one can expect nowadays from wildlife agencies in most of the states. Or less than that, for the price tag of the resident hunting and fishing license has hardly kept up with the rate of inflation; and license fees, most places, are the principal source of an agency's operating income. In times gone by, a state like Ohio could afford to purchase farmland and woodland for wildlife habitat and public hunting. And when land was cheap, most states did that. Ohio acquired a half million acres. But now, with the price of an acre calculated in thousands of dollars rather than hundreds, with legislators loath to sanction broader sources of public funding, game managers are turning to the private landowner with incentives to provide what most states cannot—more habitat, and access to it for city hunters who are not as lucky as I was, knowing this neighbor boy with a weekend farm and pheasants on the East Fork of the Little Miami River.

The Division of Wildlife of the Ohio Department of Natural Resources offers a number of incentives to landowners, as I discovered one day dropping by the department's District Five headquarters at Xenia, which covers seventeen counties in the southwestern quadrant of the state. Wildlife Management Supervisor Warren Katzenmoyer told me first about the pheasant program. "We're trading birds for habitat," he said, and then went on to explain the various formulas by which the division provides pheasants to farmers in exchange for their promise to keep a certain acreage of cover undisturbed for a period of time. Under one formula, for example, the owner of eighty acres or more may receive eight birds for every three contiguous acres of undisturbed grass or legume cover, up to a maximum of twenty-four birds, or nine acres. Under another plan, the state will release ten birds for every ten acres left undisturbed for two years, up to a maximum of fifty birds per landowner. Undisturbed pheasant cover is defined by the state as mammoth red clover, sweet clover, timothy, or brome grass. In addition, the division offers free technical assistance to enhance habitat further with food patches and brush piles. In District Five, about two hundred landowners had signed up for one or another of these pheasant restoration programs when I spoke with Katzenmoyer, with the result that some five thousand game-farm birds were strutting free in the wild. Inasmuch as a pheasant is not reluctant to leave one farm for the next one over, especially when a load of number-six shot is fanning its tail feathers, Katzenmoyer is confident that some of the planted birds will disperse and, if all goes well, multiply and replenish the state. "The wild stock now numbers about a hundred sixty-five thousand birds statewide," Katzenmoyer said. "Our goal is three million by the mid-nineties."

Still, the bird at the end of the stick may not be enough. For the long-range effort, there is a plan to lease acreage for three to five years, paying the farmer $80 to $120 per year for an acre from which he might otherwise expect to earn $180 annually, after expenses, in crops, given fair weather and a healthy market. The leased acreage would be planted to brome grass and legumes, which are as good for holding the soil in place as for sheltering pheasants. On an intensively farmed Ohio acre nowadays, erosion is taking away nine tons of soil a year. The wildlife people figure some farmers might be willing to accept a small financial loss, leasing for habitat, if they knew that for three to five years they could cut their losses of the most precious capital of all, the soil. "We've got to try something new," said Katzenmoyer. "If we wanted to *buy* all the land that's needed to restore the pheasant in Ohio, it would cost us billions."

But there is also the problem of public access, for it is not the game people's intent merely to provide the farmer with birds for his own amusement, or to encourage a bumper crop of clover and brome grass. The idea is to provide as well more hunting opportunities for Ohio sportsmen, and to supplement with private lands the state's own inventory of public hunting areas. District Five Wildlife Manager Tom Fulton said he figured the fifty-six thousand state-owned acres in his region were capable of absorbing less than 25 percent of the district's hunting pressure. "So we'd just be in one whole big mess of trouble," he said, "if we didn't have co-op hunting."

Co-op hunting is a Buckeye euphemism for the quid pro quo that prevails in Ohio between the Department of Natural Resources and farmers who have a soft spot in their hearts for landless hunters but are fed up with the vandals and trespassers. In practice, the landowner agrees to permit free hunting and fishing on his property—first come, first served—but retains the right to limit numbers and to turn away applicants of unsavory demeanor. In return, the state supplies the landowner with signs ("Hunting with permission only") bearing the state's official imprimatur and suggesting to the outlaw that there is a warden behind every tree. It does not work out quite that well for the landowner, though the state does send its game protectors around during hunting season, so that more protection is available within the co-op system than outside it. "There's not many states going after these problems the way Ohio is," Fulton said proudly. "Bet we got the lot of 'em whipped."

And I replied that one should never underestimate the power of Missouri.

Design for Conservation

With scant oscillation, the center of population gravity in the United States has been sliding west by south more or less since it was first located twenty-three miles outside of Baltimore, Maryland. That was in 1790. By 1880, the center had slipped to the Kentucky hills near Cincinnati, and the last official decadal fix placed it at a point in Illinois hard by East St. Louis and the Mississippi River. Given the gravitational pull of the

Sun Belt, the center nowadays probably falls somewhere across the Mississippi in the river-break trees of Missouri, or possibly farther out, in a fescue pasture at the edge of the Ozark Plateau. Not that population gravity should make any large difference as to how well or badly a state might handle affairs of the hunt and of wildlife management. Nor that it matters greatly, though it must matter to some degree, that Missouri is where the eastern hardwoods meet the prairie and the southern pines; or that its cities lean toward the borderline edge, with plenty of open country for creatures and crops in between; or that some people like to hunt game while others would as soon float its spring-fed rivers or poke around in its limestone caves; or that Missourians have this abiding faith in doing most things their own way. License-plate slogans proclaim it to be the Show Me State. Show me you're any better, show me you're even as good. I don't believe anyone can show Missouri, at least not in the management of things that are close to the hearts of people who, be they hunters or spelunkers, care a great deal about the out-of-doors. Other states may go their same old way, trudging along the rut of traditional fish and game management practices, seeking only to pump up the game populations and the license sales, and to hell with non-hunters. But not Missouri. For Missouri may well be the only state in the Union where wildlife managers, hunters, and non-hunting outdoor folk of every sort have fashioned an opportunity to work together for wildlife, for the land, and for their own recreational pleasure. In that sense, I think that maybe the Show Me State should be considered a center of conceptual gravity, too—a model, a point upon which public policies and private attitudes might finally achieve a measure of balance, without the bitter divisiveness that has attended the hunt in this country for so many years.

Missouri was not always exemplar of the pack. Fifty years ago, it trudged along with the other states, and probably *behind* a good number of them. Deer, otter, beaver, grouse, and prairie chicken, according to one historian, had "passed virtually out of the picture" by 1930. Each year the legislature chipped away at the game laws. For a time, fish and game revenues unexpended at the end of each biennium were impounded by the state's treasurer and locked away in the General Fund. In 1931, the Sporting Arms and Ammunition Manufacturers Institute published Aldo Leopold's *Report on a Game Survey of the North Central States.* Leopold had little praise for the situation in Missouri. Insofar as the region's lagging acquisition of public game lands was concerned, he found Missouri to be "the 'key log' in this jam." And he singled out Missouri to illustrate his conviction that public financing of fish and game projects should be spread not only among the ranks of the sportsman but across the general population as well.

"In money," wrote Leopold, "the average citizen of Missouri spends per year for game and fish production through public channels not to exceed one-tenth the cost of a box of shells, and often less than it takes to run his automobile one mile. . . . The average citizen, as well as the hunter, has a stake in wildlife. It is his property, and the social value of hunting and other recreations depending on wildlife affects his individual welfare. He supports parks, schools, museums, etc., not [only] because he uses them personally, but because of their value to society. Why should he not help support wildlife conservation?"

Leopold had already advanced a similar idea in his "American Game Policy" of 1930, in which he cited seven basic actions needed for game restoration throughout the nation. Action Number Six urged sportsmen and wildlife administrators to "recognize the non-shooting protectionist and the scientist as sharing with sportsmen and landowners the responsibility for conservation of wildlife as a whole. Insist on a joint conservation program, jointly formulated and jointly financed."

At the time, Leopold's ecumenical advisory no doubt struck a note of heresy in the minds of most of his professional peers. Join with the protectionists? Open the doors of management to the bleeding hearts? Embrace the bird watcher as brother? No. Better to go it alone and frugally, the prevailing wisdom insisted, than to get rich and bogged down in extraneous programs, such as parks, or infiltrated by anti-hunters whose laments even then could be read in the public prints. True, a few

of the states in time would begin to make a token effort on behalf of non-hunters concerned with non-game programs. In
time they would have to, for by the 1960s participants in the
so-called quiet outdoor recreations—hiking and camping and
canoeing and such—were scoring more days afield than practi-
tioners of the ancient blood sports; and a few of the quiet types,
with college degrees in some newfangled environmental science, were even beginning to infiltrate the hunter's own club-
house and last redoubt, the state fish and game agency.

Still, suspicions of heresy linger nationwide. In most states,
governors continue to lard their fish and game boards or natural resources commissions with appointees favored by rod-and-
gun constituencies. Rare on such boards is a Joan Wolfe of
Michigan, a non-hunting environmentalist, or a Raymond
Dasmann of California, an author and ecologist with creden-
tials in the Leopold vernacular. Scratch the over-forty crowd in
the typical resources agency and, as often as not, you find grad-
uates of agricultural and industrial forestry schools, whose professional reading ever since has been largely confined to field
reports and the pages of *Field & Stream, Outdoor Life,* or *Guns and
Ammo.*

The literature has a lot to do with the lingering suspicions,
as well as the divisiveness. To read some of the columnists for
the hook-and-bullet press, or their counterparts on many metropolitan dailies, is to enter a world in which ambiguity and
ecumenism are not allowed. The way these scribes see it, if
you're not for 'em, you're against 'em. More to the point, if you
are not a hunter, there is something drastically wrong with you.
You are a "twitty bird," or a "daisy sniffer." Or possibly an
"elitist." And, sure as shootin', you are out to get their *guns.* No
matter that you have no traffic with Cleveland Amory's "Hunt
and Hunters Hunt Club" or Alice Herrington's emasculating
fire brigade; go afield, unarmed, with backpack or binoculars,
and you are the enemy.

Over time, this kind of intellectual diet begins to put layers
of fat around the cerebrum. And stifles the kind of thinking
Aldo Leopold espoused for Missouri and for the nation. And, as
a matter of fact, gets in the way of some rather strong evidence

that public attitudes about hunting are not quite so dour as the alarmists of the sporting press would have us believe. Some examples . . .

In a survey of 2,500 respondents throughout the country, Yale University researcher Stephen Kellert found that a substantial majority—64 percent—approved of recreational hunting as long as the activity included utilization of the meat. Few, however, approved of hunting for "sport" or trophy values only. If one extrapolates from Kellert's cohort to the nation as a whole, and concedes that most hunters probably do utilize the flesh of the game they recreationally take afield, even though the utilization is more for ritual than need, then it must follow that Americans for the most part are tolerant of the hunter who eats what he kills. Fair enough. And a fair antidote to editorial and administrative paranoia, it seems to me.

Further ecumenical good news comes from Daniel Witter of the Missouri Department of Conservation and William Shaw of the University of Arizona. In two separate studies—one involving about 600 "nonconsumptive" wildlife enthusiasts in southern Arizona, the other polling a like number of respondents drawn from the membership rolls of the American Birding Association, Inc., Ducks Unlimited, Inc., and the Wildlife Society—Witter and Shaw found attitudes leaning strongly toward a coalition of hunters and non-hunters joined "in common action for wildlife."

Contrary to the twitty-birded alarms of the shooting press, most birders and other nonconsumptive types appear to have no particular ax to grind on the issue of hunting. Big majorities in both studies felt that a government ban on hunting would be counterproductive to wildlife; that, in fact, hunting was sometimes essential to prevent overpopulation of game species. There was evidence, too, of mutual respect, or at least tolerance, between hunters and non-hunters. Waterfowlers from Ducks Unlimited gave the birders good grades as users of wildlife; the birders themselves remained fairly neutral in their judgment of hunters, being neither wildly pro nor anti. And there was a general consensus among all groups, including the duck hunters, that an imbalance prevails between game and non-game programs, and that non-hunting wildlifers have no acceptable way to help pay the costs of non-game management. (Illustrative of the historic frustration of non-hunters: The Michigan Audubon Society once advised its members to buy hunting licenses, inasmuch as that was the *only* way they could contribute directly to state wildlife restoration programs.)

Alternatives to buying a hunting license, or to doing nothing at all to share the costs of wildlife management, are numerous in theory but rare in practice throughout the fifty states. No more than one or two of the states allow their fish and game agency to tap general revenues to finance non-game programs. Yet sizable majorities of people questioned in the Witter-Shaw Arizona study and in Kellert's nationwide survey approved of this method of funding. One or two other states offer their residents a checkoff option to contribute a part of their state income tax refunds to non-game programs. Again, majorities of the Kellert and Witter-Shaw respondents approved of a tax checkoff for non-game funding. They thought it a splendid idea. Back home in the statehouses, their legislators apparently think it is a lousy idea.

And what about special use taxes to support additional wildlife programs? Stephen Kellert put a number of options before his 2,500 people and found that majorities favored taxes on fur clothing, outdoor recreational vehicles, and both backpacking and bird-watching equipment. Perhaps of greater significance was the willingness of the special user himself to be so taxed. Both recreational vehicle owners and bird watchers, though by scant majorities, approved the idea of taxing their own hardware to help support wildlife. And trappers—no skin off their cheeks—were explicably willing to pass on a tax to the furred consumer. But the backpackers balked. The backpackers, by a slim majority, did *not* approve of a tax on their ware, hard or soft. And *why*, when all of the other types did? I have a theory. Backpackers have this identity problem. I mean, there are some people who carry backpacks so that they may go far afield in order to hunt or fish or watch birds or take photographs. But these people call themselves hunters or fishermen or birders or photographers. So what is a backpacker? Could it be he is simply an overnight hiker? Or is he someone who likes the sound of it—*backpacking*—and when he isn't testing his hips and spine and shoulders against the force of gravity, settles down with his own generic version of *Outdoor Life* or *Guns and Ammo*, in which he discovers that wildlife is somebody else's problem?

And finally, what about the use of a general sales tax increment specially earmarked for wildlife programs? The question was raised in one of the Witter-Shaw studies, but respondents rejected it. Which is a puzzlement to me, inasmuch as sales tax revenues now provide the financial base for what is probably the finest, and surely the most ecumenical, state fish and game—and *non-game*—program in America. Namely, Missouri's.

The Show Me State trudged out of the dark ages of resource management in 1936. That was the year Missourians voted to throw the patronage politicians out of the game business. By constitutional amendment, they established a bipartisan conservation commission, insulated it from statehouse interference, and empowered it to create a new department with full responsibility for all the wildlife and forestry resources of the state. Henceforth, the old fish and game office would provide no feather bed for friends of the high and mighty. And there would be no pink slips and cleared desks every time a new man moved into the governor's mansion. That the meddlers were successfully isolated is evidenced by the long tenures of those who have served as director of the Department of Conservation over the years. Since 1937, there have been only four.

Carl Noren was the third. With the commission's approval, Noren brought in a team of outside consultants to give the department an impartial checkup—no pulled punches and no rubber stamps. One of the consultants was A. Starker Leopold of the University of California (and a son of Aldo). Another was the water resource planner Irving Fox, from the University of Wisconsin. And the third was a native Missourian, Charles

Callison, then executive vice-president of the National Audubon Society. The team's findings were released in 1970. For the most part there were high marks for the department's "outstanding record of past accomplishments" and for "smooth functioning of the managerial machinery." But times and problems change, the team noted, "and we discern some issues of considerable social importance that might profitably be reevaluated." Foremost in the consultants' view was a need to provide recreational opportunities outside the traditional milieu of hunting and fishing. It was no longer enough, they warned, "to say that nature lovers profit from the establishment of waterfowl refuges, fishing lakes, and public shooting grounds. . . . Wild rivers, to provide opportunities to observe nature, are as important as intensively managed bass lakes for bait casters." And apart from the recognized objective of maintaining crops of fish, game, and sawlogs, the consultants found that the agency had a "clear obligation to protect ecologic diversity" throughout the state as well.

Out of this critical analysis came a plan. A "Design for Conservation," they called it; and it would be implemented— after a few false starts in other directions—through a new source of revenue, a one eighth of one percent override on the state sales tax. To mitigate what someone called "the relentless scrape and crunch of development," there would be acquisition of upland habitat and wetlands and prairie and forest. There would be new natural areas and stream-access sites. Public-land-poor Missouri would double its holdings, to 600,000 acres. And all of the services of the department would be expanded, especially in the areas of outdoor education and natural history interpretation. But only if an initiative petition secured the prerequisite number of signatures to get an amendment on the ballot. And then only if the people of Missouri could see their way clear to cast an affirmative vote.

The people could, and they did, by a thirty-thousand-vote plurality. Much of the credit for that, and for the signatured petitions that made the vote possible, goes directly to the heart of outdoor ecumenism, the Missouri Conservation Federation. It is not the typical rod-and-gun coalition, this federation. It is not the classic swaggering band of yokels you find in some states, always demanding ease and convenience in the pursuit of sport, and devoting their best energies to the ridicule of non-game types. It is not the kind of organization to be threatened by the awakening aspirations of little old ladies in tennis shoes and of hippies in Vibram-soled boots. If for no other reason than that quite a few non-hunters belong to the Federation through membership in one or more of its 175 diverse, and not altogether consumptive, affiliates. "We've always tried to bring the different interest groups together," Ed Stegner, the Federation's longtime executive director, told me one afternoon at his office in Jefferson City. "And that's exactly where we had them—working hard and together—for 'Design for Conservation.' But you just let the preservationists go out their own way, and the hunters go off in the other, then nobody wins."

A mill or so off the dollar does not seem a great deal at the cash register. But in a state as populous as Missouri, it can add up fast—say, to between $24 million and $30 million a year. From scratch, it can double the recipient agency's budget, as it did in the first year of the tax for Missouri's Department of Conservation. Over two years, it can purchase sixty-seven thousand acres of high-quality wildlife habitat in seventy-two counties, including the large tract known as Weldon Spring, which is only thirty miles from Gateway Arch in downtown St. Louis, and no doubt will be used more intensively by passive wildlifers than by hunters. In just one year, it can pump three quarters of a million dollars into the acquisition of two new natural areas, four tallgrass prairie tracts, two "urban wild acres" sites, and two cave systems regarded as being strategic to the preservation of endangered species, including the gray bat. It can refine and extend an ambitious conservation education program in the state's public schools, such that instructional-aid materials prepared by the department are now being used by more than six thousand elementary-school teachers. And it can take an underfinanced and understaffed natural history section and quickly turn it around into what may well be the most effective center of non-game activity conducted at a state level anywhere in the country. And all of this costs just a bit more than one mill off the sales-taxed dollar, or about $5.50 per capita per year. Which is still far less, cast in Leopoldian comparatives, than the cost of a box of shotgun shells, and barely what it costs nowadays to drive the family flivver the sixty miles from Sedalia to Jefferson City.

In Jefferson City, I spent two days poking around the Department of Conservation, looking at the uncommon bits and pieces of work that are being financed by that scant mill off the sales-taxed dollar. My guide was James Keefe, the chief information officer, with departmental tenure running back to 1951, with newspapering and zoology studies before that. Keefe grew up urban in St. Louis. He was twenty-eight years old before he took up hunting, with muzzle-loaders. Since then he has home-crafted twenty-two of them, Pennsylvanias and Hawkens, mostly, and he takes great pride in the brass platework and in the curly maple of the stocks. One gets the impression that Jim Keefe is proud, too, about the way his department is looking to the future, though the man himself leans privately toward historical things, such as old guns and arrowheads and pottery shards, and sometimes he worries that the land is closing up with too many people, and the sticker on his truck imparts the outrageous news that American Indians had lousy immigration laws. One night in his study, at home, we were talking about some of the department's new programs, and I asked if there was one huge obstacle they collectively were seeking to overcome. "The way kids get to school," he said. "Kids used to walk to school down a country lane, or across a field, or through the woods. I didn't, in St. Louis, but kids out this way did. Now look what we've got. You don't get much feel for nature riding a bus to a consolidated school."

Webster County occupies a fair piece of the Ozark Plateau just east of Springfield, which is the third-largest city in Missouri, growing so fast you'd think it would rather be first. Still, there is good country round about for raising cows and corn and alfalfa; good, too, for deer and wild turkey and cedar and oak in bluff-top and river-bottom places not yet plugged up by too many plowshares or people. Not counting the ancient ones who left their arrowheads along the headwaters of the James, Niangua, and Pomme de Terre rivers, the region was first settled to white-skin standards by Kentuckians with long rifles. Having heard that Daniel Boone stayed two jumps ahead of the nation's center of population gravity by moving to Missouri, the Kentuckians decided to jump themselves, albeit a bit farther south than the pathfinder had. Thus, when the state got around to divvying up notable names for its counties, headstrong Boone's stayed north, while Ozark migrants had to settle for Daniel Webster's. Not only that, but someone then decided to name the county seat Marshfield, after the Great Compromiser's Massachusetts home.

There was something of a compromise in my own visit to Marshfield, Missouri. I mean a compromise in the sense that I had already exposed myself to the extremes of hunting in America—the exotic, the sublime, and the banal—and now I wanted to see how the other half lived in relation to the game, these border Midwesterners in bib overalls, not pouring out of the cities in the chill dawn of Opening Day, or chartering aircraft to remote taiga camps, or riding pack horses into the mountains, but just hunting the way it used to be for most people, and still is for some—out the back door and across the fields and into the woods, for fun and the pot. And here in Missouri, where the ideological climate for hunting seemed a bit more temperately productive than in other places I'd been, I wanted to test a supposition. I wanted to see, among people of long-rifle heritage and closeness to land, whether there might now be, for whatever reasons, a falling away from the hunt, a cooling of the venatic instinct, a snuffing of the spark that has beckoned men afield since the morning Adam took a taste of the apple and thereupon decided that things go better with meat.

In Marshfield, I called on John William Brooks III, a fiftyish man, born in these parts, and said to be as knowledgeable about hunting and fishing, and as hooked on them, as any Ozark individual could possibly be and still have a family, a job, and a farm to look after. People call John William Brooks

"Bill" so as not to get him confused with his father or his own elder son, who both reside locally and share the same name as well. Bill's roots reach into Kansas; his paternal grandfather was raised there in a sod hut when Kiowas were still skulking round about. Those of his wife, Ruth, run back to Kentucky, to a man named Day who hobnobbed with Daniel Boone in the dark and bloody days, and who probably got out to Missouri even before Boone did. Bill Brooks said he'd read somewhere that Boone had run Ruth's ancestor out of the bluegrass territory. I asked how come, and Bill, faking a stage whisper since his wife was nearby, said there was only one way to figure it. Old Man Day had "too much mouth."

Bill and Ruth Brooks live with their younger son, Joe, two cats, and an indeterminate number of dogs in a comfortable ranch house on the edge of town. The place backs onto a spring-fed pond, where beavers are busy from time to time, and then rolls out across more than a hundred acres of pasture and woodland. On this, and on seven hundred acres elsewhere, Brooks raises Angus and Hereford cattle for beef. By Ozark standards, he is a middling farmer—not small, but not big either, especially since a portion of his land is much the way Old Man Day or Daniel Boone might have found it 175 years ago, all buckbrush and sage grass and black oak. Brooks likes it that way, because he's a hunter; and keeps it that way because he can afford to. The Brooks Gas Company, which Bill took over when his father retired, is Marshfield's major independent distributor of propane gas and appliances. So it is the business in town that allows Bill Brooks not only to stay down on the farm, moonlighting cows, but to keep a good part of his land coarse and scruffy for gamier crops. "Without the business," he said, "I'd have to fescue it *all* off, just like everyone else." Fescue is the current state of the art in southern Missouri for seeding pastures, and Bill Brooks doesn't much care for it. Fescue is fine for winter grazing but, according to Brooks, has scant value as food or cover for small game. Brooks would prefer all his pastures in bluestem and sage grass and lespedeza, the way it used to be out here; but then, after all, he has to think of the cows. So some of his fields *are* planted to fescue. "And that makes me feel," he said, "like the preacher who's caught on a spree with the town bad woman."

Brooks showed me around the country that first afternoon at Marshfield. The turkey season had just opened, his son Joe was out somewhere in the woods trying to call one in, and Bill himself was profusely apologetic that he had to leave his own gun at home, since he had already taken the limit, one tom, first thing Opening Day. "We'll get one up just to look at, anyway," he said in the cab of his pickup truck. And tapped his fingers on a small, hollow cedar box with a paddle-like lid—his turkey call. "They're sure coming back," he went on, meaning turkeys. "Deer, too. Now in nineteen and forty-seven, when I got out of high school, there was next to nothing round here. I remember the first deer track I ever saw in this country. I couldn't believe my eyes. So I dug all around it, lifted it like it was some kind of cast, and took it on home. I needed the proof. It was so bad then, people would have thought I was making things up." We swung off the highway onto a gravel road leading down to the Brookses' big acres along the Niangua. "Now the game's coming back but the country's not ready for it," he said. "Just in the flash of an eye, the big woods is gone. All fescued over. What's going to happen in the next twenty years? Where are we going to wind up? Is Webster County going to be like Kansas—and no room for game?" Somehow the questions did not seem to want answers. And besides, I had none.

Now we turned off the gravel and headed down along the river through a cornfield strewn with broken stalks and tall with ragweed. Brooks stopped the truck and stared thoughtfully into the disarray of the crop that had failed. "I tried it two years," he said. "But it just didn't turn out. Don't know why exactly. It's good bottom soil." Then he smiled and said, "You sure can't beat *this* for turkey and deer. That's what my wife thinks, too. Thinks I let it go on purpose, just for the game."

"Did you?"

"Not on purpose," he said. "Guess it was meant to be this way."

At the far end of the neglected field, the land tipped up out of the creek bottom along a line of hickory trees. We walked up to the largest, sat down with our backs against its bark, and waited a while for the rest of the world to settle down. There was a cool breeze in the valley, the sound of faraway crows, the smell of dry leaves. And then Brooks was holding the cedar box in the palm of one hand while he scraped the lid back and forth with the other. No answer. The paddle-lid scraped again. *Keee keeee keeeee kecow cow cow.* But still, no answer.

For another while we let things settle down and talked softly with the cool wind on our faces. I started with my supposition that there might be a general falling away from the hunt. I told Brooks of men in the East—and not all that far east, since I was thinking of men from Michigan and Kentucky—who voiced uncertainties as to whether their sons would take to hunting as they had. I spoke of the difficulties most places nowadays, the pull of other recreations competing for one's time, the need to be going farther and farther out each year from the back porch, and sometimes returning with less. The conventional wisdom, I said, was that sooner or later, hunting in America would be dead on arrival, due to attrition. And yet maybe such wisdom was too conventional for this part of the country.

On my way into Missouri I had dropped by the farm of a man named Wheaton, near Paris. Good quail country, there. We had talked about birds and cover and how pleased most hunting folk thereabouts seemed to be with that sales-tax override that had the Department of Conservation going like blazes. And then I had talked with the man's son, Jim. He was twenty-nine. He had hunted addictively to the age of seventeen, hung up his guns then, got him a hot rod, and was gone from it all, just "girlin'." And most of his friends had gone the same way. Now they were pushing thirty and hunting again. Jim Wheaton told me it was different then, being young around Paris a decade ago. It seemed that the fellas couldn't get enough girlin' and racing fast cars and grooving to rock and dudeing around in city-slick suits from St. Louis. And now? Now, he figured, these young ones just out of high school were riding in pickups and strutting the country-western steps and dudeing around in Levi's and denim jackets. And cowboy hats. Still girlin'. But still huntin', too. And Jim said he thought what it all added up to was this: a hankering to get back to the way things were when life was simpler, though probably harder; and maybe a yearning to be close again to the land.

Bill Brooks heard it all out and nodded, saying, "I don't see much reason around here to think that there's *ever* going to be an end to hunting. It's going to get harder, sure, and maybe someday—you want to go hunting, you just better own some land to do it on. But people will still want to hunt. My boys sure do. Why, there's even some people round here who've never done it, and *they* want to hunt. Retired fellow from Chicago moved down here and bought some acres, and he came into the office one day to order some gas, but ended up asking questions about what kind of shotgun he should buy. He'd never owned a gun, much less shot one. But now he was living in the country with land of his own, and by golly he was bound and determined he was going to *hunt*." So much for suppositions.

We raised one turkey that afternoon, a hen. Heard her across the Niangua somewhere in the trees. Then we walked up through some oaks on our side, and called again, and heard nothing but the dry rattle of dead leaves still clinging to the branches. And then Bill Brooks began to tell me of the drums.

"What drums?" I asked.

"The ones you hear when you're alone in the woods. As far in the woods as you can get. You've never heard them?"

I said I wasn't sure that I ever had.

"You've got to be where you can't hear cars or trains or anything," he said. "You've got to be in a place beyond hearing. Not here. But I could take you if we had the time. All of us Brookses are loners in the woods. We like to come and sit alone and listen, and only when you can't hear anything else, that's when you hear the drums. It's probably only the blood pounding in your temples, but to me it sounds like the pounding of drums."

Is there ever any message from these drums? I wondered.

"I think the message is when you *don't* hear them," Bill Brooks said. "And I haven't heard them for such a long, long time."

To a Deer Blind

When I got home from Missouri, a letter and a phone message were waiting for me. The letter was from Fred Bear, that dean of the bow hunters. Bear wrote that he was planning to return to the hunting preserve called Grousehaven, up in Ogemaw County, for Opening Day of the deer season. The *other* season, he explained, not with bows but with rifles. And he wrote that since northern Michigan was more or less where I had started this quest of mine, why didn't I join him there, to finish it off? Fred Bear has always had a jump on good ideas.

The telephone message was from Tom Davis, the elk hunter from Hell. Skunked the autumn before, when I went with him, Davis had vowed he'd return to Montana this year for another try. That's what I suspected the call was about. And it was. He was off to the Gallatin Divide, and wanted to know if I might be leaning that way myself.

Not this time around, I told him. But I might be coming a part of the way a few weeks later. Had he forgotten that November 15 was Opening Day for deer in Michigan? Would he be back from Montana by then? Would he like to head north, meet Bear and his gang at Grousehaven, and poke around in the woods for a while? And something else. Could he bring a spare rifle?

There was a long silence at the other end of the line, and then Davis said, "For you?"

"Why not?"

"You want to hunt?"

"I've been thinking about it."

"You weren't thinking about it last year. What changed your mind?"

"The last year changed my mind."

"We'll go, then," he said. "You can use the Mauser."

"Won't that be a little heavy for whitetail?"

"Not if you use it right," he said.

We discussed where to meet, and when, and I wished him the best of luck in the western mountains. Then we rang off. As things turned out, my wish would carry no weight with the gods of the chase, for in just a few days Tom Davis would be out in Montana getting skunked by bull elk for the second year in a row.

Having returned—and recovered—from that rout, Davis met me at the Detroit airport on November 14, and we drove north in a rented camper, up U.S. 23 into I-75 at Flint, and on past Saginaw and Bay City, pulled along by a thickening flood of other campers and vans all going hell-for-leather out of the cities of Down Below toward the big woods of Michigan. Davis was the skipper in our vehicle. Somewhere near Pinconning, a station wagon overtook us in the passing lane and a back-seat boy in a blaze orange cap threw him a big wave.

"Going to his first hunt, I'll bet," said Davis.

"That makes two of us," I said.

"I thought you used to hunt as a kid."

"I did, but that was nearly thirty years ago. And then only once for deer."

"Did you get one?"

"No. But I didn't try very hard."

"And you haven't been out for anything else since?"

There had been one time. I had gone to the Eastern Shore of Maryland, for geese, with a man named Doug Painter—a pro, in fact, since Painter happens to be a writer for the National Shooting Sports Foundation. We sat for two wet days in a blind sunk in a cornfield near the Choptank River, and each morning and afternoon great undulating wedges of geese had crossed the sky above us, and Painter had tried to call them down to our decoys, but to no avail. Late in the afternoon of the last day, two stray honkers did come down, easing in, looking us over, wings out flat; and Painter whispering, "Get ready now, easy, easy ..."; and I, pressing the safety in the trigger guard of the borrowed 12 gauge and looking up through the cornstalks at the birds floating into range, and feeling that everything—the geese coming down and the shotgun rising to the shoulder—was a strange, slow beat off the measure of real time; and finally wondering, as Painter thrust his own gun through the lattice of stalks, how this could come to me so easily after all these years, now, without doubt or pause, wanting my eye and hand and weapon to bring down the goose on the right. And then, maybe forty yards out, the birds broke away. Painter fired. And I fired. And missed.

"Were you sorry?" asked Davis.

"A little bit," I said.

"Would you have been sorrier if you hadn't missed?"

"Maybe," I replied. "They're a beautiful bird. They mate for life. There are hunters who tell me they are through taking geese. It got to them. I hear there are hunters who feel that way about deer, too."

"You one of them?"

I said maybe that's what we were going to find out.

And once I went afield with a friend who likes hunting ruffed grouse because it stretches his legs in pleasant country, tests his reflexes, and helps fill the time between the end of this year's trout season and the beginning of the next. And because, in his opinion, it is hunting at its very best. To this particular occasion, I came an unarmed spectator, professing no interest in renewing an acquaintance with shotguns, but then, at the end of it, going away wishing I had. I might have guessed that grouse territory in October would do that to me. I had read enough—heard enough, too, from veteran bird shooters—to know that if any kind of hunt could bring a fellow out of retirement, a good day of grouse shooting would be the likeliest one to turn the trick.

It is not my intent, while extolling grouse, to belittle those uplanders whose tastes happen to run to other birds. In any event, men must be forgiven the circumstances of geography. I can understand why, in desert country for example, bird shooters sing the virtues of the white-winged dove; why, on the plains, there is so much to be claimed for Hungarian partridge; why prairie folk praise the ring-necked pheasant; and what drives certain gentlemen down in the piney piedmont to follow their dogs to the bobwhite quail. But it is the ruffed grouse (and its migratory sidekick, the woodcock) that makes dedicated wastrels of so many hunting men in the mixed hardwood forests of the Northeast. To the devoted ones, the grouse, or pa'tridge as it is called colloquially in the precincts of New England and the upper Great Lakes, is king of the North American game birds.

"It's tough and it's native and it knows how to make its own way," my friend Pat Smith was saying on our way to his grouse beat in the Catskill Mountains of New York State. "It's not as fast on the wing as a quail, but when you flush it it's not likely to be out in the open either. You've got to reach it shooting fast through the woods. You've got less than two seconds to locate the bird and swing on it." Smith snapped his fingers to accentuate the element of speed. "There's nothing like it," he said, "except for taking a trout on a dry fly."

Any resemblance between shooting a grouse and hooking a trout on a dry fly is certain to be coincidental, if not downright mythic; yet grouse hunters of my acquaintance are forever exercising the analogy. Possibly this occurs because, during the warmer half of the year, many pursuers of grouse hunt trout with artificial flies, while in the other half, fly fishermen inclined to bear arms are likeliest to bear them against upland birds in general, and, geography permitting, grouse in particular. Some men tie trout flies with the feathers of grouse that fell to their own guns. Moreover, certain kindred qualities cannot be denied. Side-by-side shotguns, for example, deserve the company of split-bamboo fly rods, though over-and-unders are now as acceptable to the upland elite as is the limber graphite rod to the trouting aficionado of Tonkin cane. And among a fair number of trouters and grousers there is this uncommon disdain for the bag limit, not in the sense of desiring more than the law allows, but in being satisfied with less. My friend Smith told me he would be content with one bird a day, or none, if only shotgun pellets worked like flies. He said there was only one thing wrong with bird shooting—no such thing as catch-and-release.

Smith had a place staked out up near Roscoe on the Beaverkill River. It wasn't his own place; it belonged to a man who allowed him to work it over because Smith never came up with dogs, and the man was under the mistaken impression that no one could take grouse without them. The landowner himself had two English setters and a Gordon, and for a time had been considered one of the best dog men in the entire country. In fact, the man was so good with dogs, and so attentive to their training, that he had never taken time enough to learn how to shoot. Smith, on the other hand, had had nothing better to do. He was a ferocious shot, and he knew how to follow his own nose. I asked if they ever hunted together, Smith and the landowner. "Are you kidding?" Smith said. "Why spoil a perfect relationship?"

The country that Smith liked to work over starts with alder and willow along a Beaverkill tributary, rolls up an easy slope under sweet fern and sugar maples, then tops out among hemlock and beech on the crest of a cherty ridge. Nowhere is the understory so dense that one cannot snap off a fairly clean shot, though until late October the scarlet and burnt-orange leaves of the maples do tend to get in the way.

Smith moved slowly and deliberately through the woods about ten yards ahead of me. He carried his Winchester side-by-side at the port arms position, so that one easy movement would bring the butt to his shoulder in an instant. We had been moving uphill for about twenty minutes when the first grouse thundered out of the ferns at two o'clock to Smith's gun. A fast, dark blur against the bright foliage—and it was gone. "We'll get that one on the way home," he said, but I failed to detect any strong conviction in the statement. Then another bird went up and away as he swung on it without firing. "And let's save that one, too," he said. "Just in case we run out of birds in the afternoon."

We took our time on the long slope and rested a while by a stone wall near the top, and then we followed the wall into a stand of hemlocks. Halfway through, I heard a grouse get up somewhere to our right, and even before I could locate the bird, Smith's 20 gauge had caught it in a pattern of shot. The bird fell in the open, on a carpet of hemlock needles. Smith broke his shotgun open, pocketed both the spent and the live shell, and, when he reached the grouse, took it in his hand, gently. Though the bird appeared to be dead, Smith must have felt some life through the feathers. Suddenly he grasped it in both hands and broke its neck.

"That was a nice shot," I said. "Someday you've got to teach me how that's done." Smith promised he would try to do that, if I'd take the time. But I never did. And now I was on my way to a place called Grousehaven, to see what it was like to kill a deer.

Tom Davis and I arrived at Grousehaven just before dark. Bill Boyer, who has owned the place since 1926, hailed us from the door of his cabin and said there was a crackling good birch fire inside, and we were welcome to it and whatever else of a warming kind we might happen to find, if only we didn't mind putting up with the ornery critter staked out by the hearth. Davis wanted to know what kind of dog it was, and Boyer said, "Don't mean the dog. I mean Fred Bear."

He was there, all right, about as un-ornery a man as you will ever meet—the slow easy hand reaching out and the face almost breaking in half with a grin. We talked about his bow-and-arrow business down in Gainesville, Florida, and how different the labor situation was there as compared with that of Grayling, up here, where Bear Archery used to be; and then we went through some of Bill Boyer's scrapbooks, with the yellow-edged photographs of all the hunts over the years, and the men who came here sometimes Opening Day—Arthur Godfrey and the Air Force generals Twining and LeMay. Which explained why, here at Grousehaven, there was an airstrip long enough to handle the likes of a DC-3. Handled quite a few, I'd heard, back when Opening Day at Grousehaven drew nearly as many gold stars as a meeting of the Joint Chiefs of Staff. But now there just weren't that many of Boyer's old hunting friends coming up any more. The years had been culling them out.

Still, there were enough here this time around to make the dinner table crowded over at the lodge. Boyer's two sons, Alger and Harold, were up (Alger all the way from New York); and Bob Munger, who had hunted all over the world with Fred Bear in expeditionary days when Bear was a star of ABC-TV's "American Sportsman," and who now was a kind of one-man Greek chorus to the master archer's epic storytelling, especially when it seemed to Munger that his friend might be handling the facts as one handles a drawstring; and F. F. Everest, whom everyone deferred to as "the General," because that's what the man was, four stars, now retired but once the commander of all of America's tactical air bases from Prestwick, Scotland, eastward to Turkey. Not to mention a half dozen younger men, mostly from Michigan, and mightily honored, as Davis and I were, to be filling the places of those who would, or could, no longer be with us.

After supper that night, the table talk drifted from epic tales of the hunt to the deplorable qualifications of so many of the hunters who would be out in the woods of Michigan on Opening Day, men with no skill in woodscraft and little respect for a loaded rifle, and less for the game. Someone suggested that it was probably easier in some states to get a hunting license than a certified copy of one's own birth certificate. "That's exactly the point," said the General. "It's too damn easy. We've got to make it necessary in America for every hunter who goes into the woods to know what the hell the score is."

From the end of the table, Fred Bear said he'd go along with a system whereby every aspiring hunter would be exposed to sixteen hours of instruction. But that wasn't good enough for the General. "Oh hell, Bear," he said. "Sixteen hours is like pissing in the sea and expecting the tide to rise. I'd hunted all over the world, but in Germany I still had to study two weeks to pass interrogation by the *Forstmeister* of the *Revier* where I wanted to hunt red stag. That's the way it ought to be." There were a few mild dissents around the table, some saying that in America, unlike Germany, hunting was a democratic right that sort of ran with the land; and maybe if you made the standards *too* high, you'd find yourself on the indefensible side of a discriminatory situation. The argument did not impress the General. "Damnit," he said. "If a man's going to do anything— drive a car, fly a plane, shoot a rifle—he's got to be taught to do it *right.*" From the corner of my eye I could see Tom Davis nodding his head vigorously. He looked like a man who wanted to stand up and cheer.

Later, Fred Bear went back to Bill Boyer's cabin to keep our host company, Munger turned in for the night, some of the others settled down in front of a television set, and the General waved Davis and me toward his own room, where there was a bottle of fine old bourbon and some more talk about the way things ought to be, and, at my insistence, about the General himself. He sat on the edge of his cot, assembling around him all the gear he would need for the morning's hunt—the treasured .30/06 that had been with him around the world, the hand-loaded cartridges, the binoculars in their weathered case, the sturdy cane that would help take some of the pressure off his ailing leg. And there on the cot, too, was the birthday card that we had passed around the supper table for signatures, noting that Opening Day would be the third day of F. F. Everest's seventy-sixth year.

He had come out of Council Bluffs, Iowa, son of a birdshooting man; had graduated from West Point about the time Bill Boyer was first setting up camp in these Ogemaw woods; studied ordnance, flew all the early planes while the horse soldiers were pooh-poohing air power, fought a war in the Solomon Islands, moved up through the ranks to become top chief of the Tactical Air Command, then retired to South Carolina. And still the General believed in doing things only if one could do them right.

The German hunting system had greatly impressed the General. He spoke of the difficulty of obtaining a license and of how each candidate must undergo the most rigorous course of training. Figures I had come across somewhere in the literature indicated that a candidate for the hunt had to complete the equivalent of a hundred-hour course of instruction in management practices, wildlife biology, hunting traditions and ethics, and use of firearms. And I told the General I had heard that more than a third of those who attempt to qualify as hunters are rejected for failing the required tests. "You'd screen out most of the slobs," said the General, "if we did that here."

In the morning, we were up at five. There was a thin cover of snow on the ground, and small crisp flakes were still coming down out of a black sky. No one had much to say at breakfast. Davis handed me a dozen cartridges for the Mauser, then headed off with a flashlight to his appointed beat on the near side of a spruce swamp. I was directed to another place, the Horseshoe, on the swamp's other side, and the General was to be posted somewhere more or less in between. I went into the Horseshoe off a dirt track, tripping on low brush in the dark, found a tight cluster of oaks, crawled in among them, and waited for the dawn. It took its own sweet time coming. By my watch it was seven before things began to gray up enough to look around—the oaks starkly silhouetted, the understory running off close to the ground, almost park-like, a big opening in the woods, upwind, where deer might be crossing on their way to the swamp. I took a handful of cartridges out of my pocket and pressed four into the magazine, and then chambered the top one with the bolt. The safety was set. The scope sight was clear of the tissues I had wedged at either end to prevent the glass from fogging when the rifle came out of the warmth of the camper at five. Now I was ready. Were the deer?

About five minutes later I heard the first faraway shot. Too far away, I figured, to be from any of the Grousehaven guns. With the light spreading out all around, there were more shots, in singles and series, and one very close—Davis?—the General? Then I could see deer moving toward my opening in the woods. Three of them stepping high, white tails slowly a-wag, cautiously looking it all over, sniffing, going for the swamp. The butt of the Mauser was against my shoulder now and my thumb sneaked up along the bolt to flick off the safety as each of the animals moved into and across the lens of the scope. All ears and no horn. So I reset the safety, lowered the rifle, and watched the does mosey along into the swamp. Only after they were gone did I begin to wonder what I might have done, at that range, if one of the three had been a buck.

There were no deer in the afternoon. The sun went down under purpled clouds and it grew suddenly cold in the woods on the way back to camp. When I got there, two deer were hanging from the buck pole behind the lodge, and Alger Boyer was trying to convince a skeptical audience that his was as big as the General's. Then Tom Davis straggled in skunked from the swamp. "Tomorrow's the big one," he said to me later, in the camper as we turned in for the night. "I can just about feel it. Can't you?"

I could feel *something* the next morning, but it wasn't the big day. It was the numbing cold, reaching down through four layers of chamois and wool until I thought I would never stop shaking. Or maybe it wasn't the cold at all. Maybe it was staring through a cross-haired lens into the eyes of a buck at seventy paces.

Day Two had begun a little later than the first—Davis off to a new beat, to Fred Bear's own favored haunt in a part of the woods called Lost Acres; and I, back to the Horseshoe, but with just enough light this time to pick out a spot with a better field of fire across the opening where I had seen the three does the morning before. It was an old blind that hadn't been used, I guessed, for years—six black oaks in a tight ring with thick slabs of bark wedged into the spaces between the tree trunks. A little pillbox in the forest, with lichens and moss for interior decor.

The shaking started a little before eight, right after the herd came out of the brush at the west end of the clearing. I stopped counting after twenty. I had never before seen so many deer at one time in one wild place. All of them were moving slowly in scattered groups toward the swamp. Through the scope I could distinctly see one spikehorn buck, but all of the others—impossibly—appeared to be does. It was hard to tell, even with the scope, for most of them were maybe three hundred yards out. My thumb went up along the bolt, found the safety latch, snapped it down and off. I put my shoulder against the nearest tree and snugged the Mauser's barrel into a crotch between two slabs of the pillbox's bark. I brought the scope back to the spikehorn buck. And waited, shaking.

And waited, thinking, too. For there had been another letter on my desk when I returned from Missouri, a letter from a friend who had come to suspect that I was up to no good. If I was really serious about trying to "defend" hunting for pleasure, he wrote, then I would surely have to deal with the moral arguments of Joseph Wood Krutch, among others, and not be taken in by the "obscurantist mystique" of a "sophistical reactionary" such as Ortega y Gasset. To say that "one does not hunt in order to kill—one kills in order to have hunted" was not an adequate reply, my friend believed, to a clear and simple question like Krutch's "How justify the killing of any living thing for the sake of *pleasure*?" But what, after all, was so clear and simple about Krutch's question? Or was it *too* simple? How justify the killing of a carrot for the sake of holding it in your hand and admiring its color and texture, and then eating it, with pleasure? How justify the use of wood, the felling of a living giant, the saw blade dripping sap, when coal for heat, or steel for structure, would serve just as well, though not so pleasurably? If there was one line to be drawn among living things, and another between the acceptable pleasures and the damnable ones, where did one draw them? I have heard of ethical vegetarians—and I respect them—who eschew all flesh but still devour eggs, and possibly with a good deal of shame rather than pleasure, for what is the cooking of an egg if it is not abortion? Heavy thoughts for so early a morning in the Michigan woods.

I had just emerged from my sophistical reactions to Krutch and my critical friend when I saw the second buck. It was standing about sixty or seventy yards out, in the open, head down and broadside to my blind. I swiveled the rifle a few inches to the left, laid the cross hairs across a point behind and slightly under its shoulder, eased my finger around the trigger. A touch of ice. A pounding in the temples, a sound as of drums inside the heart. Easy now. Easy. Use it right. Do it right. Do it.

The buck's head jerked up and its eyes were on me. The forelegs splayed out as if to brace themselves, the nose brushed the air in an arc. The buck wasn't sure yet. I hadn't moved. The wind was to my advantage. The buck held fast. Then the eyes—the huge glistening eyes that had torn my own away from the cross hairs on the shoulder—turned in the other direction as a foreleg stiffly stamped the ground. Just once. Do it now. But do it *right*? After all these years? After all the contempt felt in the last year for the ones who do *not* do it right? If I missed, if I wounded the animal, if I should have to take more than one shot, if its dying was drawn out—would it be right? Would *I* be right?

I opened the bolt of the Mauser, ejecting the cartridge into the palm of my hand. Another touch of ice. And when I looked out again into the clearing, the buck was gone. I sat there for another hour with an empty chamber in the rifle, and the sun came over the tops of the spruce at the edge of the swamp, and the shaking stopped. Then I went out of the Horseshoe toward camp. Just short of the airstrip, on a dirt track, a car came up behind me and I stepped aside to let it pass. The car stopped, and Bill Boyer, with Fred Bear grinning beside him, leaned out from the driver's seat to inquire if I had had any luck.

"I had plenty," I said.

"You get one?"

"Not this time," I said. "I've got some learning to do first."

They both looked disappointed and I wanted to tell them not to be. But I didn't, because there was better news. Boyer and Bear had just come out from Lost Acres, and they said Tom Davis was back there now, dressing his deer.

Author's Note

Many people were uncommonly helpful to me as I put this work together, and most have already been mentioned. But a few of the names bear repeating, with grateful thanks for their contributions: Durward Allen of Purdue University, Cleveland Amory of the Fund for Animals, David Cline of the National Audubon Society, Jim Keefe of the Missouri Department of Conservation, Stephen Kellert of Yale, John Madson of Nilo Farms, Patrick Smith of Landmark Productions, and David Swan of the Northwest Alaska Native Association in Kivalina.

Other helpful people, for one reason or another, or none, were not mentioned. I do that now, again with special thanks. In Michigan, to Pete Murdick and Bob Wagner of Gaylord; in Montana, to Jim Posewitz and Bill Schneider of Helena; in Alaska, to Tony Vasca of Bethel, Harold Sparck of Chevak, and Fred Mitchell and Bob Stephenson of Fairbanks.

And a score of salutes to Kathleen Fitzpatrick, Shellie Hagan, Elizabeth Kaufmann, and Leslie Ware, all then of *Audubon* magazine; and to its intrepid editor, Les Line, who started it all.

A Note About the Author

John G. Mitchell was born in Cincinnati, Ohio, and educated at Yale University. He has written for various periodicals and served for four years as editor in chief of Sierra Club Books. His two previous books are *Losing Ground,* a collection of essays on environmental topics, and *The Catskills: Land in the Sky,* with photographs by Charles Winters. He is a regular contributor to *Audubon* and *American Heritage* magazines. He lives in Connecticut with his wife and two daughters.

A Note on the Type

The text of this book was set, via computer-driven cathode-ray tube, in a film version of a typeface called Baskerville. The face itself is a facsimile reproduction of types cast from molds made for John Baskerville (1706–75) from his designs.

Baskerville's original face was one of the forerunners of the type style known as "modern face" to printers—a "modern" of the period A.D. 1800.

Composed by American–Stratford Graphic Services, Inc., Brattleboro, Vermont. Printed and bound by American Book–Stratford Press, Saddle Brook, New Jersey. Typography and binding design by Virginia Tan.